EDMUND BURKE: HIS LIFE AND LEGACY

The Right Hon. Edmund Burke: an engraving (1791) by M. Benedetti after a painting by Sir Joshua Reynolds reproduced courtesy of the British Museum

The Right Hon. Edmund Burke: an engraving (1791) by M. Benedetti
after a painting by Sir Joshua Reynolds reproduced courtesy of the
British Museum

Edmund Burke

HIS LIFE AND LEGACY

Ian Crowe

Editor

FOUR COURTS PRESS

Set in 10.5 on 12.5 point Ehrhardt
by Carrigboy Typesetting Services for
FOUR COURTS PRESS LTD
55 Prussia Street, Dublin 7, Ireland
e-mail: fcp@indigo.ie

This edition is not for sale in North America, where a
separate edition is published under the title of
The Enduring Edmund Burke: Bicentennial Essays,
published by Intercollegiate Studies Institute, Inc.,
3901 Centreville Road, Post Office Box 4431,
Wilmington, Delaware 19807.

A catalogue record for this title
is available from the British Library.

ISBN 1–85182–306–9

Printed in Great Britain
by Hartnolls Ltd, Bodmin, Cornwall

Foreword

This volume is principally a commemoration of the bicentenary of the death of Edmund Burke, and the Edmund Burke Society is very pleased to commend it as a tribute to one of Britain's greatest parliamentary figures, whom Macaulay considered the greatest man since Milton.

When the Society began drawing up plans for the bicentenary, it was not immediately obvious that another book on Burke was needed. But this collection, unusual in concept and composition, is ample justification of the decision. Ian Crowe has brought together the widest possible range of contributors, and the essays reflect the breadth of Burke's own interests as well as the scope he left for interpretation. Appropriately, the contributors come from Britain, Ireland, America and France. Burke's writings are of interest to the historian, the philosopher, the economist, the journalist, the literary critic, the lawyer, the politician and the political thinker, each of whom will have his own approach to that legacy.

The Society hopes that the diversity of the contributions will be mirrored by a diversity of readers. This is a collection for the general reader as much as for the Burke scholar. It is a book for anyone with a keen interest in the enduring issues of politics and society, and we believe that this year's commemoration will enhance Burke's standing once again in politics as well as in schools and universities. The fundamental questions about how we are governed, about our individual and corporate responsibilities at home and abroad, about social behaviour and about coping with change, are no different now from two hundred years ago. Burke was a practical politician, not an idealist or an ideologist, but his struggle to balance principle with circumstance did not make him a cynical pragmatist. His consistent values give his writings a permanent significance.

Burke used language that may be unfamiliar to us, but his ideas remain clear and crisp. He is not hard to read, even when he presents us with those difficult concepts so important to him: natural law, morality and trust. Above all, Burke wrestled his whole life, publicly and uncompromisingly, with the issues of right and wrong.

PETER TANN
Chairman, *The Edmund Burke Society*
London, 1997

Contents

8   *Contents*

Editor's Preface

My thanks go to all the contributors to this volume for their considera-
tion and promptitude in the face of difficult deadlines, and for their
encouragement and suggestions. The committee of the Edmund Burke Society
has offered vital and unstinting support throughout the process of compilation,
and I am particularly grateful to Jim McCue and Peter Tann, who have offered invaluable help with the editing and planning, and to Sir Peregrine
Rhodes, the chairman of the Society's bicentennial committee. Any editorial
weaknesses that remain are the consequence of my having failed to act upon
their prudent advice. Christopher Lane, Christine Berry, W.-A. Burke-Miailhe
and Michel Canavaggio rescued me from awkward bottle-necks, and I cannot pass over in silence those who patiently bore my editorial mood swings
at close quarters over the year in which this project was developing: Karen
and Jeremy Dyson – and Zbigniew Volak, who gave so much support did not
see the project completed.

A Note on References

Many of the essays in this collection include extensive references that may guide the reader to appropriate sources and further material. Consequently, it has not been felt necessary to include in the volume a bibliography or list of recommended reading. The references to the editions of source material which appear most frequently are abbreviated as follows:

Works: The Works of the Right Honourable Edmund Burke (Bohn's British Classics), 8 vols (London, 1854–89).

Correspondence: The Correspondence of Edmund Burke, ed. T. W. Copeland *et al.*, 10 vols (Cambridge, 1958–70).

Writings and Speeches: The Writings and Speeches of Edmund Burke, ed. P. Langford *et al.* (Oxford, 1981–).

Reflections: Reflections on the Revolution in France, ed. Conor Cruise O'Brien, (Harmondsworth, 1968).

Parliamentary History: The Parliamentary History of England from the Earliest Period to the Year 1803 (London, 1806–20).

Introduction:
Principles and Circumstances

Ian Crowe

There is something peculiarly elusive about Edmund Burke. This is not just a practical problem, that 'to do him justice,' in Hazlitt's words, 'it would be necessary to quote all his works', or that he maintained a frustrating silence over his personal affairs and burned piles of such papers shortly before he died. It is also an intellectual problem: his career and writings present us with an abundance of apparent contrasts that are difficult to resolve satisfactorily.

These apparent contradictions were pored over by his contemporaries. Hester Thrale was forcibly impressed by domestic contrasts when she 'lived with him and his lady at Beaconsfield among dirt cobwebs, pictures and statues that would not have disgraced the city of Paris itself: where misery and magnificence reign in all their splendour, and in perfect amity'. Burke's professional face was equally bemusing. He constantly argued the case for circumspection and moderation, but in a style that was often impatient and aggressive: even his friend and great admirer William Windham was once moved to comment on a 'passion so unreasonable and manners so rude'. Burke was renowned in his own time for his political wisdom, grounded, as he was always keen to stress, on a study of human nature: yet Horace Walpole – in a judgment no less pertinent for being complimentary – said that, 'Of all the politicians of talents I ever knew, Burke has the least political art.' Burke's humanity was evident time and again, over India, the plight of Irish Catholics, the slave trade. He appealed for clemency on behalf of men arrested in the wake of the Gordon Riots, during which his own life had been threatened more than once: yet Lord Inchiquin felt that, 'He is admired by everybody, but has no friends.' He was a parliamentarian of such stature that his pall-bearers included the Speaker of the House of Commons, the Lord Chancellor and the Secretary of State for War: to Hazlitt, however, the truth was simply that this great man 'was out of his place in the House of Commons'.[1]

---

1   *The Complete Works of William Hazlitt*, ed. P.P. Howe (London, 1932), vol. VII, p. 301; *Thraliana*, ed. K. Balderston (Oxford, 1951), p. 475; *Diary of the Right Hon. William*

Over two hundred years the contrasts have persisted. Burke is remembered for his suspicion of political solutions based upon dogmas and theorems, and for his practical attention to reality; but he is known by maxims that have impact precisely because of their universal application. 'People will not look forward to posterity, who never look backward to their ancestors'; 'I am most afraid of the weakest reasonings, because they discover the strongest passions'; 'Those who attempt to level, never equalise.' Few people in history can have been quoted more frequently out of context than this man, for whom the context was everything. As a consequence, his is a confusing legacy: too much a philosopher for politicians, and too much a politician for philosophers; the father of a party he never knew, with a name he never spoke; the ideologist of an anti-ideology and a philosopher of pragmatism.

Edmund Burke moved through strongly contrasting worlds and experienced widely fluctuating circumstances. He was born in Dublin – or, perhaps, Shanballymore – but soon after he reached twenty he moved to London, where he later abandoned what security he had enjoyed there from study in the Middle Temple to try his fortune as a writer, journalist and moral philosopher. We have few records for these years, but in this competitive and hostile world Burke would have found it essential, practically and emotionally, to preserve his ties of kinship and the *mores* of his upbringing. At the same time, he would have found it essential to conceal them. He knew that his ambitions and talents were woven in with ties that would restrict as well as secure him.

These ties did not escape the notice of his political opponents, and Burke never wrestled himself loose from the ambiguity of his position. Within a year of entering Parliament, for example, he wrote in some anxiety to his old school friend, Richard Shackleton: 'I am given to understand that you had received at some time a letter from England, some way relating to me. Have you ever received such a letter?' Shackleton admitted that he had, and had replied to it, as requested, by offering personal memories of Burke and his family. The enquirer was never identified, but his motives became apparent some years later, when the piece appeared in the *London Evening Post*. This prompted a sharp rebuke from Burke to Shackleton: 'It is full of anecdotes and particulars of my life. It therefore cuts deep. I am sure I have nothing in my family, my circumstances, or my conduct that an honest man ought to be ashamed of. But the more circumstances of all these which are brought out, the more materials are furnished for malice to work upon: and I assure you that it will manufacture them to the utmost.'[2]

Windham, ed. Mrs Henry Baring (London, 1866), p. 167; *Last Journals of Horace Walpole during the Reign of George III, from 1771–83* ed. A. Francis Steuart (London, 1910), vol. I, p. 82; *The Farington Diary*, ed. James Greig (London, 1922–28), vol. I, p. 191; Hazlitt, op. cit., p. 302.
2   *Correspondence*, I, 270–71 and II, 130.

Burke entered politics in 1759. By that time he had established a sound reputation as a writer, with his works *A Vindication of Natural Society* (1756) and, more especially, *A Philosophical Enquiry into the Origin of our Ideas of the Sublime and Beautiful* (1757) – the second of which drew him into a valuable and productive communication with Adam Smith. He was also earning £300 a year for editing Dodsley's *Annual Register*, and working on a history of England. His friend William Dennis wrote to Richard Shackleton in 1757: 'Ned I fancy writes pamphlets for the great ones.'[3] Paul Langford considers as 'truly remarkable' the speed with which Burke, an outsider, moved into the highest circles of political life in Britain.[4] His first political appointment was as secretary to William Hamilton, who became Chief Secretary for Ireland in 1761, and in 1765 Burke entered the employment of the Marquis of Rockingham. Within six months, through the generosity of his 'cousin' William Burke, he secured the seat of Wendover and he first spoke in the House within days of the opening of the new session, in January 1766. His earliest speeches, delivered in his first month in the House, were on American affairs – the Stamp Act disturbances and the Rockinghamite Declaratory Resolution – and were received with great enthusiasm. Richard Burke, his brother, wrote to the painter James Barry that Edmund 'has gained prodigious applause from the public, and compliments of the most flattering kind from particulars'.[5]

Burke understood the tensions and conflicts that such rapid advancement could produce. Men of his background could rise in politics, but only usually to the level of minor administrators. Burke shot beyond this, and his studied silences over his career before entering Parliament attest to the strain. Journalism, even of the highest order, was not a training to be flaunted, and there is no reference in his hand to the pamphlets he produced to earn a living. Nor did he ever acknowledge publicly his editorship of the *Annual Register*. Instead he chose to deal with his past by analogy, readily clothing himself in Cicero's toga as the new arrival, and accepting the parvenu's rôle with its implications of quiet pride and loyal service. This was illustrated in his confrontation with Sir William Bagot on the floor of the House in 1770. William Burke recalled that, on that occasion, Edmund told Bagot that 'he took to himself the appellation of a *novus homo*. He knew the envy attending that character. *Novorum hominum industriam odisti*; but as he knew the envy, he knew the duty of the *novus homo*'; and he then warned the House of 'the impropriety and danger of discouraging new men', stating that 'rising merit stamped with virtue would indeed seek to rise [and perhaps become]

3 *Correspondence*, I, 124 n5.
4 *Writings and Speeches*, II, 4.
5 *Correspondence*, I, 238.

equal, nay ... superior to the lazy something that came by inheritance'.[6] This
was a message, a motivation, that Burke had not lost by the end of his life.
In his *Letter to a Noble Lord* (1796), he wrote that, unlike his antagonist the
Duke of Bedford, he had not been 'swaddled, and rocked, and dandled into a
legislator; '*Nitor in adversum*' is the motto for a man like me ... At every step
of my progress in life (for in every step was I traversed and opposed), and at
every turnpike I met, I was obliged to show my passport, and again and
again to prove my sole title to the honour of being useful to my country.'[7]

Burke's ambivalent attitude to his origins was heightened by the religious
issue (upon which, he noted, Shackleton had dwelt long enough in his piece
to raise suspicions). He wrote, in *Reflections on the Revolution in France* (1790),
'We are Protestants, not from indifference but from zeal', but his own background perhaps led him to add that such Protestant zealotry was no longer
a threat to Roman Catholicism.[8] His father had possibly been a convert to
Protestantism, his mother was a Catholic (who, according to Shackleton,
'practised the duties of the *Romish religion* with a decent privacy'[9]), and he
married a Catholic. His sympathies with Roman Catholicism remained strong
to the end of his life through family and friends, and were strongly apparent
in his later writings against the spread of atheistic Jacobinism in France and
Ireland; they also added a sinister shading to his political face. Just before the
appearance of Shackleton's potted biography in April 1770, Sir William
Bagot had attacked Burke in the House of Commons as a man thinking like
'one bred at St Omer's ... and fitted to be Secretary to the Inquisition'.[10] In
June 1780 Lord George Gordon's speeches against Catholic Emancipation
singled out Burke in particular. In 1796, William Miles, writing to defend the
Duke of Bedford against Burke's excoriating *Letter to a Noble Lord*, wished
Burke had taken his retirement from Parliament more seriously: 'His chaplet
and rosary, it was thought, would have exercised his meek faculties in a
species of arithmetic, very different to that which he had studied in his commerce with a profane world.' Instead, Miles continued, in his demands for a
war of extermination against the French revolutionaries, Burke had remembered his confessions of early life and endeavoured 'to replunge an emancipated world once more into ignorance, barbarism, and vassalage' through the
restoration of the power of his mother church.[11]

6 *Correspondence*, II, 128.
7 *Works*, V, 124–25.
8 *Reflections*, 187.
9 *Correspondence*, II, 129.
10 Ibid., 127.
11 W. Miles, *A Letter to Henry Duncombe*, Esq. ... (London, 1796), pp. 1–2 and 3.

In the way of *novi homines*, Burke had a burning pride in the very struggles which he found it necessary to conceal. At the same time, he sought acceptance in the world that demanded such concealment. His estate at Beaconsfield is an illustration of this conflicting drive. It was bought at heavy cost in 1768 and sustained thereafter through the accumulation of debts that must at times have strained his principles and compromised his devotion to the dogged integrity of the *novus homo*. In his will, Rockingham cancelled 'certain bonds' in Burke's name which have been estimated at £30,000 in value.[12] Despite injudicious investments in East India stock by his closest associates, the embarrassments of Lord Verney's financial difficulties (when Burke was sued in chancery by Verney for £6,000 in debts) and Horace Walpole's affected outrage at his use of patronage for the short time he was in office, charges against Burke's integrity in his financial and political affairs have simply not been proven. But the strain of a life stretched across different worlds is evident, from the passion of his reaction to criticisms of his pension in the last years of his life right back to the outburst that accompanied his break with William Hamilton in 1765. Burke had acquired a much needed pension through Hamilton, but had then become agitated when it appeared that Hamilton unreasonably expected to be able to draw on his secretary's services at his pleasure. 'Mister Hamilton is begged to consider,' Burke wrote in his own defence, 'that no obligations which include the whole life and existence of a man are valid in any country from which actual servitude is excluded.' This tortuous self-justification runs to several pages, but no word in it carries more import than *servitude*.[13]

Burke's experiences, in their complexity and obliqueness, arose from the need to hold on to principles while learning to adapt to changed and changing circumstances; that is, to distinguish, as Burke himself put it, between the principles themselves and the forms in which they were variously manifested.[14]

It is, then, no surprise that his early political career concerned, in Paul Langford's words, 'the construction of a rational defence for the principle of party'.[15] He committed himself early to a group of men in Parliament who claimed ties of impartial duty and civic virtue above those of patronage and personal connection, and his defence was articulated in his highly praised tract, *Thoughts on the Cause of the Present Discontents* (1770). The concept of 'party' that he propounded there, of 'a body of men united for promoting by their joint endeavours the national interest, upon some particular principle in

12 Earl Fitzwilliam to Burke, 3 July 1782. *Correspondence*, V, 8.
13 See *Correspondence*, I, 182–86.
14 See *Writings and Speeches*, VI, 345.
15 *Writings and Speeches*, II, 12.

which they are all agreed',[16] provided a means by which Burke, and people from his social background, could best influence political decisions. At the same time, he professed himself a strong advocate of the aristocratic system, insofar as the landed interest was best suited, by independence, upbringing and the responsibilities of trusteeship, to combine private with public good and so to preserve liberty. When, later, aristocracy itself seemed under threat from Jacobinism, he wrote: 'The strong struggle in every individual to preserve possession of what he has found to belong to him and to distinguish him, is one of the securities against injustice and despotism implanted in our nature.'[17] Within the British constitution, however, party could cut across the exclusive ties of social groupings and cliques. It was grounded in the great land-owning interest, but its non-sectional aims and flexible social base could provide opportunities for rising talent to perform its service to the state. This in itself was a great benefit to government, for, as Burke wrote in his *Reflections*, 'there is no qualification for government, but virtue and wisdom, actual or presumptive'.[18] In his embittered last year he made the same point rather differently in a letter to his friend Thomas Hussey. Here he spoke of a Jacobinism more dangerous than that 'which is speculative in its origin, and which arises from wantonness and fullness of bread': it was the Jacobinism 'which arises from penury and irritation, from scorned loyalty, and rejected allegiance'.[19]

Party also appealed to Burke because it combined principles with political action. He believed that a party should be a moral body, but one which existed only in particular circumstances and for particular goals. By combining philosophy with action it nurtured that 'first of all virtues', prudence,[20] and embodied Cicero's great dictum in his work *On Duty*: 'the whole glory of virtue is in activity'.[21] This was Burke's element: the philosopher in action, striving to reconcile those potentially conflicting elements, principles and circumstances, by means of party.

The troubles in the American colonies provided the first test for this virtuous mechanism. Was the Rockingham party, within which Burke soon acquired considerable influence, to stress the principles that bound it, and which it saw as threatened by British policy in the American colonies, or to stress the need for a pragmatic approach within the practical limitations of British rule there? Burke certainly declared himself persuaded by the crisis 'that

16 *Works*, I, 375. Compare Burke's words in the House of Commons in 1791, *Parliamentary History*, XXIX, 421.
17 *Reflections*, 245.
18 Ibid., 139.
19 Burke to the Rev. Thomas Hussey, *post* 9 December 1796. *Correspondence*, IX, 162.
20 *Reflections*, 153.
21 Cicero, *De Officiis* (Loeb Classical Library), p. 21.

government was a practical thing'.[22] Policies of successive administrations, such as the Stamp Act, Townshend Duties or Tea Act, were attacked by the Rockinghamites for failing to take account of the circumstances existing in America at the time of the dispute over taxation and imperial policy. In 1766, Burke asserted that the rule of the imperial constitution should be 'taken from its own circumstances and its local aptitudes', not based on theoretical imperial rights, and he praised the year-long Rockingham administration of 1765–66 for its treatment of 'the passions and animosities of the colonies' over trading interests, which were allayed and composed 'by judicious and lenient measures'.[23] Over the next decade his position did not change. In 1772, on a different parliamentary matter, he reminded John Cruger, the Speaker of the General Assembly of the Province of New York (for which Burke was the London agent at the time) that 'everything in political conduct depends upon occasions and opportunities',[24] and five years later he mused, of the growing unrest in America, that, 'instead of troubling our understandings with specula-tions concerning the unity of empire ... it was our duty ... to conform our government to the character and circumstances of the several people who composed this mighty and strangely diversified mass'.[25]

And yet, at the same time as advocating the politics of circumstance, Burke's American writings were filled with the language of principles. The Rockingham ministry of 1765–66 itself passed a Declaratory Act which had as its purpose the reassertion of full British sovereignty over the colonies, and Burke re-ferred in his speech in support of this measure to 'the principles of the British constitution', that could make particular distinctions between America and Britain 'vanish into air'. These were the 'principles of freedom', upon which an empire should be governed. In 1774, he begged the House to 'revert to your old principles', and the next year his plan for conciliation with the colonies was constructed upon his assertion that America was 'devoted to liberty ... on English principles'.[26] It became clear in 1790, on the publication of his *Reflections*, that even his closest political friends had been convinced, wrongly, that his sympathy with the colonists had been grounded, like their own, on abstract principles of liberty.

In 1782, the Rockingham party had its second, brief spell in power, during which Burke was Paymaster-General. The administration was brought to an end by the death of Rockingham in July of that year. From that time, and perhaps earlier, Burke showed himself to be disillusioned with party as a

22 *Works*, II, 29.
23 *Writings and Speeches*, II, 46, 55–56.
24 Burke to J. Cruger, 30 June 1772. *Correspondence*, II, 309.
25 *Works*, II, 28–29.
26 *Writings and Speeches*, II, 46 and *Works*, I, 432, 464.

means of restoring virtue to public life. With the dismissal of the Fox–North Coalition at the end of 1783, on the defeat of Fox's East India Bill, he became increasingly isolated, and his prudence, certainly, deserted him. However, he remained loyal to the principles that had bound him to his party, and, if he had been unable to secure the supremacy of those principles, he could now, at least, fight to avoid their being overwhelmed by the murky alliance of political expediency and corruption.

In this frame of mind Burke began to concentrate on an exhausting campaign against misrule in India, which had been agitating him increasingly since his appointment to a select committee on Indian affairs in 1781. The campaign culminated in the impeachment, for 'high crimes and misdemeanours',[27] of Warren Hastings, the Governor-General of Bengal, whom Burke, as the chief prosecutor, believed had presided over a corrupt and arbitrary government on behalf of the East India Company. This clear and passionately held brief offered a prospect for Burke's contemporaries to clarify the apparent ambiguity in his thought between principles and circumstances.

His charges against Hastings were of a similar nature to those which he had levelled against British policy in America, although he recognised a wide difference of degree. British rule in India, he argued, had become little better than despotism, where the interests and goals of the governors were in direct conflict with those of the governed, and where a policy of exploitation and extortion broke the social and political bonds of that community. Prudence was no quality of the Hastings régime, as he explained in his speech in support of Fox's East India Bill: 'All this vast mass, composed of so many orders and classes of men, is again infinitely diversified by manners, by religion, by hereditary employment, through all their possible combinations. This renders the handling of India a matter in a high degree critical and delicate. But oh! it has been handled rudely indeed.'[28] Burke pointed out that Indian communities could not be regulated according to principles appropriate to the circumstances of English villages and estates, but he feared that even reformers of the government of India had forgotten this basic rule of prudence.

However, Burke's plan of prosecution could only work – before a British court on behalf of Indian subjects – if he could elevate the issue above the distinguishing circumstances of widely different continents. Hastings' crimes had to be ones against humanity, not Indians, or Hindus, and so the laws invoked had to rest on principles that were universal: 'The sun in his beneficent progress round the world does not behold a more glorious sight than that of men, separated from a remote people by the material bounds and barriers of nature, united by the bond of a social and moral community, all the

27 *Parliamentary History*, XXV, 1394.
28 *Works*, II, 182–83.

Commons of England resenting as their own, the indignities and cruelties
that are offered to all the people of India.'[29] For Burke, the process of impeachment, which reached the Lords in 1788, had become the means whereby
the constitution of the empire could rescue a sense of those principles which
it had been the purpose of party to promote. It is not surprising, then, to see
the *novus homo* take on, again, the mantle of Cicero, who had led the impeachment of Verres, the corrupt governor of Sicily, in 70 BC.

In this light it might appear, ironically, that Hastings had broken the
bonds of the moral community by fitting his power too closely to the circumstances he had found in India: 'Mr Hastings ... says: I had an arbitrary
power to exercise; I exercised it. Slaves I found the people; slaves they are.
They are so by their constitution; and if they are, I did not make it for them.
I was unfortunately bound to exercise this arbitrary power, and accordingly
I did exercise it. It was disagreeable to me, but I did exercise it, and no other
power can be exercised in that country.'[30] Burke's contrary belief that, 'the
laws of morality are the same everywhere', echoes his words two years earlier,
in his speech on the Rohilla War: 'It was a tenet in politics which he ever
had, and ever would hold, that all British governors were obliged to act by law.
In India to be sure it could not be expected that they could practise Magna
Charta. But there they had the law of nature and nations, the great and fundamental axioms on which every form of society was built.'[31] A British governor
should 'govern upon British *principles*, not by British *forms*';[32] but even
Burke's parodies of Hastings' position failed to clarify to the full satisfaction
of his audience the distinction he was trying to make.

Burke's thought on empire was very much more than an *ad hoc* extension
of domestic political conflicts. Certainly these principles seem to form a constant theme running back to his writings on the Irish issue which date from
before his entry into Parliament. In his *Tracts Relative to the Laws against
Popery in Ireland* ('completed' by 1765 but unpublished in his lifetime), Burke
described the damage that laws restricting the freedom of the Catholic majority
were having on the prosperity of the country and explained that 'a law against
the majority of the people is in substance a law against the people itself'. This
was so, he continued, because such laws infringed 'a superior law, which it
is not in the power of any community, or of the whole race of man, to alter
– I mean the will of Him who gave us our nature, and in giving impressed
an invariable law upon it'.[33] Any principles enshrined in that superior law

29 *Writings and Speeches*, VI, 457–58.
30 Ibid., 346–47.
31 Ibid., 346, 109.
32 Ibid., 345 (my italics).
33 *Works*, VI, 20, 21.

bound imperial government as surely as they bound individuals in their ordinary, private relations. It was, indeed, a shared belief in those principles that
secured the empire, with ties as 'light as air [and] as strong as links of iron'.[34]

The French Revolution of 1789 broke into the impeachment proceedings
and here, too, Burke concentrated first on the danger of implementing political programmes in defiance of circumstances. This applied both to the support offered to the French revolutionaries by British radicals and Whigs and
to his attack on what he saw as the 'false principles' of the revolutionaries: 'I
cannot stand forward, and give praise or blame to any thing which relates to
human actions, and human concerns, on a simple view of the object, as it stands
stripped of every relation, in all the nakedness and solitude of metaphysical
abstraction.'[35] Whereas he had fought to uphold liberty in America and India,
for the French he spoke contemptuously of their *liberté* as poised perilously
upon 'abstract principles' and 'pretended rights'. Real liberty, he had written
at the time of the American Revolution, 'inheres in some sensible object' – that
is, it is a principle only to be enjoyed when tempered by circumstance. In its
abstract purity it is a curse; it must be 'limited in order to be possessed'.[36] Now,
in the *Reflections*, the point is sharply made by analogy: 'Is it because liberty
in the abstract may be classed amongst the blessings of mankind, that I am
seriously to felicitate a madman, who has escaped from the protecting restraint
and wholesome darkness of his cell, on his restoration to the enjoyment of
light and liberty?'[37]

But Burke also identified the French Revolution's false principles in order
to contrast them with true ones, and his anti-revolutionary writing refers ever
more frequently to the latter, from 'sacred principles of property' to the 'first
principles of law and natural justice'. As the Jacobin threat spread, the stress
he placed on these principles became stronger because they appeared in danger not merely of being ignored but of being totally subverted. The Jacobin
menace heralded, for Burke, an apocalyptic battle between true and false principles. In these circumstances, practical and prudential considerations meant less
and less to him. From 1791 he began to agitate for the invasion of France on
behalf of principles of international law and, it seemed, in defence of a system
that had outlived its purpose. Consequently, as Burke lay dying at Beaconsfield,
with the Jacobin forces poised to invade his homeland, the resolution of principles and circumstances seemed as far away as ever.

It is possible to conclude from some of his own writings that Burke was not
unaware of the continuing ambiguity of his position. In 1791 he published

34 *Works*, I, 508.
35 *Reflections*, 89–90.
36 *Works*, I, 464 and II, 30.
37 *Reflections*, 90.

A Letter to a Member of the National Assembly to clarify a number of points he had made in the *Reflections*. Here, his repeated and sincere refusal to offer specific advice on political developments in France – 'I must see with my own eyes, I must, in a manner, touch with my own hands, not only the fixed, but the momentary circumstances, before I could venture to suggest any political project whatsoever'[38] – was contained within some of the most confident, rich comments on human nature, learnt presumably in Britain and Ireland and yet deployed to pull apart the aspirations of the French revolutionaries.

If it is true that Burke was ultimately unable to reconcile these apparently conflicting stresses, it is hard to see what value his writings have for anyone but the historian of eighteenth-century British politics, and difficult to refute the argument that exploring his legacy is a futile and even disingenuous exercise. This has, indeed, been a favoured response of a number of political theorists and commentators in recent years.[39]

A modification of this bleak conclusion has been to circumvent the problem by firmly subordinating one side of the perceived conflict to the other. Thus, to some, Burke was a supreme pragmatist – more or less sincere – who either used principles as a movable rhetorical device for pursuing particular short-term political aims, or accumulated and modified principles in a committed but confused fashion. Alternatively, his thought presents us with a set of consistent principles propounded through circumstances that were cleverly or unintentionally shaped to fit the point: this was a process that took him further away from the reality of politics and frustrated his record of political achievement, but made him a man for all time.

Neither approach really leads to a richer appreciation of Burke's legacy. In the first case, his thought collapses into a 'pick and mix' arrangement for literary pragmatists. It becomes a resource for sound-bites. In the second, Burke's principles will be seized upon by those who are inclined to believe them already, but they will be insufficiently rooted in neutral ground to persuade the open-minded. They might strengthen conviction, but they will never convince. Both are popular approaches, but each supposes that a resolution of the problem of circumstances and principles is not possible, at least in the terms that Burke bequeathed. There are, however, two points that they overlook, which Burke might have deployed in his own defence and which, taken together, offer a more optimistic and productive approach to his thought.

One of these was a practical defence, which he laid out in his *Appeal from the New to the Old Whigs*. This tract was published in 1791, as a direct response

---

38 *Works*, II, 549.
39 There is an invaluable survey of literature on Burke in *Edmund Burke. A Bibliography of Secondary Studies* to 1982, eds. Clara I. Gandy and Peter J. Stanlis (New York, 1983). See also Conor Cruise O'Brien, *The Great Melody* (London, 1992), pp. xxxi–lxxv.

to the charges of his former Whig allies that his views on liberty in America and France were inconsistent. He protested that changing circumstances required different stresses in argument to counter different threats, and that there had once been a time when people had been able to 'distinguish between a difference in conduct under a variation of circumstances, and an inconsistency in principle'.[40] *This* is the reason why we need to remember that all of Burke's political writings after 1759 were written in response to specific political issues, not so that we can prove his inconsistency by forced comparisons of language.

The other defence is an intellectual one. It could be argued that the distinction between principles and circumstances has often been drawn too sharply by his critics. Burke, after all, clearly believed that principles vary in degree according to different departments of activity, with some naturally more or less rigid in their application than others – principles of charity, principles of rhetoric, commercial principles, or principles of political action broadly appropriate to common and anticipated circumstances. Most are conditional by their nature, being constructs either of abstract theory or of past experience, and the rôle of the statesman, as we have seen, is to act prudently in marrying these principles with the new realities of existing circumstances. But this art does not, in itself, make the statesman *merely* a pragmatist in Burke's eyes: there are two further points to consider.

First, Burke did hold to a belief in certain 'first principles', implanted in our nature by God, and expressed in our 'untaught feelings'.[41] These principles, he believed, are the basis of those contingent principles of action by which we regulate our social and political life. They do not change. They are Burke's articles of faith, and we shall not resolve any riddle in his life unless we accept unequivocally his sentiment, as expressed in the *Reflections*, that 'man is by his constitution a religious animal'.[42] This was a proposition he had made clear in his early thoughts on 'Religion'[43] and the *Tracts Relative to the Laws against Popery in Ireland*, and he made it clear again at the end of his life, when he focused on the atheistic nature of Jacobinism as the fundamental threat to society. It is precisely when Burke's writings are taken as a whole, as Hazlitt recommended, that this underlying consistency appears, and it is one that is based, inescapably, on the belief that there is a common law of morality that binds all human beings.

Second, these 'first principles', like the true rights of men, are 'incapable of definition, but not impossible to be discerned'.[44] Such principles are transmit-

---

40 *Works*, III, 27.
41 *Reflections*, 183.
42 Ibid., 187.
43 See Ian Harris (ed.), *Burke: Pre-Revolutionary Writings* (Cambridge, 1993), pp. 78–87.
44 *Reflections*, 153.

ted through the circumstances of history, but they are not created by history. We certainly do not learn them from the schoolbook or decide upon them in the debating chamber, but neither are they the accumulated wisdom of the much vaunted University of Life: 'My principles enable me to form my judgment upon men and actions in history,' Burke once explained, 'just as they do in current life; and are not formed out of events and characters, either present or past.' In other words, 'history is a preceptor of prudence, not of principles'.[45] We do, indeed, learn about principles by observing circumstances, but this is because those circumstances are working upon our 'untaught feelings'.

Early in his career Burke wrote – as so often, in self-justification – 'The principles of true politics are those of morality enlarged, and I neither now do or ever will admit of any other.'[46] There is no evidence to show that Burke ever went back on his word. They were the principles that Burke attempted to defend against Jacobinism; they were the law before which he tried to bring Hastings to justice; they were the proper links of empire; they were the aim of party.

As these principles of morality were universal, but dealt with the particular circumstances of man, they were also vital guides for the *novus homo*. For the same reason they can guide us today. They have never provided aspiring politicians with plans of action, because they do not run ahead of circumstances, and for this reason they are ill-suited to promoting the career of any man who holds to them. But they have alerted people to injustice, and made them keen in sensing danger to their liberties and well-being, and sometimes they have vested their defenders with a prophetic and timeless wisdom that has benefited future generations.

45 Burke to William Markham, *post* 9 November 1771, *Correspondence*, II, 282. This part of the manuscript is in William Burke's hand. See ibid., 252.
46 *Correspondence*, II, 282.

Edmund Burke and British Views of the American Revolution: A Conflict over Rights of Sovereignty

Peter J. Stanlis

From 1763 to 1783, British views of the American Revolution varied widely. There was no monolithic conviction among Tories, Whigs or radical eighteenth-century Commonwealthmen, nor among various segments of the British population at large. The central political principles at issue between Britain and her American colonies were perceived by only a few men, and even when such men agreed in basic political theory, and held the same conception of empire, they differed in regard to practical policy. Undoubtedly, the broad range of British views of the American Revolution reflected the usual differences men have about complex social, political, religious and economic problems. But three significant viewpoints can be identified in what was probably the fundamental conflict over the nature of government between Britain and America – the question of British rights of sovereignty. These differences were manifested in practical politics in conflicts over such matters as taxation and representation, revenue and regulation, freedom and subordination.

Perhaps no one understood the central issue of legal and political sovereignty more clearly than Francis Bernard, royal governor of Massachusetts Bay from 1760 to 1769. In a letter from Boston, on 23 November 1765, he wrote:

> The question [is] whether America shall or shall not be subject to the legislature of Great Britain ... All the political evils in America rise from the want of ascertaining the relation between Great Britain and the American colonies. Hence it is, that ideas of that relation are formed in Britain and America so very repugnant and contradictory to each other. In Britain the American governments are considered as corporations empowered to make bye-laws, existing only during the pleasure of Parliament, who hath never yet done anything to confirm their establishments, and hath at any time a power to dissolve them. In America they claim ... to be perfect states, no otherwise dependent upon Great Britain than by having the same King, which, having complete legislatures within themselves, are no way subject to that of Great Britain,

which in such instances as it has heretofore exercised a legislative power over them, has usurped it. In a difference so very wide, who shall determine? The Parliament of Great Britain? No, say the Americans ... that would be to make them judges in their own cause. Who then? The King? He is bound by charters, or constitutions equal to charters, and cannot declare against his own grants. So ... there is no superior tribunal to determine upon the rights and principles of the American colonies.[1]

Historically, the 'superior tribunal' which determined the rights of sovereignty over America was the War of Independence.

The issue of sovereign rights was precipitated by the Stamp Act, which the Grenville ministry passed in 1765, and by the Townshend Act of 1767, which followed its repeal. The Americans resisted both these acts and so forced a resolution of the question of sovereignty. British responses to American resistance assumed three possible courses of action: to grant the colonies outright independence; to compel colonial obedience to Parliament through force; or to conciliate the colonies by granting each colonial legislative assembly considerable legal sovereignty over its internal affairs, including the right of taxation, while maintaining British imperial sovereignty in external affairs.

I. BRITISH DECLARATIONS IN FAVOUR OF AMERICAN INDEPENDENCE

During 1774–75, Josiah Tucker, Dean of Gloucester, preached in favour of granting the American colonies immediate independence from Britain. After hostilities began, Tucker argued in a series of pamphlets that it was impossible for Britain to conquer her colonies, that a protracted civil war would be an economic disaster for the mother country, and that, since the Americans refused to submit to the jurisdiction of Parliament, it was best 'to separate totally from the colonies'. Tucker, a moderate Tory and severe critic of Locke's theory of a revocable social contract, in effect applied that thinker's theory by asserting that it was in Britain's economic self-interest to break her historical, contractual relationship with America. Later, in *Four Letters on Important National Subjects* (1783), Tucker expressed satisfaction that America was independent and lamented that Britain had not 'totally cast them off' without war, as it would have 'saved both them and us ... blood and treasure'. But at the time, Tucker's views were dismissed by Samuel Johnson as a 'wild proposal' and by Edmund Burke as 'childish'.

---

1   Francis Bernard, *Select Letters on the Trade and Government of America* (London, 1774), pp. 31–32.

Other Britons privately shared Tucker's views. Horace Walpole, an ardent Whig, wrote to Horace Mann in 1770: 'The tocsin seems to be sounded in America. That continent ... is growing too mighty to be kept in subjection to half a dozen exhausted nations in Europe.'[2] David Hume, a Tory, expressed a similar view to William Strahan in 1771: 'Our union with America ... in the nature of things, cannot long subsist.' In October 1775, Hume upstaged Jefferson with his own declaration of independence: 'Let us, therefore, lay aside all anger, shake hands, and part friends. Or if we retain any anger, let it only be against ourselves for our past folly; and against that wicked madman, Pitt, who has reduced us to our present condition.'[3] On 19 June 1775, James Boswell recorded a conversation with Hume: 'He said, It was all over in America. We *could* not subdue the colonists ... He said we may do very well without America, and he was for withdrawing our troops altogether.'[4] Hume's close friend Adam Smith, an independent Whig, advanced, in his *Wealth of Nations* (1776), economic, political and psychological reasons why the Americans should be independent in all internal affairs, including the right of taxation, with or without an imperial union with Britain.[5] Hume and Smith may have expressed the views of Francis Hutcheson, Professor of Moral Philosophy at Glasgow from 1730 to 1746, who advanced a theory that it was 'unnatural' for self-sufficient colonies to remain in subjection to a mother country, and unwise, for economic and humanitarian reasons, for nations to maintain 'grand unwieldy empires'. In his *System of Moral Philosophy* (1755), Hutcheson utilised the 'natural rights' theories of the classical republican Robert Molesworth, and argued that if a mother country passes 'oppressive laws ... with respect to ... colonies so increased in numbers and strength that they are sufficient by themselves ... they are not bound to continue in their subjection'.[6]

Arguments for American independence based upon metaphysical 'natural rights' were advanced by a heterogeneous group of Calvinist nonconformists, political revolutionaries, ideological radicals and Commonwealthmen, such as Richard Price, Joseph Priestley, 'Junius', John Cartwright, Brand Hollis, Tom Paine, Mary Wollstonecraft and Catherine Macaulay. Their revolutionary theories derived from Milton, Algernon Sidney, Molesworth, and especially

2 *The Letters of Horace Walpole*, ed. Helena Paget Toynbee (Oxford, 1903), vol. VIII, p. 449. Walpole's pro-American views are well described by J.C. Reily, 'Horace Walpole, Friend of American Liberty', in *Studies in Burke and His Time*, XVI, no. 1 (1974), pp. 5–21.
3 *Letters of David Hume*, ed. John Y. Greig (Oxford, 1946), vol. II, pp. 237 and 300–01.
4 *The Letters of James Boswell*, ed. Chauncey Brewster Tinker (Oxford, 1924), vol. I, p. 233.
5 See Davis Stevens, 'Adam Smith and the Colonial Disturbances', in (ed.) A.S. Skinner and T. Wilson, *Essays on Adam Smith* (Oxford, 1975), pp. 202–17.
6 Francis Hutcheson, *System of Moral Philosophy* (1755), vol. II, bk. II, p. 308.

John Locke, and were championed by such politicians as Wilkes, Shelburne and Pitt. Typical of this group was John Cartwright (1740–1824), who, in a series of letters in the London *Public Advertiser* in the spring of 1774, rejected the recognition by both Burke and Tucker that Britain enjoyed prescriptive legal sovereignty over America:

> Parliament hath not the rights of sovereignty over his majesty's American subjects. We have no need of profound learning ... nor even of the history of the respective provinces and their different origins; neither do we want copies of grants, charters, or acts of parliament, in order to judge of the question before us ... Let us then hear no more of a right in our present-constituted parliament to govern the Americans, as being derived from any former exercise of this sovereignty, from the original dependency and protection of the emigrants and infant colonies, or from the tenour of grants and charters! The respective governments in America are no longer dependent colonies; they are independent nations.

On a simple appeal to inherent and unalienable abstract rights held to be original in every one, and with complete indifference to historical origins and chartered legal rights of British sovereignty, twenty-seven months before Jefferson's celebrated document was revised and adopted by the Continental Congress, Cartwright declared the American colonies independent. As Bernard Bailyn has shown in *The Ideological Origins of the American Revolution* (1967), in America, between 1750 and 1776, Cartwright's type of ideological argument was expressed in over four hundred pamphlets.

Clearly, even before hostilities began in 1775, a variety of British Tories, Whigs and radical Commonwealthmen, for reasons that were very different and even contradictory, favoured independence for America. But their views were either privately held or dismissed as impractical by the dominant powers in the British government and by the public. As the war continued, however, and especially after Burgoyne's defeat at Saratoga late in 1777, many who had favoured a policy of force or of conciliation became advocates of immediate American independence.

II. PUBLIC OPINION, KING AND MINISTRY:
A POLICY OF FORCE

During the 1770s, public opinion, King George III and a substantial majority in Parliament backing the North ministry, remained adamantly opposed to independence for the colonies. After important concessions failed to satisfy the Americans, they favoured the use of military force to maintain British sovereignty over the colonies. In February 1775, after North's proposal for transferring the exercise of the right to tax to the colonial assemblies had been rejected, King George and his ministry believed the Americans left Britain no choice but to use force. On 18 February 1775, Horace Walpole, a severe critic of the North ministry, wrote to William Mason that a great majority in both Houses favoured war, and that they believed the colonies would submit in three months. He told friends in France that the war was 'fashionable' in England. In September 1775, the *Gentleman's Magazine* noted that 'no plan of reconciliation will ever be formed that will content the present ministry and the present Continental Congress'. In December, the same publication reported: 'It is now the declared design of Government to employ the whole national force ... to compel them to acknowledge the supremacy of the British legislature.' In March 1776, it lamented the unreasonableness of the Americans, and noted that in Britain: 'The temper and spirit of the nation are so much against concessions, that if it were the intention of administration, they could not carry the question.'[7] Edward Gibbon, a staunch supporter of the North ministry, has testified that the policy of force remained popular in England until the second session of the 1781–82 Parliament:

> In the first session of the new parliament, administration stood their ground; their final overthrow was reserved for the second. The American war had once been the favourite of the country: the pride of England was irritated by the resistance of her colonies, and the executive power was driven by national clamour into the most vigorous and coercive measures. But the length of a fruitless contest, the loss of armies, the accumulation of debt and taxes, and the hostile confederacy of France, Spain, and Holland, indisposed the public to the American war, and the persons by whom it was conducted; the representatives of the people followed, at a slow distance, the changes of their opinion, and the ministers who refused to bend, were broken by the tempest.[8]

The original unanimity between public opinion, King and ministry, that a policy of force would soon defeat the American rebels, evaporated as the war continued.

The policy of force rested upon the solid, legal foundation of constitutional law as propounded in William Blackstone's *Commentaries on the Laws of England* (1765–69). Blackstone based constitutional law on 'ethics, or natural law', which gave a moral foundation for the legal and political sovereignty of

7   *Gentleman's Magazine* (1775), pp. 445, 597, and 1776, p. 136 respectively.
8   *Memoirs of the Life of Edward Gibbon*, ed. George Birkbeck Hill (London, 1900), pp. 212–13.

all established governments. He argued that 'the power and jurisdiction of parliament ... is absolute'. Ultimate power must rest somewhere, and Parliament
was the place entrusted by the English constitution for that sovereignty.
Blackstone denied that any 'state of nature', prior to the existence of organised society, provided a moral basis for judging the legal and political uses of
power in society, because 'man was formed for society', and only historically
developed societies provided the constitutional norms and means for judging
practical legal sovereignty. Blackstone specifically noted and rejected the
'rights of man' doctrines which derived from Locke's social contract theory,
because he believed that such doctrines dissolved society. They introduced
anarchy by making the very existence of government depend upon the arbitrary will of each individual, or the collective will of numbers of individuals,
rather than the corporate reason and will of many generations of men embodied in the constitution.

Practically all of the pamphlets written in defence of Parliament's sovereign rights over the American colonies rested upon assumptions similar to
Blackstone's constitutional principles of government. Soame Jenyns, in *The
Objections to the Taxation of Our American Colonies, briefly Considered* (1765),
rejected the popular thesis that taxation without representation was tyranny,
and argued that the Americans should be satisfied with 'virtual' representation. Jenyns concluded that Parliament had a perfect 'right' to tax America
as it saw fit.

By far the most powerful and profound defence of Britain's unqualified
'rights' of sovereignty over America was written by Samuel Johnson (1709–84),
in four pamphlets: *The False Alarm* (1770); *Thoughts on ... Transactions
Respecting Falkland's Islands* (1771); *The Patriot* (1774); and *Taxation No
Tyranny* (1775). Johnson believed in limited constitutional monarchy as prescribed by England's common law. In *The False Alarm* he argued against
Lockean 'natural rights', which made the popular will and rights of electors
supreme over constitutional authority and legal precedents. In his three other
pamphlets, despite his very harsh opinion of the North ministry, Johnson defended the administration's American policy against such critics as Wilkes,
'Junius', Mrs Macaulay and the Rockingham Whig opposition. Indeed, Johnson
came close to being the official spokesman for the King and the North ministry.

Johnson's political theory presupposed that government is a matter of
moral necessity for man, and not a voluntary relationship between rulers and
subjects. Government evolves through history, and is not derived from any
pre-civil 'state of nature' or original social contract. Therefore it cannot be
legally dissolved by disaffected citizens. These ideas applied to the bonds between Britain and America. Britain held undoubted dominion over her colonies
by 'prescriptive tenure'; she had 'natural and lawful authority' because the
colonies 'were settled under English protection; were constituted by an English

charter; and have been defended by English arms'.[9] These empirical facts of history and law made the American colonies constituent parts of the British empire, with Parliament and King supreme in all rights of sovereignty throughout the whole. By accepting British protection, the Americans assumed British rule. Legislative powers had indeed been granted to the colonial assemblies by Britain, but, as Johnson noted, these assemblies had 'acted so long with unquestioned authority' that they had 'forgotten whence that authority was originally derived'.[10] To Johnson, the colonies owed their political existence to their royal charters, which bound them to Parliament as the source of all legal sovereignty. Like King George III, Johnson believed the colonies had conspired to become independent before Parliament had taxed them. By denying British sovereignty, the Americans now made it necessary to subdue them. The conflict was not over money or taxes, but over legal power, and the Americans were the aggressors: 'They consider themselves as emancipated from obedience, and as being no longer the subjects of the British crown. They leave us no choice but of yielding or conquering, of resigning our dominion, or maintaining it by force.'[11] The American revolutionaries appealed to abstract slogans about 'rights' in order to justify exempting themselves from taxes under British sovereignty; but to Johnson such ideological appeals, based on a revocable social contract in a supposed state of nature, destroyed all historically developed constitutional governments and made even the existence of institutionally organised society impossible.

Johnson's social and political arguments, officially approved by the North ministry, were also popular with the British public. As Boswell noted, they were 'congenial with the sentiments of numbers at that time'. They were taken to reinforce the mercantile economic theory, held by great numbers of Englishmen, that colonies were founded and existed for the economic benefit of the mother country. Johnson's pamphlets on America provided a strong rationale for the British policy of force.

III. EDMUND BURKE'S POLICY OF CONCILIATION AND THE TRANSITION FROM COLONIAL TO FEDERAL EMPIRE

When we turn to Edmund Burke, we find that historians have generally limited their study of his speeches and writings on the conflict between Britain and her colonies to his best known works: *A Short Account of a Late Short Administration* (1766); *Observations on 'The Present State of the Nation'* (1769);

---

9 *The Works of Samuel Johnson*, ed. Arthur Murphy (London, 1850), vol. II, p. 612.
10 Ibid., p. 617.
11 Ibid., p. 626.

Thoughts on the Cause of the Present Discontents (1770); *Speech on American Taxation* (1774); *Speech on Conciliation with the Colonies* (1775); and *A Letter to the Sheriffs of Bristol* (1777). On the basis of his themes and arguments in these works, historians have concluded that his conception of legal and political sovereignty never went beyond what he called 'the constitution of the British empire'.[12] But it would be a serious error to assume that this conclusion adequately reflects his final views, since he later modified them in important respects.

For a greater understanding of Burke's final beliefs regarding the constitution of the British empire, it is necessary to study these works in conjunction with his less well-known writings on American colonial affairs: *A Bill for Composing the Present Troubles in America* (16 November 1775); *Address to the King* and *Address to the British Colonists in North America* (1776); and *A Letter to the Marquis of Rockingham* (6 January 1777). A careful reading of these somewhat obscure pieces reveals some important changes in Burke's conception of the British empire and the nature of sovereignty within it – changes that foreshadow the latter-day concept of a British commonwealth of independent nations.

The conflicts between Britain and her American colonies may well be said to have commenced on the Heights of Abraham in Quebec, when the Marquis de Montcalm surrendered French Canada to the British in September 1759. The politically keen-witted Montcalm prophesied that, with this military victory, Britain would lose her American colonies. With the conquest of Canada in the French and Indian Wars (1754–63) – the American counterpart of the European Seven Years War – the realisation of a world-wide colonial empire was given an enormous impetus in the minds of the British public and its government. Up to this time, the American colonists had necessarily looked to the mother country for protection against the Spaniards to the south and the French to the north; but with the removal of any military threat from the French, the Americans felt much less need to look to Britain for defence against external enemies, and began to feel much more self-reliant.

This process was reflected in their demands for greater legislative power for their royally chartered and popularly elected colonial assemblies. Within a decade or so, all of the colonies had acquired a considerable degree of self-government. As Burke was to note in 1774, looking back on the origins of the crisis, America had acquired by 1763 'every characteristic mark of a free people in all her internal concerns. She had the image of the British constitution. She had the substance. She was taxed by her own representatives. She chose most of her own magistrates. She paid them all. She had in effect the sole

12 Edmund Burke, *Speech on American Taxation*, in *Works*, I, 435.

disposal of her own internal government.'[13] In the light of this vital development in colonial self-rule, the practical exercise of British sovereignty over
America clearly required greater prudence and equity than ever before, and
these qualities, Burke went on to argue, were found wanting in government
policy.

For example, he pointed out that, in the very year that the Treaty of Paris
officially gave Canada to Britain and removed any military danger to the
colonies, a 'huge increase of military establishment was resolved on' by the
Grenville administration, to be financed through 'revenue to be raised in
America'.[14] Burke believed that the conflict over sovereignty began when
Parliament decided to establish a standing army in the colonies and to tax them
to pay for it and for the recent war with France. Many Americans suspected
that the standing army of 26,000 men and seventy ships of war was aimed at
their chartered liberties. They also regarded the claim of Parliament to tax
them as an attack upon their constitutional rights.[15] As the conflicts over
these issues became more and more intense, the grand design of British im-
perialism pushed the colonies towards full independence.

To Burke, 1764 was the turning point in Britain's policy towards her
American colonies, because in that year, for the first time, Parliament was not
content to control America through commercial regulations, but instead sought
to secure revenue through taxation. This fatal policy was briefly reversed
under the Rockingham administration from July 1765 to July 1766. During
that year the Rockingham Whigs combined the repeal of the Stamp Act,
which gave the colonies particular freedom from taxation by Parliament, with
passage of the Declaratory Act, which affirmed that Parliament had 'full
power and authority ... to bind the colonies ... in all cases whatsoever'. Burke
noted that the Stamp Act was repealed 'on principles, not of constitutional
right, but on those of expediency, of equity, of lenity'. The Declaratory Act
was passed 'not from any opinion they entertained of its future use in regular
taxation', but because 'the general reasonings which were employed against

13   Ibid., 404.
14   Ibid., 405–6.
15   Later, in his speech in support of a motion to repeal the tax on tea, Burke observed
     in retrospect that 'at the close of the last war large additions were made unnecessarily
     to the English army'. See *Burke's Speeches on American Taxation, on Conciliation with
     America and Letter to the Sheriffs of Bristol*, ed. F.G. Selby (London, 1956), Intro-
     duction, p. xxxi. Also, in his *Speech Introducing a Motion for an Enquiry into the
     Causes of the Late Disorders in America* (9 May 1770), he noted that 'the Stamp Act
     was to go to the pay of the army; but this struck at the root of their assemblies'. He
     added: 'They deny your right to send out an army to them. They have resolved that
     the establishment of a standing army is an invasion of the rights of the people.' See
     Edmund Burke on the American Revolution, ed. Elliott R. Barkan (New York, 1966),
     pp. 11 and 14.

that power went directly to our whole legislative right; and one part of it could not be yielded to such arguments, without a virtual surrender of all the rest'.[16] Burke recognised that legal sovereignty could not be divided. But in 1769, when he wrote these words, he was prepared to sacrifice Britain's 'right' of taxation in order to retain her legal sovereignty over America.

Two important themes run through all of Burke's writings and speeches on the conflicts between Britain and her American colonies: the violation of historical experience, and the lack of moral prudence in the uses of political power by Parliament. In place of these two basic requirements for peace and equity, the King's ministers, Grenville and North, engaged in *a priori*, ideological speculations about their abstract 'right' to tax the colonies. In sharp contrast, Burke believed that the royal charters of each colony, the Navigation Acts of 1651, 1660, and 1663, and the Declaratory Act of 1766, were the 'corner-stone of the policy of this country with regard to its colonies'.[17] Until hostilities took a military turn, he paid little attention to the colonial charters. Instead, he reiterated the theme in the work he had published with his kinsman William Burke, *An Account of the European Settlements in America* (1757), and stressed the need to maintain the long-established mercantile economic system by which Britain regulated the trade and commerce of the colonies. But even in this early work, he had warned against excessive control of the colonies and, although he admitted that Britain derived the greater advantage under mercantilism, he stated that the colonies also benefited from that economic arrangement. Until the early 1770s he argued that Parliament should consult and follow past experience – the system that had prevailed up to 1764. In addition to historical experience, moral prudence taught that governors should rule in accordance with the temper and beliefs of the governed, with full regard to circumstances, and not by abstract theories of government or the mere arbitrary will and reason of those in power.

When the contrary policy was resumed, after the fall of Rockingham's government, under the Chatham and North administrations, it led to the series of conflicts which culminated in war and the independence of the colonies. It is noteworthy that Burke never referred to these events as 'the American Revolution', but only as 'the American war'. The conflict was not over rival theories of government, such as democracy and monarchy; rather, it was a *civil war* within the British empire, brought on initially by the political imprudence of Parliament. He regarded the colonies as wholly on the defensive in this war, and he did not believe that their original intention was to secure independence from Britain. On 19 April 1769, he stated in Parliament that

16 *Works*, I, 279.
17 Ibid., 401.

irrational fears, backed by sincere convictions on both sides of the Atlantic, were creating and accelerating a mutual distrust between Britain and her colonies that had led to a disastrous psychological impasse: 'The Americans have made a discovery, or think they have made one, that we mean to oppress them; we have made a discovery, or think we have made one, that they intend to rise in rebellion. Our severity has increased their ill behaviour. We know not how to advance; they know not how to retreat ... Some party must give way.'[18]

Although Burke refused to discuss any theory of sovereignty in the abstract, in his early response to colonial resistance he clearly accepted the legitimacy of Parliament's sovereignty over the colonies. Even in his *Speech on American Taxation*, he argued that Parliament 'as from the throne of Heaven ... superintends all the several inferior legislatures, and guides and controls them all, without annihilating any. As all these provincial legislatures are only co-ordinate to each other, they ought all to be subordinate to her.' But he then added a significant principle: 'She is never to intrude into the place of the others, whilst they are equal to the common ends of their institution.'[19] This added principle clearly differentiated between the 'idea of the constitution of the British empire, as distinguished from the constitution of Britain'.[20] In short, while Burke continued to recognise the general sovereignty of Parliament, at the same time he came to hold that it should 'never ... intrude' into the sovereignty of the chartered rights of colonial legislatures as long as they fulfilled 'the common ends of their institution' in domestic affairs. The function of Britain as the superior central government in its empire was to supervise, not to supersede, colonial governments.

Burke was convinced that the Grenville and North policies had encouraged conflict because they had been based not on historical experience, nor on a strict regard for the character, temper and beliefs of the Americans, nor on the infinitely complex circumstances of their historical development, but on 'mere abstract principles of government'. He believed that this form of ideology was a kind of political and metaphysical insanity; it applied speculative abstract concepts to practical social and political affairs. In his *Speech on American Taxation*, he attacked the ministry's appeal to an abstract 'right' of sovereignty in order to justify their 'right' to tax the colonies as fatal in its practical consequences:

18 *Sir Henry Cavendish's Debates of the House of Commons*, ed. John Wright (London, 1841–43), vol. I, 398–99. See also *Writings and Speeches*, II, 231–32.
19 *Works*, I, 434.
20 Ibid., 435.

Leave America, if she has taxable matter in her, to tax herself. I am not here going into the distinctions of rights, nor attempting to mark their boundaries ... Do not burden them by taxes; you were not used to do so from the beginning. Let this be your reason for not taxing. These are the arguments of states and kingdoms. Leave the rest to the schools; for there only they may be discussed with safety. But if, intemperately, unwisely, fatally, you sophisticate and poison the very source of government, by urging subtle deductions and consequences odious to those you govern, from the unlimited and illimitable nature of supreme sovereignty, you will teach them by these means to call that sovereignty itself in question ... If that sovereignty and their freedom cannot be reconciled, which will they take? They will cast your sovereignty in your face. Nobody will be argued into slavery.[21]

In refusing out of moral prudence to enforce sovereignty as an abstract absolute 'right' without regard to the empirical circumstances in America, or to the political consequences of ideological theory, Burke was following a precept laid down by his party chief, the Marquis of Rockingham: 'Such a right was irrelevant unless the Americans chose to acknowledge it.'[22] Burke saw that the attempt by the ministry to enforce its 'rights' of sovereignty in America would result in the loss of the colonies.

By 1775, Burke realised that the problem of harmonising British sovereignty and American freedom was at a critical stage. He noted later in his *Letter to the Sheriffs of Bristol*: 'I am ... deeply sensible of the difficulty of reconciling the strong presiding power, that is so useful towards the conservation of a vast, disconnected, infinitely diversified empire, with that liberty and safety of the provinces, which they must enjoy.'[23] On 16 November 1775, in his proposed *Bill for Composing the Present Troubles in America*, Burke told the House that Britain should officially give up her rights of sovereignty in taxation to the colonial assemblies, thus granting the Americans full constitutional rights in representation, taxation and all of their domestic affairs. He observed that 'sovereignty was not in its nature an abstract idea of unity, but was capable of great complexity and infinite modifications'. Thus Burke proposed a giant step towards granting American nationhood, freedom without independence, and came close to the nineteenth-century concept of a British commonwealth of free nations. Parliament rejected his Bill. Yet within two years, after Britain's defeat at Saratoga, North's administration offered the

21   Ibid., 432–33.
22   Rockingham to William Dowdeswell, 13 September 1774, in Wentworth Woodhouse MSSR–1504, Rockingham Papers, Sheffield Public Library.
23   *Works*, II, 31.

Americans substantially the same proposal, only to have it rejected. By the end of 1775, and irrevocably after the Declaration of Independence, Burke was convinced that North's insistence upon 'unconditional submission' guaranteed American independence, which he himself preferred to conquest by force.

It follows that, after military conflict had begun between the colonies and Britain, Burke felt compelled to change his original position regarding sovereignty within the empire. The first explicit sign of his transition from empire to federalism occurs in the provisions of *A Bill for Composing the Present Troubles in America*, in November 1775. This Bill and his speech of about three and a half hours in support of his motion on how to conciliate America have been largely ignored or minimised by historians, and even by Burke scholars. Yet, together with his *Address to the King* and his *Address to the British Colonists in North America* (1777), it sets forth the major change in his conception of sovereignty within the empire.

Burke first laid it down as a principle that 'sovereignty was ... capable of great complexity and infinite modification, according to the temper of those who are to be governed and to the circumstances of things: which being infinitely diversified, government ought to be adapted to them and to conform itself to the nature of things, and not to endeavour to force them'.[24] In essence this is Burke's principle of moral prudence, the first of political virtues, applied to sovereignty. It stands in total contrast to King George's declaration on 18 November 1774, that 'blows must decide whether they are to be subject to this country or independent'. Neither the King nor North's majority in Parliament could conceive of any modification in sovereignty as an alternative to unconditional submission to Britain or independence for America. This narrow and rigid conviction illustrated what Burke meant by his aphorism that 'magnanimity in politics is not seldom the truest wisdom; and a great empire and little minds go ill together'.[25] Conciliation through moral prudence and a change in sovereignty within the empire meant that Britain should grant total self-rule to the colonial assemblies and limit its sovereignty to foreign affairs. Burke's proposal was a giant step towards granting the Americans nationhood within a federated British empire that retained this limited authority. It provided constitutional freedom but not legal independence, and it had the basic rudiments of the concept of a commonwealth of free nations united through the Crown to Britain.

A more refined measure of Burke's vital change in his conception of sovereignty is apparent in the companion pieces addressed to the King and the

24 Edmund Burke: *On Conciliation with the Colonies and Other Papers on the American Revolution*, ed. Peter J. Stanlis (Lunenburg, 1975), p. 165.
25 *Works*, I, 509. The first half of Burke's aphorism is carved on the pedestal of his statue in Washington, D.C.

American colonists. In both works, Burke reviewed the 'misconduct of government' which resulted in the alienation of America, and noted the 'repeated refusals to hear or to conciliate' colonial complaints, followed by the British use of force. Parliament constantly oscillated between enforcement and concessions. In both addresses, he emphasised 'the vital principles of the British constitution' contained in the colonial charters, and their violation by statutes of Parliament, often without cause or provocation. In the *Address to the King*, he observed that 'the cause of inflaming discontent into disobedience, and resistance into revolt' was centred in 'the subversion of solemn fundamental charters, on a suggestion of abuse, without citation, evidence, or hearing'.[26] He referred to the policy of taxing the colonies for revenue as 'an attempt made to dispose of the property of a whole people without their consent'.[27] This violated the provisions in the colonial charters, and resulted in rebellion.

In his *Address to the British Colonists in North America*, Burke again lamented 'the invasion of your charters'. Quite distinct from his position early in the conflict with the colonies, he now argued that the constitutionally established chartered rights of each colony took legal precedence over parliamentary statutes: 'Because the charters comprehend the essential forms by which you enjoy your liberties, we regard them as most sacred, and by no means to be taken away or altered without process, without examination, and without hearing, as they have lately been.'[28] In this work, Burke treated the colonial charters as the constitutional foundation for colonial liberties and rights. In essence, this is his case against the 'arbitrary' and 'unconstitutional' acts of Parliament in American colonial affairs.

In retrospect, as the troubles in America mounted, Burke's reiterated appeals to past historical experience and to moral prudence on the part of Parliament became increasingly inadequate to quiet the fears and resistance of the colonies. A new arrangement in legal and political sovereignty was urgently required. Between 1774 and early 1778 Burke gradually developed a plan for a federal type of sovereignty within the British empire. On 2 December 1777, the day before news reached London that Burgoyne had surrendered at Saratoga, he said in the Commons: 'We must and ought to treat with [the colonies] on the terms of a federal union.'[29] But by the time the North administration repealed the punitive legislation of 1774, amended the Declaratory Act, and gave up the 'right' of taxation, many colonists had declared in favour of independence. This development was confirmed when the Continental Congress rejected the

26 *Works*, V, 465.
27 Ibid., 462.
28 Ibid., 479. He added that the colonial charters 'ought by no means to be altered at all but at the desire of the greater part of the people who live under them'.
29 *Parliamentary History*, XIX, 517.

offer made by the Carlisle Commission of a greatly enlarged colonial sovereignty, and by April 1778 Burke favoured an end to the war and independence for America. After news of Cornwallis's surrender reached London three years later, and Parliament knew that America was lost, Burke bitterly and ironically reminded his colleagues in the House: 'We did all this because we had a right to do it: that was exactly the fact.'

Yet Burke never arrived at a full-fledged theory of a commonwealth incorporating independent nations that would be legally connected with Britain. The closest he came to such a concept was in his second speech on conciliation in his appeal for 'a federal union'. That appeal remained in a rudimentary form. He failed to follow up the obvious necessity to maintain the legal connection of the colonies to Britain through the monarchy. Apparently, he could not imagine that the rôle of Britain's limited constitutional monarch could be extended to an overseas empire. Moreover, behind his omission was his long-standing fear as a Whig that the monarchy might again aspire to absolute power, and that too much patronage in the hands of the Crown would corrupt Parliament. Despite this serious restriction in his revised conception of empire, Burke was far more perceptive than any of his British contemporaries regarding the political problems of empire and the need for a new conception of sovereignty. That historical development remained to be worked out during the nineteenth and twentieth centuries.

This essay, which includes new material, is based on one which appeared in *Early American Literature*, vol. XI, 1976. Copyright © 1976 by the Department of English, the University of North Carolina at Chapel Hill. Used by permission of the publisher and the author.

Burke and India

P.J. Marshall

Burke would probably have considered the question of how political philosophy should be applied to the practicalities of politics as wrongly posed, at least in regard to India, which was the issue that absorbed by far the largest amount of his time and energy. In a properly ordered world, he would have argued, there should be no conflict between practicality and philosophy in its highest form, that is, morality; but if conflict did occur, practicality must always be subordinated to moral imperatives.

In an engagement with India that lasted for some thirty years, there are certainly practical achievements to record, but they are dwarfed by a record of failure of which Burke was only too aware. The India Bills of 1783 – his plans for regulating the government of British India – were rejected, and Warren Hastings, whom Burke pursued for more than fifteen years, was acquitted at the end of his impeachment. Claims have sometimes been made for the importance of Burke's influence on the subsequent evolution of British rule in spite of such failures; whether Burke himself would have endorsed them is very doubtful. Nevertheless, India had elicited from him statements about the moral basis of politics which are of universal significance. For Burke, no considerations of political practicality could be allowed to compromise these principles.

I

In the early part of his career, Burke had considered India a political issue like any other. He had engaged in the defence of the East India Company's autonomy against what he saw as attempts to strengthen the executive government at its expense. In the mid-1770s, however, he began to take an interest in the way the Company discharged its responsibilities for governing its Indian territory. His sources of information were inevitably self-interested and even tainted, but there can be no question that Burke's judgment was influenced by his own personal or political advantage. From the 1780s, indeed, India became a political millstone round his neck. His conviction that the Company was guilty of serious abuses of power outweighed other political calculations.

His attention was initially directed to events in the south of India, but later shifted to Bengal. His knowledge of Bengal was in the first instance gathered through a parliamentary Select Committee, which sat from 1780 to 1783 and issued eleven reports, several of which can be attributed to Burke. On the basis of these enquiries, he became convinced that Warren Hastings, as Governor-General of Bengal, bore a heavy responsibility for what Burke himself saw as the corrupt and predatory administration of Bengal and its neighbouring provinces. In a brief tenure of office in 1783 Burke persuaded his colleagues to adopt his chosen remedy for misgovernment through Fox's Bills, which advocated the replacement of the East India Company by a parliamentary commission to regulate the government of British India. This was a politically vulnerable proposal which provided the pretext for the defeat of the government. Formally in opposition for the rest of his life, Burke resorted to attempts to make an example of Warren Hastings through the process of parliamentary impeachment. He achieved a remarkable success in persuading the Commons to adopt his charges and send Hastings to trial before the Lords in 1787. The trial began in 1788 and ended, to Burke's despair, in the acquittal of the defendant in 1795. Burke died two years later.

A huge body of published writing and recorded speeches survives from Burke's involvement with India. He drafted parliamentary reports. He made innumerable contributions to Indian debates in the House of Commons. Shorthand writers recorded every word that he uttered over the seven years of the Hastings impeachment. Some of his major speeches in the Commons and at the trial were published, either under his direct authority or posthumously by his literary executors.

In spite of the failure of Fox's India Bills and of the impeachment, all this outpouring of argument certainly had an effect on the shaping of Indian policy by others if not by Burke himself. In matters of detail, Burke could be a skilled and persuasive lobbyist of men in power. On wider issues, his vigorous championing of measures such as the recognition of what seemed to be the property rights of Indian landowners helped to create the climate of opinion in which the Permanent Settlement of the Bengal revenues came to be enacted in 1793. Above all, he articulated the deeply felt disillusionment of his generation with the immediate consequences of the British acquisition of territory in India. Instead of gaining riches and reputation from India, Britain was faced with scandal and financial crisis. No government could have ignored calls for reform; but Burke gave these demands coherence and a high moral tone, and the ferocity and persistence of his assaults on selected culprits no doubt had some deterrent effect in later years.

Although Burke's programme for the reform of what he had then regarded as an irredeemably corrupted East India Company was rejected in 1783, he accepted the possibility of at least limited subsequent improvement. After his great outburst in 1785 against the decision to sanction payment of the debts of the Nawab of Arcot without inquiry, he generally acquiesced in the new order of Indian management under Pitt and Dundas. He evidently saw it as some advance on what had gone before, and, in any case, he needed the support of ministers for the impeachment of Hastings. Burke spoke warmly of 'the beneficent government of Lord Cornwallis' as Governor-General from 1786 to 1793.[1] When he disapproved of Cornwallis, as he evidently did over the war with Mysore from 1790 to 1792, Burke kept silent.[2] Yet to see the later Company raj, with its wars, its high fiscal demands on its own provinces and its manipulation of the surviving Indian states, as the fulfilment of Burke's ideals goes against all the evidence of his writings and speeches. His younger followers were later to mount parliamentary attacks on Wellesley. Burke would surely have joined in and found much else to condemn. His vision of what an empire should be and his sense of the moral imperatives underlying it could not be permanently accommodated to any conceivable pattern of actual British rule in India.

Burke told the electors of Bristol in 1774 that their city was 'part of a great *empire*, extended by our virtue and our fortune to the farthest limits of the East and of the West'.[3] This empire was a single entity, subject to the sovereignty of the British King and Parliament. Yet it was an empire composed of very diverse societies, all requiring fundamentally different treatment. 'I never was wild enough,' Burke wrote, 'to conceive, that one method would serve for the whole; I could never conceive that the natives of *Hindostan* and those of *Virginia* could be ordered in the same manner; or that the *Cutchery* Court and the Grand Jury of *Salem* could be regulated on a similar plan.'[4] The art of imperial statecraft was to let diversity flourish by intervening as little as possible. The members of the empire had developed systems of government appropriate to their own circumstances: the elected assemblies of the North American and West Indian colonies, the Irish Parliament and the political institutions of the Mughal empire. All these must be respected.

Although, like most contemporary Europeans, Burke believed that eighteenth-century India had declined sadly from the height of Mughal power, he still compared the rulers of the successor states of the empire to the kings, electors, princes, dukes and other ruling nobility of contemporary Germany.[5] He insisted that even when late Mughal rulers had oppressed their subjects, they had still left 'a Hindu policy and a Hindu government' intact. Hindu

1   *Works*, VIII, 101.
2   *Correspondence*, VII, 139.
3   *Writings and Speeches*, III, 70.
4   Ibid., 316–17.
5   Ibid., V, 390.

institutions had throughout recorded history made 'a people happy and a government flourishing' under 'the paternal, lenient, protecting arm of a native government'.[6] There was no place in such a world for British collectors, magistrates or judges. Indeed, wherever the British had intruded they had produced conditions even worse than those in the 'troubled and vexatious era' of the last Muslim rulers of Bengal. A British empire in India must be based on the preservation of Indian authority at every level. The British must respect the complete independence of the rulers allied to them and scrupulously preserve the rights of landowners and other subordinate authorities within their own provinces. The functions of British government should be strictly limited to protection. Indians must above all be protected from the British themselves. The primary function of British metropolitan authority was to do precisely that by vigilant enquiry into the doings of the British in India and by exemplary punishment of individuals when necessary. This was the rôle of Parliament, the sovereign authority of the whole empire. Although Burke was responsible for what was called the Bengal Judicature Act of 1781, he saw Parliament's functions in Indian governance essentially in judicial, not in legislative, terms. The parliamentary commission to be created by Fox's India Bills was intended 'to regulate the administration of India upon the principles of a court of judicature'.[7] The impeachment of Hastings was the supreme expression of Parliament's inquisitorial functions. It was an act of 'the imperial justice which you owe to the people that call to you from all parts of a great disjointed empire'.[8]

II

Needless to say, Burke's vision of a 'great disjointed empire' had little in common with the British empire that was emerging and was to be consolidated in the nineteenth century. Burke's model of empire was the Roman one. In discussing the problem of 'calling governors to a strict account' in order to protect peoples who had 'no distinct privileges secured by constitutions of their own and able to check the abuse of the subordinate authority', he gave the House of Commons a disquisition on Roman history.[9] His personal model was, of course, Cicero in his prosecution of Verres for extortion in Sicily. Like Cicero, Burke saw it as his duty to protect the rights of the dependent peoples throughout the empire.

6   Ibid., VI, 312, 305.
7   Ibid., V, 444.
8   Ibid., VI. 277.
9   Ibid., 93–94, 105–06.

Again like Cicero, Burke saw this duty as an obligation enforced by divine law. However dubious its origins might be, he believed that a British empire in India was ordained by God. 'All power is of God,' and 'conquest ... is a more immediate designation of the hand of God.'[10] There were great difficulties to 'our attempting to govern India at all. But there we are; there we are placed by the Sovereign Disposer: and we must do the best we can in our situation. The situation of man is the preceptor of his duty.'[11] Even if the British had acquired their superiority by 'fraud or force, or whether by a mixture of both', duties inescapably followed.[12]

In the first place, British imperial government must be government according to law. Burke's Indian speeches contain some of the clearest enunciations of his belief that all men are bound by a universal law emanating from God. 'We are all born in subjection, all born equally, high and low, governors and governed, in subjection to one great, immutable, pre-existent law, prior to all our devices, and prior to all our contrivances, paramount to our very being itself, by which we are knit and connected in the eternal frame of the universe, out of which we cannot stir.'[13] All human law was derived from this source. This proposition was true not only of the common and statute law of England but it was true of the legal systems of Asia. They, too, were derived from a higher, natural law. Theories, embodied in the ancient and powerful European stereotype of 'oriental despotism', that Asian rulers were in no way bound by law but exercised absolute power, were abhorrent to Burke. 'I do challenge the whole race of man to show me any of the Oriental governors claiming to themselves a right to act by arbitrary will.'[14] He spent a great deal of time in demonstrating that sophisticated systems of law existed in both the Hindu and Islamic traditions. 'I must do justice to the East. I assert that their morality is equal to ours as regards the morality of governors, fathers, superiors; and I challenge the world to show, in any modern European book, more true morality and wisdom than is to be found in the writings of Asiatic men in high trusts.'[15] Everywhere in Asia the ruler was bound by the law and, as the inheritors of obligations of indigenous rulers, the British were equally bound by them. 'Every person exercising authority in another country shall be subject to the laws of that country; since otherwise they break the very covenant by which we hold our power there.'[16] Men

10 Ibid., 350–51.
11 Ibid., v, 404.
12 *Works*, VIII, 307.
13 *Writings and Speeches*, VI, 350.
14 Ibid., 353.
15 Ibid., 361.
16 *Works*, VIII, 5–6.

like Hastings were bound to govern 'the people of India ... according to the largest and most liberal construction of their laws, rights, usages, institutions and good customs'.[17]

Imperial rule for Burke must not only be rule according to law, but, like all government, it must be rule in the interests of the ruled. 'All political power which is set over men ... being wholly artificial, and for so much, a derogation from the natural equality of mankind at large, ought to be some way or other exercised ultimately for their benefit.'[18] When the East India Company accepted the *diwani* of Bengal, 'Great Britain made a virtual act of union with that country, by which they bound themselves as securities for their subjects, to preserve the people in all rights, laws and liberties, which their natural original sovereign was bound to enforce'.[19] 'The sovereign's rights are undoubtedly sacred rights, and ought to be so held in every country in the world; because exercised for the benefit of the people, and in subordination to the great end for which alone God has vested power in any man or any set of men.'[20]

Since empire in India was the gift of divine providence, however inscrutable, Burke never contemplated withdrawal from Britain's imperial responsibilities. Moreover, he believed that Britain could legitimately derive benefits from its Indian dominions. A properly conducted empire would be advantageous to both Britain and India: practicality and morality could coincide. The British could expect to trade profitably in India and, as rulers, could receive a reasonable return in a surplus of Indian taxation. But they could only attempt to do these things on the terms that Burke had laid down. Government must be regulated by law at every point and the interests of the governed must be uppermost at all times. In any conflict of interests those of the imperial power had to give way.

Burke never exercised executive responsibility for Indian government. There are, however, strong indications in his writings and speeches as to how he felt such responsibilities should be discharged in practice. Like so many of his contemporaries, Burke believed that international trade was a benign force for improvement throughout the world. Trade between Britain and India had the potential to do good for both partners. This potential had, however, been frustrated and the trade as conducted by the East India Company had turned into an engine of oppression. His main explanation for this appeared in the Ninth Report of the Select Committee of 1783. Burke argued that a mutually beneficial trade had existed before 1765. The Company had

17   Ibid., VII, 482.
18   *Writings and Speeches*, V, 385.
19   Ibid., VI, 281–82.
20   *Works*, VIII, 5.

exported silver, which had 'encouraged industry, and promoted cultivation in a high degree' in India. In return for its silver, the Company had obtained commodities 'essential for animating all other branches of trade, and for completing the commercial circle ... The English Company flourished under this exportation for a very long series of years. The nation was considerably benefited both in trade and in revenue.'[21]

This happy situation of mutual benefit came to an end when the East India Company acquired political power in Bengal. The Company then ceased to export silver to India, paying for its cargoes out of the territorial revenues that it was now able to collect. Political power enabled the Company to control the production of Indian textiles, fixing prices at artificial levels to its own advantage and eliminating competition from other merchants. This amounted to an 'annual plunder' of Bengal. The province was inevitably impoverished.

But while Indians suffered, the Company lost as well. Its revenue declined and goods obtained by control and coercion proved to be of poor quality. Not only was the economic exploitation of India an immoral departure from the inviolable principle that the benefit of the ruled must always be put first, but its results demonstrated that 'all attempts' which 'tend to the distress of India, must, and in a very short time will, make themselves felt, even by those in whose favour such attempts have been made'. Any extraction of wealth from India could only take place after ensuring that an 'influx of wealth shall be greater in quantity and prior in time to the waste'.[22] But in Burke's view, 'the principles and economy of the Company's trade have been so completely corrupted by turning it into a vehicle for tribute' that it required radical reform to return it to 'a bottom truly commercial'. By that he meant respecting 'the main spring of the commercial machine, the *principles of profit and loss*'.[23] Had Fox's India Bills come into force, control of the textile trade would have been forbidden by law, as would the monopolies of salt and opium operated by the East India Company.

III

Burke's prescription for the Company's government of its Indian provinces was the strictest non-intervention. The Company had no business to attempt to administer them at all. However, before the Company could leave well alone there was much work of restoration to be accomplished. Burke accepted that some changes could not be reversed. The Mughal Emperors or the

21 *Writings and Speeches*, V, 222–23.
22 Ibid., 258.
23 Ibid., 241.

Murshidabad Nawabs could not be put back on the throne of Bengal. But others who had been the victims of oppression, such as Raja Cheit Singh of Benares or the Begams of Oudh, must certainly be compensated and restored. Landowners, such as the Bengal zamindars, must also be restored; provisions to this effect were included in Fox's India Bills. Once the social hierarchy had been put back in place, it must be left inviolate. Burke had always believed that Hindu society was a closely knit organic whole, each part dependent on the others. The 'native princes' of south India, for instance, ensured that 'all ranks of people had their place in the public concern, and their share in the common stock and common prosperity'.[24] By the closing stages of the impeachment events in France had made Burke even more fervent in his insistence that aristocracy must be cherished in India. 'Men of great place, men of great rank, men of great hereditary authority, cannot fall without a horrible crash upon all about them. Such towers cannot tumble without ruining their dependent cottages. The prosperity of a country that has been distressed by a revolution which has swept off its principal men cannot be re-established without extreme difficulty.'[25] The British must leave well alone. Intervention in so complex a social mechanism, about whose workings they must be ignorant, could only lead to disaster.

Protected from invasion by British arms, but otherwise left to themselves, Indian provinces would flourish. Just as they were entitled to a beneficial trade, so the British were entitled to dispose of some part of the taxation that passed upwards through the landowners and nobility. But the same principles applied to revenue as to trade. The wealth of India could only be appropriated by the British on a scale that would do no harm to Indian society. For Burke, the purpose of empire was not primarily either the acquisition of wealth by Britain or the enhancement of British power; it was for Britain to win honour. 'For to increase its commerce without increasing its honour and reputation would have been thought at that time, and will be thought now, a bad bargain for the country.'[26] Honour and reputation came from ruling according to law in the interest of the governed.

In Burke's time and since, many men entrusted with power in India, including Warren Hastings, strove to acquire honour and reputation by governing in what they conceived to be the interests of the governed. But none of them could follow Burke's prescriptions to anything like the letter. Although none denied that the British should govern benevolently, all perforce made compromises.

24   Ibid., 423.
25   *Works*, VIII 59.
26   *Writings and Speeches*, VI, 282.

British economic interests could not be disregarded. The Company's monopolies and controls survived. When most of them were replaced by a system of free trade, the operations of the market could still be tilted against the Indian cultivator or artisan. Imperial rule had its necessities which might not coincide with a strict interpretation of Indian welfare. Revenue could not be kept at minimum levels. Tax rates were increased to help meet rising government expenditure. The Company spent heavily, largely because it could not live at peace with neighbouring Indian rulers. It maintained a huge army and conquered more and more territory. Those Indian states that survived were not treated as independent allies. In the interests of British security, they were subjected to the interference of Residents and required to maintain British troops.

Restoration of an old order followed by strict non-intervention were impractical guidelines for future policy. There was never any question of restoring rulers who had been deposed in the past. Nor did the Permanent Settlement in Bengal or other revenue systems guarantee that an ancient aristocracy would control the land. Even were this possible, the British began to doubt whether it was desirable. Administrators increasingly came to believe that they could not leave well alone, but must intervene to protect peasants against landlords. Intervention to bring about 'improvement', whether through schools, Christian missions or new legal codes, also began to appear on the agenda of British India.

Those who ruled India found Burke's insistence on the maintenance of that rule incompatible with his insistence that British government must never deviate from the strictest interpretation of what was lawful and what was in the interest of the governed. Whether Burke could have resolved these conflicting imperatives in practice can never be known. It was perhaps fortunate for him that he did not have to try. Without power, he remained the self-appointed conscience of British India. He left behind him an uncompromising statement of the priority of moral principles that applied not only to India but to all government. In deep depression about the state of the world in 1794, Burke consoled himself with what were virtually his last words delivered against Hastings: 'There is one thing, and one thing only, which defies all mutation; that which existed before the world, and will survive the fabric of the world itself; I mean justice.'[27]

27 *Works*, VIII, 440.

Rereading the French Revolution:
Burke and the Paradoxes
of History

Steven Blakemore

When Edmund Burke responded to the French Revolution two centuries ago, he and it seem immediately to have acquired opposing, mythical status, like Manichean forms of energy. As the iconoclastic power of the revolution erupted into the European consciousness, Burke realised that the inherited, traditional European world – a world which he contended had evolved over two thousand years – was forever changed. In his *Reflections on the Revolution in France*, he saw the revolution ironically reproducing the 'past' it was supposedly burying. Subsequently, he argued that as the revolution reproduced the ideologies and fantasies of the past, so, at the same time, it turned into something that was suddenly quite new and indefinable. He struggled to describe what was radically new about it in the traditional language of *tyranny* and *despotism*, in an effort to identify the French Revolution as the first *totalitarian* event in history. Therefore his own original insights are instructive for an understanding not only of what a revolution is, but what it may become.

I

In his counter-revolutionary writings, Burke often depicts the revolutionary forces as a conflicting assortment of opposing components, all jumbled together and possessing a kind of paradoxical life of their own. Indeed, he argues strongly that one of the distinguishing characteristics of the revolutionaries is their fatal attraction to political paradoxes which they attempt to resolve. He traces this attraction to the Enlightenment and particularly to its patron saint, Rousseau, who informed David Hume that he purposely cultivated paradoxes to create 'new and unlooked-for strokes in politics and morals' as a way of attracting attention now that the 'marvellous' machinery of heathen mythology had lost its power. By replacing heathen mythology with a new paradoxical mythology, Burke suggests, Rousseau created a new, modern superstition for frenzied supporters of the revolution, 'who in their paradoxes are servile imitators; and even in their incredulity discover an implicit faith'.[1]

In the *Reflections* and subsequent anti-revolutionary works, Burke explores the consequences of revolutionary ideology and produces a critique of what he contends is the paradoxical nature of the revolution. When he uses the words *paradox* or *paradoxical*, he does not primarily mean a seemingly contradictory statement or phenomenon which is nonetheless true or authentic, although that sense did exist in the eighteenth century. What Burke means by *paradox* can be gauged from the *Oxford English Dictionary*: 'A statement or tenet contrary to received opinion or belief; often with the implication that it is marvellous or incredible; sometimes with unfavourable connotation, as being discordant with what is held to be established truth, and hence absurd or fantastic.' In a further definition, the word is 'often applied to a proposition or statement that is actually self-contradictory to reason or ascertained truth, and so, essentially absurd or false'. The 1755 *Dictionary* of Burke's great friend, Dr Johnson, gives only the pejorative denotations: 'Paradox – a tenet contrary to received opinion; an assertion contrary to opinion; a position in appearance absurd.' Likewise, the adjective *paradoxical* means: 'Having the nature of paradox' and 'inclined to new tenets, or notions contrary to received opinions.'

Burke uses the word primarily in the sense of a deviation from received truth or opinion – truth or opinion that is traditional, inherited, and prescriptive – and hence his critique focuses on the iconoclastic thinking that he sees assaulting the established parameters of the eighteenth-century world. The icons were, of course, to be smashed by the force of pure reason – reason freed from the inherited and 'irrational' codes of thinking rooted in the past. But, as Burke emphasises time and time again, reason employed independently of these inherited codes is folly – groundless metaphysical abstraction that creates nothing more substantial than 'delusive plausibilities' – and its vacuity is illustrated by the paradoxes to which such thinking necessarily gives rise. 'I do not vilify theory and speculation,' Burke stresses, 'No; whenever I speak against theory, I mean always a weak, erroneous, fallacious, unfounded, or imperfect theory; and one of the ways of discovering that it is a false theory is by comparing it with practice.'[2] Thus, the proliferating contradictions that result from the revolution are the consequences of the fundamental discrepancy between revolutionary rhetoric and reality.[3]

---

1 *Reflections*, 283–84.
2 See M. Freeman, *Edmund Burke and the Critique of Political Radicalism* (Oxford, 1980), p. 28.
3 Cf. Burke, *Letters on a Regicide Peace, Letter One* (1796): 'The foundation of [France's revolutionary] Republic is laid in moral paradoxes.' *Works*, V, 209.

What, precisely, are the revolutionary paradoxes that Burke identifies? First, he argues that the new, liberating knowledge celebrated by the revolution – knowledge once supposedly suppressed by a consortium of popes, priests and kings – is actually knowledge based on old errors previously refuted by the European world. In the *Reflections*, he contends that this knowledge is disguised in a language of novelty and revelation. His criticisms of Richard Price and other British supporters of the French Revolution reveal how the fantasies and fallacies of Levellers, regicides and Fifth Monarchists – the jumbled and discredited past of fervid fanatics – are resurrected by the revolutionaries and yet disguised and suppressed, as the real implications of this intellectual ancestry, and its drive to fanaticism and oppression, dawn across Europe. Richard Price resembles Hugh Peters, the Puritan minister and chaplain of the Parliamentary army in the Civil War, in his glorification of the 'king led in triumph', and the trial of Charles I is played out again in the ordeal of Louis XVI. One of Burke's main purposes in his anti-revolutionary works is to reveal what the revolutionary writer is repressing.

In his analysis of Price's sermon, which had been delivered to the Revolution Society in support of the National Assembly in November 1789, Burke shows that there are clusters of verbal echoes of the English King's overthrow, especially from the regicide texts of the State Trials – echoes which Price either consciously or unconsciously represses. Burke's findings are akin to Marx's well-known observation, in *The Eighteenth Brumaire of Louis Bonaparte* (1852), that revolutionary 'tradition' oppresses revolutionary 'imagination', resulting in perverse parodies of the past. Burke fleshes out the resemblances between the revolutionaries and their ideological ancestors, and his images of intellectual incest (as the revolutionaries lose themselves in mutual quotations) turn into metaphors of monstrous mutations. For Burke, the revolutionaries' assault on the past ironically exposes another, suppressed past now emerging in the present and future they are creating. Revolutionaries proclaim a radical break from the past that they ineluctably replicate.

Moreover, and this is a point Burke makes repeatedly, in their efforts to force their paradoxical ideology on the world, the revolutionaries not only resuscitate their ideological ancestors, but breathe new life into the old 'oppressive' forces that they want to destroy. Thus, the National Assembly institutionalises revolutionary repression by proceeding 'exactly as their ancestors of ambition have done before them. Trace them through all their artifices, frauds and violences, you can find nothing at all that is new. They follow precedents and examples with the punctilious exactness of a pleader. They never depart an iota from the authentic formulas of tyranny and usurpation.'[4] The

4   *Reflections*, 277.

'precedents and examples' refer to both the oppressive forces of the old order and the regicidal forces of persecuting Puritans. In Burke's paradoxical formula, revolutionary power is old tyranny writ new.

Burke also insists that the revolutionaries' faith in paradoxical theories constitutes the very spirit of superstition and fanaticism which they claim they are exorcising. The result is a militant, Messianic state governed by 'atheistical fathers' with 'a bigotry of their own [who] have learnt to talk against monks with the spirit of a monk'.[5] Burke repeatedly connects the revolution and its supporters with the religious fanaticism of intolerant Puritans, inquisitorial Catholics, dogmatic priests, and pagan 'oracles'. The revolution is seen as a new fanatical superstition that also mirrors the past it claims to exorcise. The revolutionaries 'are waging war with intolerance, pride, and cruelty, whilst, under colour of abhorring the ill principles of antiquated parties, they are authorising and feeding the same odious vices'.[6] His point is not merely that the revolutionaries enact hypocritically what they supposedly suppress, but that their obsession with expunging the past from men's minds, exterminating the old order and imposing total conformity to their own principles results in their becoming, *mutatis mutandis*, the very things they aim to destroy.

Hence Burke confronts the revolutionaries and their supporters with a series of specific paradoxes they themselves produce: they destroy the Bastille and create a Bastille for kings; they promote a 'democracy' based on the economic distinction between active and passive citizens; they extol a doctrine of equality predicated on a new inequality of dispossessed classes: 'Instead of better principles of equality, a new inequality was introduced of the most oppressive kind.'[7] Such contradictions and discrepancies arise inevitably out of the obsessive rationalist rhetoric of the revolution, which becomes increasingly detached from reality and increasingly driven by the same forces as the oppressive order it is replacing.

In this context, Burke argues that revolutionary ideology perpetuates old errors and that its critique of the old order is essentially a polemical *caricature* of oppression because, while he acknowledges that this system had grievous flaws and defects, he suggests that the critique is based on nothing more than old radical fantasies of oppressive régimes. He is intent on showing that revolutionary ideology is obsessed with what it criticises, and that this obsession turns into a monstrous travesty of what it opposes. It promises deliverance from tyrannical kings and mystifying superstitions, but it can only produce its own parodic version of these because its *raison d'être* is based not on reality but on its relation to a theoretical 'difference' – a difference embodied in the

5 *Reflections*, 212.
6 Ibid., 249.
7 Ibid., 355.

'counter-revolutionary' opposite. It constitutes itself by its opposition to this difference; it defines and reifies itself in pristine abstractions like 'the people' – a 'people' that must be purged of all identifiable 'enemies'. Thus, while it projects a vague, fabricated future cleansed of the pernicious past, in practice revolutionary ideology is incapable of creating an authentically new present because, enforcing itself through the very repetitive, oppressive power it supposedly resists, it reproduces the evil it is trying to repress. Burke notes that 'those who are habitually employed in finding and displaying faults, are unqualified for the work of reformation: because their minds are ... unfurnished with patterns of the fair and good'.[8]

It is a commonplace that revolutionary ideology characterises itself as stripping off the 'masks' and 'disguises' and revealing the oppressive machinery of the old order,[9] but Burke unravels revolutionary rhetoric in turn to reveal its latent will to power, and he probes the way in which this power perpetuates itself in the practices established by the revolution. For example, he aims at enmeshing the revolution in the contradictions of an ideology – an *'armed doctrine'* – that impels Jacobin armies into the heart of Europe. He notes that the expansionist ideology that promotes death to kings and liberation of 'the people' must necessarily be repressed once the revolution has become entrenched. In Burke's terms, radical ideology must necessarily be suppressed by its radical proponents because potentially it can destroy the very power that releases it. Hence, when the revolution is consolidated, revolutionaries must deny the principles they initially promoted. The principles of freedom and democracy are redefined; 'the people' are subsumed into a totalising 'general will' enforced by revolutionary vanguards. But this discrepancy between what the revolution promises and what it performs must be disguised. Thus, the language of the 'rights of man' and the revolutionary duty to confront oppressive force is explained away by new 'duties' entailing 'revolutionary' discipline. So, as Burke notes, the very leaders who 'teach the people to abhor and reject all feodality as the barbarism of tyranny ... tell them afterwards how much of that barbarous tyranny they are to bear with patience'.[10] Michael Freeman calls this Burke's 'Kronstadt thesis': 'Leaders provide followers with a 'rights' ideology suitable for destroying the old society but incompatible with the reconstruction of the new because subversive of all society. Leaders therefore call in troops to suppress the assertion of the very rights which are supposed to be the *raison d'être* of the new

8   Ibid., 282–83.
9   See Steven Blakemore, *Burke and the Fall of Language: The French Revolution as Linguistic Event* (Hanover and London, 1988), pp. 72–73.
10 *Reflections*, 345.

order.'[11] In this discrepancy between revolutionary ideology and reality, the revolutionaries become what they accuse the old order of being.

In an intentionally subversive passage in the *Reflections*, Burke attempts to ensnare the revolutionaries in their own paradoxes by suggesting that French peasants should overthrow the new oppressive order by acting on the very principles that the revolution initially promoted. Again, he is contending that revolutionary ideology produces the very monster it has supposedly slain, for the revolution turns into an inquisitional force that suppresses 'counter-revolutionary difference' in ways suggestive of the old order's persecution of 'heretics' and other 'enemies' of the state. He hopes to turn the militant ideology in on itself, like a monster which, to modify Vergniaud's dictum, recognises in its children the image of the enemies it obsessively devours.

Burke's vision of the revolution suggests that for the first time in Western experience an insane logic of contradiction ('insane' because divorced from the reality of inherited codes of thinking) is being forced on the world by a paradoxical ideology and the power that sustained it. In the *Reflections* and subsequent works, the revolution looms as the greatest assault on reality in the world's history. The revolutionaries impose a paradoxical power and enforce it through illusions of novelty, driven by an obsession with past power and oppression and legitimised by terror. In the end, however, reality has its revenge, as the revolution engenders a counter-revolution and takes upon itself what it has parodied in the old order: possession of total ideological and physical power.

II

In his subsequent anti-revolutionary works, Burke continued to explore the paradoxes that gave the revolution its subversive energy. Seeing the French Revolution as a parodic repetition of the past, he sought to explain what was simultaneously new and exceptional in the experiment. At first, he continued tracing the revolution's ideological roots to heresies and rebellions in the past that had been contained or suppressed: the Peasants' Revolt of 1381, the Anabaptists in sixteenth-century Münster, the radical Enlightenment, and the English Civil War. These iconoclastic historical events were, for Burke, radically anti-historical – hostile denials of European history and tradition and, more significantly, hostile denials of human nature. He saw the revolution as a procrustean endeavour to 'regenerate' human nature with an anti-human

11 M. Freeman, op. cit., p. 89. In *Preface to the Address of M. Brissot to his Constituents* (1794), Burke made this point specifically.

theory. While supporters of the revolution insisted that it was destined to expunge the past, Burke identified its historical pedigree. The forceful injection of alien powers inimical to Europe's historical essence and hence its real existence signified that the revolution imitated earlier movements that had been successfully opposed and resisted, and yet, in its triumph, became radically different from them. For the first time, people were allowing these powers and forces to play themselves out with the result that their trajectory could not be predicted or extrapolated in terms of past events. What Burke pointedly called 'philosophy' – the self-congratulatory term of Enlightenment *philosophes* – was, in its pejorative sense, a hostile, radical ideology at war with human nature.

Thus, while Burke initially identified the revolution with the past it had supposedly transcended, he also insisted that it subsequently constituted a new form of power resembling nothing in human history, and that historical models consequently provided no explanatory terms for the phenomenon Europeans were witnessing. In *Thoughts on French Affairs* (1791), he warned that the new French state resembled no other country and that examples drawn from ancient or contemporary history were 'wholly delusive'. Likewise, in *Remarks on the Policy of the Allies* (1793), he noted that 'examples drawn from history in occasions like the present will be found dangerously to mislead us'.[12]

Burke was, in effect, trying to describe a new species of tyranny for which he had no corresponding vocabulary. We can begin to understand Burke's quandary by considering what historical models were available to him as he tried to comprehend a revolution that had no historical parallels. In the eighteenth century, *tyranny* and *despotism* were the strongest words available for what Burke was straining to describe and explain. Tyrannies had first been discussed by Aristotle in his *Politics.* He focused on the way they were consolidated: the tyrant kept people docile by destroying their independent spirit, spying on them, leaving them poor, and waging wars in order to keep them preoccupied with mere survival. The tyrant endeavoured to ensure that opponents could not conspire against him, just as he tried to keep his subjects docile and indisposed to revolt. He openly used force to oppress his people, and sometimes he disguised it. Historically, however, tyrannies faded quickly – the tyrant could only delay his eventual overthrow.[13] The Roman historians continued this classic critique by describing a variety of tyrants nakedly imposing their wills on their oppressed populations or diverting attention with the proverbial bread and circuses. In the seventeenth and eighteenth

12 *Works*, III, 375 and 425.
13 Aristotle, *Politics*, trans. T.A. Sinclaire (Penguin Classics, 1988), pp. 343–47.

centuries, Niccolo Machiavelli (1469–1527) was considered to have described a variety of ways a tyrant could maintain power by concealing it. While Aristotle's brief analysis of tyranny was expanded and extrapolated, eighteenth-century writers continued to reinscribe the classic and humanist critiques in terms of *private* individuals or cliques selfishly violating the *public* good.

Dr Johnson's definition of *tyranny* and the synonym *despotism*, with their correspondent adjectives, encapsulates the meanings of oppressive power available to Burke and his contemporaries. Tyranny: 'Absolute monarchy imperiously administered'. Despotism: 'Absolute power'. Absolute: 'Not limited; as absolute power'. Absoluteness: 'Despotism'. Thus, the words dealing with tyranny comprised a series of confined, circular definitions at odds with what Burke was trying to articulate – not the idea of a person or a clique, but an unprecedented ideological force empowered by people who were imposing their collective will on the bodies and minds of Europe in the name of the people and the public good. Consequently, the traditional examples underlying the usage of *absolute*, *tyranny* and *despotism* neither sufficed to describe nor corresponded to this new phenomenon. Burke had to write and think within the traditional vocabulary, even though he realised that it belied precisely what he was describing. That phenomenon was what we would recognise today as *totalitarianism*, and, in this context, Burke was the first to formulate the revolution's significance as an event in the history of civilisation.

So what was the closest approximation available to him of our adjective *totalitarian*? One paradigm that did offer Burke the nascent terms with which he initially described the totalitarian nature of the French Revolution was Protestant representations of dark, oppressive, 'papal' Catholicism deployed in the polemical discourse of the radical Reformation. Militant Catholicism was depicted as a conspiratorial union of state military power and the Church's ideological coercion, with an ensuing imposition of belief into people's minds and bodies through the Church's inquisitorial torture and ideological indoctrination. This 'black legend' of Protestant Europe was repeated by Enlightenment writers hostile to '*l'infâme*'. In the early 1790s it is this model that Burke reapplied to revolutionaries who, in his understanding, had turned into the monsters they previously conjured up and demonised – that is, the absolute ideological and physical power embodied in the 'Gothic' and 'feudal' institutions of Catholic Europe.

In the *Reflections*, Burke refers to revolutionary enthusiasts, such as the Protestant Dissenter Richard Price, making revolutionary pronouncements with the absolute power and assurance of despotic popes in the twelfth century.[14] In various other works, he applies the adjective *inquisitional* to revolutionaries in

14 *Reflections*, 96.

France. Burke is, on one level, appealing to the prejudice of his British audience by attacking the revolutionaries and their British supporters with an
anti-Catholic vocabulary that had been dominant in England since the sixteenth century, and which had been used by the British to define themselves
against the Catholic 'other'.[15] But, on another level, he is subtly suggesting
that the Catholic oppression caricatured by Protestants, the imaginary spirit
of the hostile, alien 'other', did really exist in the rhetoric and practices of the
revolutionaries and their admirers. This is not to raise again the debate over
Burke's alleged Catholic sympathies, but to suggest that Burke was ambivalent
about the Reformation, which, as a radical event, he perceived as a partisan,
polemical spirit that tragically split European Christendom – a spirit he now
saw reincarnated in the French Revolution. In *Thoughts on French Affairs*, he
specifically compared the Reformation and the revolution as expansionist,
ideological movements that introduced 'interests into all countries [other]
than those which arose from their locality and natural circumstances'. In the
Reformation, like the French Revolution, 'the spirit of proselytism expanded
itself ... upon all sides; and great divisions were everywhere the result'.[16]

While the black legend of expansionist papal Catholicism still resonated in
the political writings of the 1790s, this proto-totalitarian thesis had been un-
wittingly modified in Protestant works such as John Foxe's *Book of Martyrs*
(1563), which depicted the Church as ultimately failing to conquer the minds
and spirits of the Protestant faithful, who died defiant and pristine, usually in the glorious flames of their martyrdom. Similarly, the anti-Catholic
Enlightenment writers reformulated the classic and humanist critiques of
tyranny to show that physical intimidation and mental terror were futile in
such an enlightened age and effective only against the enslaved minds of
Catholic Europe. While some Enlightenment writers continued to stress the
Church's institutional, ideological control, most emphasised the Church and
State's 'illusions' and 'superstitions' and went on to propagate corresponding
psychic and political liberation. These ideas were reinforced by Anglo-
European supporters of the French Revolution, who insisted that the old
order's illusions and superstitions were being stripped away and that even the
benighted minds of Europe's oppressed would soon be awakened and freed.

This historical background is pertinent because, as the revolution acceler-
ated, Burke recognised that, while the resemblance to the Reformation still
obtained (specifically the spirit of proselytism), the revolution had changed into

15   See Linda Colley, *Britons: Forging the Nation*, 1707–1837 (New Haven, 1992),
     pp. 11–54.
16   *Works*, III, 350. Burke's antipathy towards aspects of the Reformation is discussed by
     Bruce James Smith in, *Politics and Remembrance: Republican Themes in Machiavelli,
     Burke and Tocqueville* (Princeton, 1985), pp. 142–43.

something more radically compelling in terms of power and ideology. After 1790, the revolution had turned into a force that was successfully entrenching itself in the hearts and minds of Europe. It had mutated from a latter-day Reformation-cum-Enlightenment fantasy into the first *'complete* revolution' – a revolution that 'seems to have extended even to the constitution of the mind of man'.[17]

In his later works, Burke argued that the revolution was a form of unprecedented power: 'It is not a new power of an old kind. It is a new power of a new species.'[18] *Power* is a thematic word, appearing frequently in Burke's anti-revolutionary writings, where he contends that while the revolutionaries did not initially understand the nature of power and its physical and psychological consequences, they soon comprehended both. For Burke, revolutionary power was a new species of expansive energy; it was a combination of physical and ideological forces for oppressive ends. It affected everything, transforming society and the French mind. His metaphors of fragmentation and chaos depict this new power sundering the European world – shattering states, splintering men's minds, severing man's allegiance to the prescriptive authority of Europe's traditions.

III

In his anti-revolutionary writings, Burke maintains that the French Revolution is unprecedented in three specific ways. First, he contends that it surpasses any previous revolution in scope: it is a 'total revolution' that radically transforms everything, including the mind of man. Second, the revolution is aggressively expansionist, intending not only the conquest of France but the conversion of European states into revolutionary clones. The revolution proliferates by converting ideological force into physical power: French armies pouring into Europe are prepared for in advance by revolutionary ideas dissolving the soft tissue of European discourse, the traditional but vulnerable values of European thought. The two forms of revolutionary power complement each other, for the revolution is, above all, a militant, expansionist ideology. It is *'a revolution of doctrine and theoretic dogma'*, a 'philosophical revolution', an aggressive 'empire of doctrine'; in short, an *'armed doctrine'* that assaults with 'epidemical fanaticism' the established order of Europe.[19] Burke therefore sees the military battle for Europe as an extension of the

17   *Letter to a Noble Lord*, in *Works*, V, 111 (Burke's emphasis).
18   *Letters on a Regicide Peace, Letter Two* (1796), in *Works*, V, 244.
19   *Thoughts on French Affairs, Reflections, Letters on a Regicide Peace, Letter One* (1796), in *Works*, IV, 319; III, 407, 423; V, 290, 164.

ideological battle. Third, he argues that the fatal combination of unprecedented physical and ideological power ensures that the revolution will perpetuate itself solely through terror and force. This is, indeed, Burke's central
thesis throughout his anti-revolutionary writings: the revolution is an unprecedented extension of a potentially absolute power by a militant ideological state. In the second of the *Letters on a Regicide Peace*, he contends that
the individual in France has been subsumed into the war state and that the
revolutionaries have totally militarised society: 'Individuality is left out of
their scheme of government. The state is all in all. Everything is referred to
the production of force; afterwards, everything is trusted to the use of it. It is
military in its principle, in its maxims, in its spirit, and in all its movements.
The state has dominion and conquest for its sole objects; dominion over
minds by proselytism, over bodies by arms.'[20] In these haunting lines, Burke
is adumbrating for the first time the spectre of the modern totalitarian state,
the expansionist ideological state of the twentieth century.

This thesis, of course, can be resisted on various grounds, but Burke insists
that the revolution is totally unprecedented, and he struggles to explain a
phenomenon for which he lacks a correspondent political vocabulary. In his
Remarks on the Policy of the Allies, he states that the nationalisation of power
results in a new assault on private thought and individual liberty: 'Committees,
called of vigilance and safety, are everywhere formed: a most severe and scru-
tinising inquisition, far more rigid than anything ever known or imagined.
Two persons cannot meet and confer without hazard to their liberty, and even
to their lives. Numbers scarcely credible have been executed, and their property confiscated. At Paris, and in most other towns, the bread they buy is a
daily dole – which they cannot obtain without a daily ticket delivered to them
by their masters.'[21] Burke thus warns against a revolution waged in the name
of 'the people' that actually establishes unprecedented state oppression against
the very people it purportedly liberates – a revolution enforced by committees of security and surveillance and the new concentrated power of the state.

There are striking similarities here with J.L. Talmon's thesis that modern
totalitarianism has its roots in doctrines and practices central to the French
Revolution.[22] Some scholars have asked whether the revolution was, really,
in any way totalitarian. Ostensibly, with regard to the scale and scope of
twentieth-century examples in Germany and the Soviet Union, it wasn't; but
it is also true that the state had by then had 150 years to perfect the technology of repression. While the French Revolution does not approach the
millions killed in exercises of state genocide in this century, it did have an

20 *Works*, V, 255.
21 Ibid., III, 420.
22 J.L. Talmon, *The Origins of Totalitarian Democracy* (New York, 1960).

ideologically genocidal component in the massacres in the Vendée and the federal cities, the forced drownings at Nantes, and other political executions constituting the Terror.[23]

Nazi Germany is relevant because Burke's critique has commonly been applied to left-wing revolutions in this century. Reductive Left/Right positions, however, obscure the relevance of Burke's thinking to so-called right-wing revolutions as well. There are parallels to be explored, for instance, between Nazi Germany's *Volk* and revolutionary France's *peuple*. Despite the differences, both ideologies produced massacres and rationalisations of expansionist state power. Once the Jacobin state enshrined an abstract *peuple* as an even more nebulous 'general will' or Nazi Germany celebrated a mythical *Volk*, all 'enemies of the people' (a catch-all phrase originating in the French Revolution), all those definable 'others' – aristocrats, royalists, traitors, hoarders, Jews and counter-revolutionary schemers – could be ideologically isolated and targeted for detention or extermination.

Burke's analysis of the French Revolution is also pertinent in that he crystallised a critique of what can be characterised as the revolutionary romance – the axiomatic association of revolutionary movements with total, exhilarating liberation – with an apocalyptic regeneration of the human race. It is Burke's strength that he not only formulated a critique of what he perceived to be a paradoxically self-fulfilling ideology, but also provided an analysis of the appeal of that ideology – an appeal that has been with us for two centuries. Burke remains pertinent for the debate he provoked, for in many ways both admirers and critics of the revolution have been responding to Burke for two centuries. In this context, Burke continues to represent not merely one side but rather a constant reference point for the continuing Anglo-American debate on the significance of the French Revolution. To read the revolution's first Anglo-American commentators – Mary Wollstonecraft, Thomas Paine, James Mackintosh and hundreds of other revolutionary admirers in the 1790s – is to read the same explanations and rationalisations that have subsequently been applied to other revolutions as well. On the Right, Burke has often been used unhistorically and reductively to oppose forces of modernity associated with the French Revolution. On the Left, Burke is the spectre that still haunts the revolutionary imagination.

Until recently, the dominant academic discourse contributed to a politicised climate in which Burke could not be discussed without partisan labels.

---

23 In *Letters from France* (1796), Helen Maria Williams first documented the charge of genocide – a charge that until recently has been ignored or dismissed. See Jean-Clement Martin, *La Vendée et la France* (Paris, 1987); Reynaud Secher, *Le génocide franco-française: La Vendée-Vengée* (Paris, 1986); Rene Sedillot, *Le Coût de la Révolution* (Paris, 1987).

To take a position on the French Revolution was to risk being immediately assigned a political label based upon that position. One principal reason for this was the Left's historical identification with the French Revolution as 'the Mother of us all'.[24] Even Marx, who saw the revolution as defective in being captured by the bourgeoisie, believed it was a crucial event that prefigured the pristine future. In the twentieth century, Lenin identified strongly with the revolution, and Bolsheviks like Trotsky were obsessed with historical parallels, fearing the possibility of a 'Thermidor' reaction that would destroy the Russian Revolution. On 7 December 1988, Mikhail Gorbachev, in an address to the United Nations, underscored a parallel that the Left had been making for over half a century: 'The French Revolution of 1789 and the Russian Revolution of 1917 exerted a powerful impact on the very nature of history and radically changed the course of world development ... To a large extent, those two revolutions shaped the way of thinking that is still prevalent in social consciousness.'[25]

In *Interpreting the French Revolution*, François Furet explains how left-wing historians incorporated the French Revolution into the macrocosmic Russian Revolution, making the former 'the mother of a real, dated, and duly registered event – October 1917':

> The Russian Bolsheviks never – before, during or after the Russian Revolution – lost sight of that filiation. But by the same token the historians of the French Revolution projected into the past their feelings or their judgments about 1917, and tended to highlight those features of the first revolution that seemed to presage or indeed anticipate those of the second. At the very moment when Russia – for better or for worse – took the place of France as the nation in the vanguard of history, because it had inherited from France and from nineteenth-century thought the idea that a nation is *chosen* for revolution, the historiographical discourses about the two revolutions became fused and infected each other. The Bolsheviks were given Jacobin ancestors, and the Jacobins were made to anticipate the communists.[26]

Similarly, eighteenth-century identifications of the revolution with the 'progressive' movements of history (the Enlightenment, the Glorious Revolution

24 R. Darnton, 'The History of Mentalities: Recent Writings on Revolution, Criminality, and Death in France', in (ed.) R. Harvey Brown and S.M. Lyman, *Structure, Consciousness, and History* (Cambridge, 1978), pp. 107–08.
25 M. Gorbachev, quoted in *Time*, 9 December 1988, p. 18.
26 François Furet, *Interpreting the French Revolution*, trans. Elborg Forster (Cambridge, 1981), p. 6.

and the American Revolution) had begun in the 1790s, when it was, at first, read back into the past and provided with its political pedigree and then, when the revolution suddenly stopped resembling the past, redefined as a crucial historical stage that would be consummated in the future.[27]

Two centuries later, the protean paradoxes of history confront us with a problem first crystallised by Burke. By 1792, he had recognised that his assumptions about the revolution's course – assumptions drawn from the received classical and contemporary discourses of the day – were not, in fact, relevant. If one of the abiding interests in Burke is a general recognition that the French Revolution still impinges on the modern mind, that its echoes still resonate in the development of revolutionary movements and in the very language by which we continue to debate democracy and dictatorship, the example Burke presents us is that we must also be on our guard to recognise and assess any new reality contradicting the familiar contexts by which we read our contemporary world.

---

27 Cf. Burke's comment, in 1790, on the concrete implications of deferred utopian politics: 'I have no great opinion of that sublime abstract, metaphysic reversionary, contingent humanity, which in *cold blood* can subject the *present time*, and those whom we *daily see and converse with*, to *immediate* calamities in favour of the *future and uncertain* benefit of persons who *only exist in idea*.' *Correspondence*, VI, 109.

Burke's Irish Views and Writings

L. M. Cullen

Edmund Burke presents problems for people studying his writings and political thought largely because he was primarily a politician and his voluminous writings and speeches were dictated by the exigencies of public life. That he spent almost all of his political life in opposition aggravates the problems. In conjunction with his own excitable cast of mind, it accounts for arguments which are directed less to analysing problems in all their dimensions than to advocating, on the prompting of personal or party commitment and often under pressure of time, a path for those politicians who had to deal with them. Burke's surviving papers reflect these circumstances: they are rich in public and private letters that broach matters of public interest, but rather ruthlessly pruned of family, financial and personal correspondence.

This imbalance certainly applies to Burke's Irish contacts, though not, as is sometimes suggested, any more so than in other areas of his life. As a man making and then keeping a place in British politics, his Irish public interests were perforce intermittent, and, except in rare instances such as the survival of his letters in the O'Hara papers, the Irish dimensions of his thought and his world lack a sustained and intimate documentation. However, these dimensions are worth exploring as they may modify the impressions of Burke's principles and political method that are frequently drawn from his more famous writings. After all, his public life began and ended with Irish preoccupations.

I. BURKE'S IRISH EXPERIENCES

Our understanding of Burke's writings suffers from the tendency of commentators – even recent Irish ones such as Foster and Beckett – to consider him as Anglo-Irish or even virtually an Englishman, although the case for Burke's Irishness as made by William O'Brien and Conor Cruise O'Brien is compelling.[1] Conor Cruise O'Brien's highly effective introduction to his edition of the *Reflections on the Revolution in France* is better on this point than his

---

1 William O'Brien, *Edmund Burke as an Irishman* (Dublin, 1924); Conor Cruise O'Brien, *The Great Melody* (London, 1992).

recent biography, where his arguments depend at times on hypothesis and supposition.

Burke was sensitive to surroundings, and loyalty to kin was a marked feature of his career. On the last of his four visits to Ireland, in 1786, when he was unable to visit Munster, he recalled Munster scenery in evocative terms. His youth, which was spent partly on the Blackwater with his Nagle and Hennessy cousins, left a permanent imprint on him. The Nagles and the Hennessys had hard memories of anti-Catholic plots concocted in County Cork in 1731–32 and in 1733. These had followed the discovery that a recruiting rôle had been granted to a member of the Hennessy family, a high-ranking officer in French service, in 1730. Later, Burke's reaction to the Jacobite expedition to Scotland in 1745 was to delve into Irish history, responding with sympathy and understanding to the '45. A letter of July 1746 noted: 'I have read some history. I am endeavouring to get a little into the accounts of this our own poor country.'[2] This was the beginning of an interest in Irish history which eventually grew, in the 1760s, into serious study of the massacres of 1641. Searing experiences encountered again by his Blackwater relatives in the early 1760s can only have further excited his interest, and his later correspondence is shot through with references to these years.

Burke's presence in Ireland in 1761–62 and 1763–64, as private secretary to the Chief Secretary of Ireland, William Hamilton, coincided with alarms about Catholic plots in Munster. His own presence and rôle at Dublin Castle, both as a man with a Munster background and specifically as a relative of the Nagles, may have contributed to the thrust of the charges: but whether this was the case or not, the plots were either devised or taken up by Nagle enemies in County Cork, and it was local and national politicians from Cork who made the running against any attempts to grant political concessions to Catholics. His Irish political views were formed during this period, and his observations about Ireland in later decades are simply recollections of the period and its personalities, not informed insights drawn from later evidence. Coinciding with, or even preceding, his arrival in 1761, charges against alleged Catholic conspirators in Munster had surfaced because the prospect of concessions to Catholics nationally was in the air. In 1761, William Fant, a County Limerick attorney, informed Dublin Castle about an alleged meeting the previous year, of which 'the Nagles and Hennessys were the promotors' and at which Fant thought he had seen the Pretender disguised as a woman.[3] As in 1733, the allegation surfaced before the start of the parliamentary session, the question of permitting the recruitment of Irishmen for foreign service being the catalyst.

2   Burke to Richard Shackleton, 12 July 1746. *Correspondence*, I, 68.
3   *Correspondence*, I, 147–48, n.5.

The object of such allegations was to provide material for an enquiry which would establish that Catholics were unreliable subjects and hence that concessions to them could not be contemplated. In 1761, the lobby in the Irish Parliament was conducted by what the Lord Lieutenant, the Earl of Halifax, identified as 'Lord Shannon's friends', and the circle was soon to widen from Cork, where the banner was first raised, to embrace the Protestant interest in neighbouring south Tipperary. If the alleged plots focused on the little enclave on the Blackwater, long the sole centre of active Catholic opinion in County Cork, the point of the accusations was given added force by Burke's presence in the Halifax administration. Fant's letter, which was addressed to Halifax and dated 18 October, four days before the parliamentary session opened, was clearly politically inspired and carefully timed.[4]

The Cork political interest, though speaking for conservative Protestants, did not feel strong enough to carry the Irish House of Commons with them in a direct confrontation with a popular administration, but they were able to prevail in the end. Defeated crushingly in the Lords on 5 April 1762 in an effort to force a debate on the recruitment issue, they transferred their action to the Commons, where their proposed address to the Lord Lieutenant was rejected on 12 April by a vote of 113 to 63. This was a result gained apparently through a remarkable speech by Hamilton, which seems to have been drafted by Burke, and presumably, then, was the first public expression of the powerful logic behind all of Burke's future exposition of the Catholic question. It was clearly to this speech, and with Burke as the anonymous source, that Lord Charlemont was referring when he wrote, 'an intimate friend of his assured me that he [Hamilton] had repeated to him no less than three times an oration which afterwards he spoke in the House, and which lasted near three hours'.[5]

However, anticipating a vote favourable to the government, the opposition had already laid preparations for the defeat of the government by the simple device of proposing in the House, earlier the same morning, a committee of enquiry into the 'popish insurrections' in Munster. This committee was set up without a division. When it reported on 16 April, its resolutions were carried

---

4   L.M.Cullen, 'Burke, Ireland and Revolution', in *Eighteenth Century Life*, vol. 16, n.s., no. 1 (February 1992), pp. 27–28.

5   H.M.C. *Charlemont Papers*, vol. I, p. 145. According to Charlemont, 'all his [Hamilton's] speeches, however long, were written, and got by heart'. If the speech was written out, the likelihood that it was drafted by Burke becomes all the greater. It is also likely that it provided the first formulation of the ideas for his later unpublished paper in the 1760s on the Penal Laws. The speech made a large impact on Charlemont, and he refers to it elsewhere (ibid., p. 19). This speech has sometimes been assumed, wrongly, to be the speech which earned Hamilton his nickname of 'Single-speech'. See *Scots Magazine* (1797), p. 646.

on a division by 58 votes to 44, and the committee was recommitted, although it was the end of the session, to continue its work.[6] No administration could dare to act in support of recruitment as long as a committee with such a serious remit was in being, and so all the work of the administration was now undone. Halifax, writing to London on 17 April, revealed in a lame dispatch his awareness that he had been outwitted.[7] The opposition had already circulated scare stories in London about a rising, and even in reporting to London Halifax was on the defensive, trying to deny their substance.[8] It had become impossible for the government to take the arming issue further.

Thomas Copeland expresses understandable surprise at finding among Burke's papers the letter from Fant to Halifax, actually endorsed in Burke's hand.[9] In fact, this simply illustrates Burke's central position in the whole matter. The survival of the letter in his papers, and not in the state papers, shows that he had handled the affair, and the contents must have been discussed in the Dublin privy council. Indeed, one suspects that it was lobbying by Burke that resulted both in the issue being slow to come up in the Commons and, when the committee of enquiry into the 'popish insurrections' made its report, in the absence of many members from the House and the resulting, slender majority.

In 1762, a search for firearms in the houses of Catholics in the city of Cork and the surrounding country was organised, but there were found 'no more than thirty unserviceable firelocks and a few hangers'. This episode has been interpreted as an example of the enforcement of the Penal Laws.[10] However, the action had been authorised by the Lord Lieutenant, prompted by Burke,[11] and its purpose was actually to disprove the assertions of the anti-Catholic interest in the Commons in their own political power base of County Cork.

Such overriding of local interests by the authorities in Dublin could be repeated. In a response to the Commons' attempt to uncover a plot in Munster, and after a consequent purge in the locality, the executive took the trials of the Whiteboys out of the hands of the local gentry, and gave the task to a

6   *Journals of the House of Commons*, vol. VII, p. 161.
7   *Calendar of Home Office Papers 1760–65*, p. 174.
8   Ibid., pp. 173–75.
9   *Correspondence*, I, 147, n.5.
10   W.E.H. Lecky, *A History of Ireland in the Eighteenth Century* (London, 1892), vol. II, p. 31n.
11   *Correspondence*, VII, 285. In this letter, addressed to Richard Burke, Jr., and dated 6, 7, 10 November 1792, Burke gives the date as 1764, and this is the date followed in Cullen, 'Burke, Ireland and Revolution', op. cit., p. 41, n.26. A slip of memory, citing 1764 in error for 1762 seems far more probable, especially in the context of the many actions in Cork that spring, and the administration's own intervention in the county.

special commission of two law officers, John Aston, chief justice of the common pleas, and (of all men) Anthony Malone, who was one of the Commons' most respected members and, though holding one of the chief offices of law as sergeant in 1761, was the son of a convert. The commission itself took the form of an astonishing procession across Munster with crowds often heralding these two men as saviours. When leaving Cork, however, Aston was 'grossly insulted by the prosecutors of the Whiteboys for his lenity, or, rather, impartiality', and stones were thrown at his carriage.[12] Again, the fact that Aston's much-quoted report has survived not in the state papers but in Burke's illustrates the crucial rôle Burke was playing in these manoeuvres.[13]

When he was private secretary again, in 1763–64, Burke had to confront a similar situation. As early as April 1763, several months before the session, reports were in the air that information was to be lodged against 'men of property'.[14] Burke was alive to the issue at the very outset: 'I see by Williamson's last paper that they are reviving the rebellion stories; and have produced a second song, indeed more plausible as to the manner than the former; they asserted it was proved on the trial of Dweyr [*sic*] at Clonmel.'[15] On this occasion, the opposition in the Commons was much better organised than in 1761–62, when it had become effective only late in the session. More seriously, the administration lost its ability to manage the Lords. On 11 February, the Earl of Carrick (Lord Shannon's son-in-law) seems to have been the instigator of a Lords committee appointed to enquire into 'the insurrections', and in the report he made on behalf of the committee on 14 February he implied criticism of the two judges' commission in 1762. Not only was the report agreed, but the Lords decreed the following day, in an unprecedented order, that it should be put up in market towns and public places throughout the kingdom. The Commons committee, in existence since the preceding session, also reported on 15 February, and a motion against its findings was lost by 26 votes to 80.

In the next parliamentary session, 1765–66, the focus of enquiry was more sharply on propertied Catholics, and, in all, about forty Catholics were arrested in that time. They included James Nagle of Garnavilla in Tipperary. Garrett Nagle, the eldest son of the Ballylegan branch, apprehensive for his own safety, conformed formally to the Established Church twice inside seven

12 *Scots Magazine*, October 1786, p. 512.
13 Chief Justice Aston to Hamilton, 24 June 1762, *Correspondence of the Right Honourable Edmund Burke between the Year 1744 and the Period of his Decease in 1797*, eds. Charles William, Earl Fitzwilliam and Sir Richard Bourke (London, 1844), vol. I, p. 38.
14 *Glasgow Journal*, 14/21 April 1763.
15 Burke to John Ridge, 23 April 1763. *Correspondence*, I, 169.

months.[16] James Nagle of Garnavilla conformed in December 1765, no doubt in the vain hope of protecting himself, as did Robert Nagle at Clogher in the same month.[17] Burke's letters in the spring of 1766 are full of references to what was afoot in Ireland. His visit there in the second half of that year, from August to October, is, at first sight, a little puzzling as it occurred in a time of crisis in the career of his patron, the Marquis of Rockingham, and the full scale of its purpose does not emerge in the few letters which survive. This purpose was, however, to organise the defence of the Catholics, and one of the persons he met was John Fitzgibbon, father of the future Earl of Clare.[18]

His mission was remarkably successful. He organised a powerful defence team, and engaged in discreet lobbying of politicians in an effort to prevent any effective parliamentary action. The day immediately after, or before, meeting Fitzgibbon (Burke did not recollect twenty-six years later), he dined with the Lord Chancellor of Ireland, John Bowes, obtaining an assurance that, 'by no forwardness of his, any further mischief should be done by the Penal Laws'.[19] The Lord Chancellor's authority in the Lords and over the judicial machinery at large had, of course, a vital rôle to play in undoing any sinister legal and political manoeuvres. When he had returned, well-briefed, to London, Burke hastened to advise his relatives that 'the plot is laid deep; and the persons concerned in it are very determined and very wicked'. Significantly, those who had already been brought to trial in early 1766, before Burke began to organise the defence, did not fare well: Burke's visit had itself been prompted by the execution of three minor gentlemen and the priest Nicholas Sheehy in the spring.[20] The defence council for the Catholics was highly talented, including, among others, John Fitzgibbon himself, Sir Lucius O'Brien, John Scott and Barry Yelverton – all young men destined to establish themselves as great names at the Irish Bar, and even in some cases to advance beyond it.

---

16 O'Byrne, *Convert Rolls*; *Correspondence*, I, 216; O'Connell, 'The Nagles of Garnavilla', in *Irish Genealogist*, vol. III, no.1 (1956), p. 22.

17 O'Byrne, *Convert Rolls*; *Correspondence*, I, 276n; O'Connell, op. cit., pp. 21–22. James Nagle's conversion has sometimes been given incorrectly as December 1766.

18 Burke's sole and retrospective recording of this meeting is noteworthy. 'My last conversation with him [Fitzgibbon] was at Milltown in 1766 – we dined tête-à-tête, and he spoke to me like a good Irishman. Religion, as such made no part of our conversation then, or at any former time – but the condition of his countrymen and blood, on account of that religion, from the insane prejudices, and furious temper then raging, in the lower part of the prevailing faction seemed to make a proper impression on him ... His mind was right, both as a lawyer, and as a man that wished well to his country.' Letter to Richard Burke, Jr., 20 March 1792. *Correspondence*, VII, 101.

19 *Correspondence*, VII, 102.

20 L.M. Cullen, 'Burke, Ireland and Revolution', op. cit., p. 33. See also O'Connell, op. cit., p. 22.

Edmund Burke felt consistently that Catholics should be prepared to assert themselves when necessary. He may well have acquired this belief originally from his Nagle relatives, who had a tradition of such behaviour, whether by lobbying Parliament (in the early 1730s) or, in Nano Nagle's case, in founding a religious order of nuns in the 1750s. In 1777, when Catholic Relief was in the air, Burke's reaction to reports of the visit to Ireland of Charles James Fox (who met the Nagles there) was one of pleasure that, 'the old spirit and character of that country is fully kept up which rejoices me beyond measure'.[21] In retrospect, he felt that his own firm action in 1766 had achieved the suppression of the judicial menace threatening Catholics then, and this belief in the importance of vigorous assertion was to remain the wellspring of his advice on Irish affairs from his early unpublished writings to his dying days.

II. SPEECHES AND WRITINGS ON IRELAND

We know very little about the detailed circumstances of Burke's writing and we know little more about his method of composition: we even lack drafts of some of his texts and early speeches. The speech by Hamilton mentioned above, which is supposed to have created a sensation by its effectiveness, must have been Burke's first attempt to order his thoughts on the Catholic question. In the following session, he drafted his celebrated, long account of the Penal Laws, unpublished in his lifetime, which appears to have been a preparatory document for a petition and address drawn up at the time. The Catholic activist John Curry later reminded Burke that the petition of 1778 was based on 'that address and petition which you may remember you drew up and left with me in the year 1764'.[22] Aware that the charges in 1764 were much broader and better orchestrated than in 1761–62, Burke seems to have been party then to efforts to refute the accounts of the 1641 massacres which were being used as an argument against making concessions to Catholics. He cooperated with Curry in the latter's publication of a book on the massacres, and he also regarded himself as responsible for persuading Dr Leland to write his *History of Ireland* (1773), though with results which were to disappoint him.[23]

In fact, Burke's task lay not simply in encouraging others to do this work, but in doing much of it himself. Later, in a letter to Bishop William Markham,

---

21 Burke to Garrett Nagle, 26 October 1777. *Correspondence*, III, 391. Burke's letter to Fox, dated 8 October, is also immediately relevant to this point. See ibid., 381.
22 Curry to Burke, 18 August 1778. *Correspondence of the Right Honourable Edmund Burke between ... 1744 and ... 1797*, vol. II, p. 238.
23 Burke to Dr Markham, *post* 9 November 1771. *Correspondence*, II, 285.

he observed of Irish history, and of the 1641 rebellion in particular: 'I have studied it with more care than is common, and I have spoken to you on the subject, I dare say twenty times.'[24] With Leland, he went over some of the 1641 depositions in the library of Trinity College, and made himself familiar with a good deal of the other materials for the times.[25] Burke's own unpublished tracts on the Popery Laws, written at this time, are a formidable piece of work – not a literary, but a political piece, characterised by the full flow of Burkean logic and exposition, and consistent with arguments he had developed in 1762.[26] In 1763–64 Burke had perceived, in association with Curry and O'Connor, the two ablest members of the Catholic Committee, that the Catholic case would advance only if Protestants could be convinced that their fears, based on the legends of the 1641 massacres, were groundless. Putting together small details from his correspondence at this time, it is easy to come to the conclusion that Burke's parliamentary circle was a very wide one during both sessions of Parliament, and that Burke had also made a close acquaintance with the members of the Catholic Committee during that period.

It has been suggested that Burke hid his Irishness as far as possible, through guilt (at family conformity) or through caution (in the interests of his career),[27] and that he only once publicly departed from this tactic, in 1780.[28] This is not correct. Burke's public interest in the army augmentation issue, the major issue in Irish politics in 1767–69, related exclusively to the Catholic question. One of the arguments used in the British Parliament in support of the Enabling Bill, which would permit the Irish Parliament to take a decision on augmentation, was that army augmentation was a popular measure among the Irish gentry, 'because the country was, in a great degree R. Catholic, and therefore a rotten part of the British dominions'. By this time, Charles O'Hara could report from Ireland that 'the subject [Catholic conspiracy] is dead amongst

24 Ibid.
25 Burke to Richard Burke, Jr., 20 March 1792. *Correspondence*, VII, 104.
26 *Tracts Relative to the Laws against Popery in Ireland*, in *Works*, VI, 5–48. In January 1780, Burke stated that he had 'desisted' from his writing fourteen years previously (*Correspondence*, X, 6). This round dating would put the work into this period. By force of circumstances, Ireland was not greatly on his mind when he left there in 1764, and in 1766 his Irish thoughts and his visit there were concerned exclusively with the legal defence of the Irish Catholics. The tracts could be seen as part of a whole range of work including the drafting of a Catholic petition (not acted upon at the time) in 1764.
27 The former argument is reinforced by the claim that Burke was secretive about his Irish background and sympathies (Conor Cruise O'Brien, op. cit., pp. 58–69 and *passim*), destroyed his papers for this reason (pp. 38, 63), and may even have given his place of birth as Dublin to conceal his birth in rural Ireland (p. 14). There is no evidence for these suppositions.
28 Conor Cruise O'Brien, op. cit., pp. 201, 476, 481.

us. What little existence it has, is in Cork.' But it was vital for Burke to dis-
abuse the British Parliament of the truth of arguments so often made in
Ireland, and now asserted publicly in London, to the effect that Catholic dis-
loyalty made an increased army necessary:

> As to the rottenness of the country; if it was rotten, I attributed it, to
> the ill policy of government towards the body of the subjects there.
> That it would well become them, to look into the state of that king-
> dom; especially on account of a late black and detestable proceeding
> there, which reflected infinitely either on the justice or the policy of
> English government in ruining and putting to death many for carrying
> on a rebellion at the instigation of France, whilst the throne assured us
> we were in the most profound peace with that nation.[29]

When the Bill came up for a third reading in February 1768, 'I spoke to it
very fully and I believe for an hour together.'[30] It would seem that it was at
this time that he wrote an account of the events that had occurred in Munster
in 1762, and this finally saw the light of day in the nineteenth-century edition
of Burke's correspondence as, 'an unpublished paper of Mr Burke's, relative
to the disturbances in Ireland at the beginning of the reign of George III'.[31]

Despite his other preoccupations, Burke's attention had become fixed on
the Penal Laws again by the mid-1770s. We know that by 1780 he had drawn
up a 'most elegant abstract of our penal statutes'.[32] This has not been published, but a copy survives in the Fitzwilliam papers.[33] It is largely factual,
devoid of the emotive language of Burke's earlier or later writings on the
issue, and this illustrates its immediate practical purpose. Indeed, it was copied
out, with a good deal of minor revision, from what Burke described in 1780
as 'a preliminary part, upon more general grounds, and a sort of popular
abstr[act] of that body of statutes' which formed a part of the unfinished account of the Penal Laws he had written in the early 1760s. It is, in fact, with
much rewording, the substance of the second chapter of that original work,
of which, apart from the preliminary section, Burke noted, 'I found nothing

29 Burke to Charles O'Hara, 27 November 1767. *Correspondence*, I, 337.
30 Burke to Charles O'Hara, 20 February 1768. *Correspondence*, I, 343.
31 The editors suggest the date 1768 or 1769. It is more likely to have been written be-
    tween November 1767 and February 1768. See L.M. Cullen, 'Burke, Ireland, and
    Revolution', op. cit., p. 40, n.22.
32 Viscount Kenmare to Burke, 18 February 1780. *Correspondence*, IV, 203. The title is
    confirmed as 'The View of the Penal Laws', in *Correspondence*, X, 7.
33 Sheffield City Archives, WWM R103, 'A View of the Penal Laws of Ireland in the
    Affair of Religion'.

at all in such order, as could make it of the least use'.[34] Copies were certainly circulated among politicians in Britain when the Relief Bill was before Parliament in the spring of 1778.[35] However, the section appears to have been revised in or before 1776 – that is, at about the time when Arthur Young, the famous agriculturalist and traveller, paid his first visit to Ireland – and Burke's abstract, while ostensibly concerned with religion, deals in essence with property.

III. BURKE AND ARTHUR YOUNG

Arthur Young's visit to Ireland became an occasion to mount a broad defence of the Catholics. Burke's correspondence with Young is not very informative here, but the two men almost certainly had conversations reaching far beyond agriculture before Young actually set off for Ireland.[36] In a letter to Lord Charlemont, informing him of Young's arrival, Burke states in a telling phrase that 'examples may be given, that hereafter will be useful, when you can prevail on yourselves to let *the body of your people into an interest in the prosperity of their country*' (my italics). This can only refer to the Penal Laws, and must account for the remarkable sections on religion and on the tenantry that later appeared in Young's account of his visits to Ireland.[37] (There is also a section on the labouring poor, with an astonishing subsection dealing with 'oppression'.) The section on religion reflects Burke's outlook time and again, even repeating key phrases from the tracts on the Popery Laws and other writings which were at that time unpublished. It is just possible that Burke wrote this section, and that there is a missing paper (very different in tone from the Sheffield manuscript) which forms the link between the writings of the two men and which passed hands when they met in 1776. Such a paper would have had to have been written before 1778, because Young's book,

---

34 Burke to Lord Kenmare, 22 January 1780. *Correspondence*, X, 7.
35 Ibid. On Burke's admission, 'much the greater part were employed on the subject of these restraints on property: and all reflections on that matter are rendered nearly unnecessary by the wise Act of our last session [the Catholic Relief Act]'.
36 Burke offered to write letters of introduction for Young: 'if letters to them ['Lord Charlemont and one or two more'] would be of any service to Mr Young, Mr B. would with great pleasure write to them' (Burke to Young, *ante* 4 June 1776. *Correspondence*, III, 270). Something further transpired, as Burke's reply had left matters hanging on a further communication from Young. His letter to Charlemont, finally written on 4 June, observed that '*in conversing with this gentleman* you will find, that he is very far from having exhausted his stock of useful and pleasing ideas'. (Ibid., 270–71, my italics.)
37 Arthur Young, *A Tour in Ireland with General Observations on the Present State of that Kingdom* (Dublin, 1780).

which appeared in 1780, takes no account of the changes brought about by the Catholic Relief Act in its sections on laws and property-holding.

Moreover, Young argues at one point that it was necessary to enfranchise Catholics if their property was to be secure – a theme that Burke had included in his tracts on the Popery Laws around 1764 – and quotes Burke as an authority on the Penal Laws against Anthony Foster, one of the most bitter political opponents of the Catholics. It is also worth noting that there are passages in Adam Smith's *Wealth of Nations*, published in 1776, that seem framed in Burkean language, suggesting, similarly, access to a paper by Burke that is now lost.

IV. BURKE'S OTHER IRISH CONTACTS

Burke's Irishness is certainly a key to much of his outlook, and this extends even to his knowledge of France and to the glowing impressions of that country's *ancien régime* which we read in the *Reflections*. Many of Burke's contacts there arose, directly or indirectly, from a Nagle marriage into the French family in the west of Ireland in the middle of the century. Burke's sister Julia married a French of Loughrea, and his mother, visiting the region in 1766, was impressed by the affluent lifestyle of Catholics there. That marriage also gave Burke an entrée into Irish business circles in London and, through them, to the speculative group that surrounded the Irish financier Thomas Sutton in Paris, his associate Patrick Darcy, and their crony Isaac Panchaud, a Paris-based banker handling Anglo-French payments. Burke's contacts with Panchaud arose out of speculation in East India stock from 1769 to 1772 – a highly unethical episode in Burke's career.

One of Sutton's daughters married Andrew French, a Galway merchant resident in London in 1771, who had become a key London figure in the varied and complex transactions of the Sutton-Panchaud interest. When he visited France early in 1773, Burke lost no time making contact with Panchaud. Almost immediately after he had arrived in Paris, Burke reported that 'Panchaud arrived on Sunday night. I had a note from him immediately on his arrival; I called on him last night, but I have not yet seen him ... Panchaud has been hunting me ... since I began this letter without any effect.' Fifteen days later, one of Burke's letters was written from Panchaud's house.[38]

The evidence of Burke's contact with Patrick Darcy, a member of the French Academy of Science, which is seen by the editors of the *Correspondence* as a sign of his links with figures of the Enlightenment, simply refers back to the Paris visit, with Burke recalling 'your most obliging remembrance of an old friend'.[39] On Darcy's death in 1779, his widow married an Irishman from Thomas Sutton's Wexford circle, and in 1782 Sutton's wife wrote to Burke in warm terms referring to their acquaintance in Paris and to Richard's having met the Sutton sons.[40] It seems to have been in this company that Burke had visited the Irish College and made himself acquainted with its affairs: there is a moving passage on the visit in his letter to Lord Kenmare in 1782.[41] Thus, Burke's introduction to Paris life and to Madame du Deffand's salon came not from his English background but from his Irish contacts in France, and the dazzling Paris he saw was their circle in high society.

The years from 1782 to 1792 are the lost decade in Burke's Irish links. His interest there fades in this period. He was opportunistic on the Commercial Propositions, put forward in 1784–85 to regulate Anglo-Irish trade, (expressing views that were hardly those of a majority of Irish politicians) and his Irish circle of correspondents had narrowed. He was prey to the conspiracy theory of history, and he saw opposition to Catholic rights as stirred up by scheming politicians rather than as something deeper. The goodwill of those Irish politicians who helped him in the 1760s reinforced his attitudes at the time and it is possible that he had lapsed into complacency as early as 1767. He was uneasy again in 1775–76 on the Catholic question, perhaps privy to fears such as those entertained at the time by the McCarthys and the Wyses, rich Munster families, or aware of Arthur O'Leary's tragic experiences as a propertied Catholic experiencing legal harassment from zealot magistrates in Cork in 1771–73.[42] If so, his unease may have been dispelled once more by his contacts with such prominent politicians as the Commons speaker Sexton Pery, Luke Gardiner and Hely Hutchinson, all of whom possessed remarkably open minds.

The County Cork political interest had weakened enormously in its effectiveness from the 1770s, and Burke, with little and dubious knowledge about other regions in Ireland, may not have sensed the significance in the 1780s of the new grouping around John Foster and the Beresfords. This group was working from within Dublin Castle, not from outside, as had been the case

39 Burke to Darcy, 5 October 1775. *Correspondence*, III, 228.
40 Sheffield Public Library, WWM BKI /1652, May 1782 (Phyllis) Masterson de Sutton. Thomas Sutton was absent in Rochefort at the time, and the letter was a plea to Burke to use his influence on behalf of Luke Ryan and 'Macatar' (Macateer), two privateering masters held in London.
41 *Correspondence*, IV, 410–11. As a semi-public letter, this document is also revealing of a readiness on Burke's part not to conceal his Irish and Catholic feelings.
42 See L.M. Cullen, 'The Contemporary and Later Politics of the Caoineadh Airt Ui Laoire', in *Eighteenth Century Ireland*, vol. 8 (1993), p. 38, and L.M. Cullen, 'Blackwater Catholics ... ', pp. 579–80.

with the old Shannon interest. In addition, the fact that Luke Gardiner, with his very liberal views and his public commitment in 1782 to encouraging further Catholic advances, was a prominent member of the Beresford interest, may have misled Burke about the real nature of Irish developments. Complacently, Burke did not advert to disturbing and rising anti-Catholic undercurrents in Irish politics, and when he did refer to disturbances of the peace in the mid-1780s, he added that they were 'not at all to the degree to which the Irish, *in their exaggerating manner*, have represented the disorder to have mounted' (my italics).[43] Other comments at the time suggest that he did not fully appreciate the depth of Irish opposition to the Commercial Propositions. The same lack of insight in another context, nearly ten years later, made it impossible for him to comprehend how anti-Catholic feeling among Protestants had acquired a political rationale which appealed far beyond the self-interest of a half-dozen politicians in Dublin Castle.

Nevertheless, Burke's visit to Ireland with his son in October 1786 was an important one. Arranged on an impulse – 'How unpredicted our expedition was,' as Richard Burke put it – and with the intention of 'shewing to my son something of the country from whence he originated and to make him a little known there', it was curtailed by the prospect of an earlier resumption of Parliament than had been anticipated.[44] If visits to Cork or Galway were no longer possible, at least the Burkes fitted in a night in Ballitore, which had at first been ruled out. Social contacts with liberal Irish politicians seem to have been hectic; but in making the son familiar with Ireland, Burke foreshadowed Richard's involvement in the affairs of the Catholic Committee in 1791–92. This involvement was entered upon with the father's close support and advice, and also on the basis of his dangerous simplification of the strength of political opposition to Catholic claims.

CONCLUSION

Burke's views on Ireland reflect the intellectual weaknesses of the *Reflections* in a number of ways: a greater strength in logical deduction than in the facts themselves, and an abiding belief that a small number of public figures conspired against the common good. However, they also restore a balance to Burke's thought, upset as it was by views on the French Revolution which were little more than a powerful and excessive logical plea prompted at the outset by domestic political expediency. If events in France led him to wish

43   Burke to O'Beirne, 29 September 1786. *Correspondence*, V, 282.
44   Ibid., 282, 289.

to preserve or restore the status quo, events in Ireland produced the reverse approach. Whatever the risks, he could see, in 1796, that it was 'plain enough, that Catholic *Defenderism* is the only restraint upon Protestant *Ascendency*'.[45] He was aware of the dilemma posed by advocating reform in Ireland in 1796: the danger that it might lead to results that reformers abhorred on the one hand, and, on the other, the risk of being 'annihilated and disgraced in their country'.[46] This is not the language of a conservative: it is the view of a man who had maintained that Catholics had been too timid, and who saw in assertiveness both a brake on arbitrary power and a way forward in political life.

45 Burke to Thomas Hussey, 18 January 1796. *Correspondence*, VIII, 378.
46 Burke to Fitzwilliam, 7 December 1796. *Correspondence*, IX, 149.

Edmund Burke and the Conservative Party in the Nineteenth Century

James Sack

I

In January 1833, three years after the 'Conservative Party' received its formal baptism in the pages of the *Quarterly Review*, the *Dublin University Magazine* commenced its substantial career as the literary voice of Irish conservative opinion. The wider Conservative Party, in the wake of the passage of the 1832 Reform Bill, had just experienced its broadest electoral defeat of the nineteenth century. In an article on 'The Present Crisis', the magazine bemoaned the current state of the party, divided on the great issues of the period, reform, Catholic emancipation, the currency, free trade, the poor laws, and obviously lacking 'one such mind as that of Burke', that 'great providential instrument', who 'would set all to rights'. The author admitted, however, that Burke's 'authority is not very great at present. Look at any of the journals which influence extensively public opinion and see the contempt with which he is treated.'[1] Unfortunately for Burke's reputation, any of such journals would include the great Tory quarterlies and monthlies which, in terms of circulation and measurable impact, stood at or near the top of the heap. Indeed, one might argue that the first three decades of the nineteenth century, unlike the subsequent five, saw the flowering of a Pittite and Tory political, literary, religious, and philosophical tradition which usually superseded, if it did not entirely overwhelm, its liberal and utilitarian rivals. Yet, as the author of 'The Present Crisis' implied, the legacy of Edmund Burke had become strangely muted in realms where one might have expected it to be paramount.

I have discussed elsewhere[2] the rather ambivalent attitude of pre-1830 Pittite politicians and their press to Edmund Burke, and questioned whether British Tory opinion, particularly during the generation after Burke's death in 1797, was prepared to claim his legacy as theirs. This Tory (or Pittite) equivocation concerning Burke's importance – so strikingly at odds with the party's idealisation of the legacy of William Pitt the Younger – was widely

1 *Dublin University Magazine*, January 1833, pp. 4–5.
2 James J. Sack, 'The Memory of Burke and the Memory of Pitt' in *Historical Journal*, 30, 3 (1987), pp. 623–40; *From Jacobite to Conservative* (Cambridge, 1993), pp. 90–99.

reflected in the pre-Reform Tory press. For example, the monthly *British Critic*, founded in 1793 to combat atheism and infidelity, attributed treasonable motives to his support for the American colonists and asserted that the trial of Warren Hastings was a 'master of cruelty and injustice'. It even maintained that Burke's peroration on the French *ancien régime* 'was an outrage on common sense and decency'.[3] The monthly *Blackwood's Edinburgh Magazine*, established by the early 1820s as the Tory voice in Scotland, declared in 1825 that 'the ashes of Burke slumber almost without notice' and while the 'nation annually heaps new honours on the tomb of Pitt ... that of Burke is forgotten'.[4] John Wilson Croker, a very loyal follower of Edmund Burke, regretted in 1826 in the *Quarterly Review* (arguably the leading Tory journal in the United Kingdom) that, because of the neglect of his friends, Burke's 'mighty name was for a time obscured.'[5] The *Standard*, the chief organ of the ultra-Tory London newspaper press after its founding in 1827, claimed during the emancipation and reform crises that Burke grovelled before popery, should never have entered Parliament in the first place, and was deep into Irish financial corruption.[6] Some of Burke's political friends were chagrined that no public honours had been paid at his funeral in 1797; others noted that while Pitt and Fox clubs dotted the countryside, Tories had established no Burke clubs. *Blackwood's* asserted in 1825 that the statesman's ideas were no longer even discussed by anyone in Parliament.[7]

There were, no doubt, many personal and political reasons for this rather widespread Tory neglect of Edmund Burke. There may have been an especially serious difficulty in grafting Burke's generous sympathy for Irish Catholics and native Indians upon the trunk of early-nineteenth-century Toryism. While Burke's pro-American views were long ago and far away, and thus perhaps more easily forgotten, he was most wrapped up in his Irish and Indian activities during the last decade of his life, simultaneous with his assaults upon the French Revolution. In his *Second Letter to Sir Hercules Langrishe* (1795), Burke wrote, 'I think I can hardly overrate the malignity of the principles of Protestant ascendancy, as they affect Ireland; or of Indianism, as they affect ... Asia; or of Jacobinism, as they affect all Europe, and the state of human society itself.'[8] The vigorous ideological edge to such an argument, despite Pitt's own private votes against Warren Hastings and his resignation from office in 1801 over Catholic emancipation, set up an implicit

3 Sack, 'Memory of Burke ... ', pp. 627–28.
4 Ibid., p. 626.
5 Ibid.
6 Ibid., p. 629.
7 Ibid., pp. 623–24, 639–40, 626.
8 *Works*, VI, 58.

rivalry within Tory ranks between Burkean and Pittite loyalists – a conflict quickly won by the more pragmatic Pittites. As a contributor to *Blackwood's* maintained in 1833, in the midst of a generally positive account of Burke's principles, while Pitt was followed by many, 'no man has followed Burke'.[9]

II

It is hard to generalise about the reputation of Burke in the post-1832 conservative press or among Conservative politicians. It appears that much of the anger so clearly expressed against Burke in the Tory press of the first three decades of the century was not a factor in the longer term. However, there was the occasional heavy criticism. The *Protestant Magazine* in the 1850s, not surprisingly, thought Burke's sense of Christianity defective and hence capable of a baneful effect upon modern statesmen and governments.[10] The imperialistic *National Observer* in the 1890s, again not surprisingly, denounced Edmund Burke for his persecution of Warren Hastings.[11] Negative comments about Burke, however, are not frequent enough after 1832 to hold much significance. His name was most often cited in the Tory press in a positive way. Sometimes his considerable authority, like Bacon's or Locke's, would be used to buttress arguments, as in the 1850s in Disraeli's weekly *Press* or in the ultra-Protestant *St James's Chronicle*.[12] At other times, enormous respect would be exhibited for Burke's solid personality or his general world view. For example, *Blackwood's* defended Burke's French perspectives in 1834 and even his Indian ones in 1841.[13] In 1845 the conservative *Bell's Weekly Messenger* found Burke, while inferior to Samuel Johnson, 'one of the greatest and wisest men of modern times'.[14] The *Dublin University Magazine* in 1853 praised the Burke of the *Reflections*.[15]

But there was relatively little effort to connect Burke, like Bolingbroke or the Younger Pitt, or even George III or Canning, with a Tory or conservative interpretation of history, or to see Burke as a particular progenitor of the nineteenth-century Conservative Party. For example, a contributor to the *Quarterly* in 1881 attributed to Bolingbroke, not Burke, 'that great revolution which transformed the Toryism of Filmer and Rochester into the Toryism

9   *Blackwood's Edinburgh Magazine*, March 1833, pp. 277–78.
10 *Protestant Magazine*, July 1850, pp. 106–07.
11 *National Observer*, 30 April 1892, p. 615.
12 *Press*, 28 January 1854, p. 84; *St James's Chronicle*, 7 August 1858.
13 *Blackwood's Edinburgh Magazine*: February 1834, p. 248; May 1841, p. 653.
14 *Bell's Weekly Messenger*, 17 February 1845.
15 *Dublin University Magazine*, March 1853, p. 388.

of Johnson and Pitt'.[16] That press which was particularly loyal to the Tory democratic leanings of Lord Randolph Churchill saw little place for Burke in its pantheon. The weekly *St Stephen's Review* was emphatic, in 1885, that Tory Democracy came from Bolingbroke and Disraeli, and in 1887 it enlarged that list to include the Younger Pitt.[17] The weekly *People* maintained that the key to Churchill's political system lay in the 'traditional continuity of the policy of the Tory party', which it associated with 'the policy of Pitt, of Canning, of Peel, and of Beaconsfield'.[18] In the monthly *National Review*, Ernest W. Beckett, in a defence of Churchill after his controversial resignation from the Cabinet in December 1886, traced the pedigree of Tory Democracy through Churchill and Disraeli 'back to Pitt and Bolingbroke'.[19]

This late-nineteenth-century conservative neglect of Burke has not gone unnoticed by modern British historians. John Fair and John Hutcheson, Jr., when discussing the ideological traditions which underlay recent British Conservatism, found it 'remarkable' that T.E. Kebbel, in his influential *History of Toryism* (1886), while upholding as Tory heroes, Pitt, Liverpool, Canning, Wellington, Peel, Derby, and Disraeli, 'made only scant reference to Burke'. They also observed that in F.E. Smith's *Toryism* (1903), Burke 'receives slight recognition'.[20]

Part of this conservative neglect no doubt originated from the same over-riding issue which made Burke's ideas unpalatable in certain Tory circles in the early nineteenth century: Ireland. In fact it was sometimes more histori-cally comfortable to ignore Burke's Irish legacy, as some Tory journals and sympathetic biographers did,[21] than to espouse a bogus version of it to make Burke's ideas fit in with a prevailing Tory Protestant world view. Hence, dur-ing the Catholic emancipation struggle in the late 1820s, the Tory bishop of Exeter asserted in print that, were he alive, Burke would not favour the lift-ing of Catholic disabilities.[22] The *Standard* maintained in 1839 that if only Burke had lived a few years longer he would have repudiated the whole para-phernalia of his pro-Catholic opinions.[23] *Blackwood's*, in 1844, in an article favourable to Burke on the occasion of the publication of four volumes of his

16 *Quarterly Review*, April 1881, p. 179.
17 *St Stephen's Review*: 4 July 1885, p. 11; 8 January 1887, p. 11.
18 *People*, 7 June 1885, p. 8.
19 *National Review*, March 1887, pp. 24–25.
20 John D. Fair, John Hutcheson, Jr., 'British Conservatism in the Twentieth Century', *Albion*, Winter 1987, p. 553.
21 For example, see *Blackwood's Edinburgh Magazine*, September 1834, pp. 324–39; or George Croly's *Life of Burke* (1840), for which see Sack, *From Jacobite to Conservative*, p. 135.
22 G.C.B. Davies, *Henry Phillpotts, Bishop of Exeter, 1778–1869* (London, 1954), p. 73.
23 *Standard*, 27 November 1839.

correspondence, bemoaned the fact that the great man had not 'lived till our day', when he would have thrown off his pro-papal 'delusions' and, like the 'lion of the desert shaking the forest with his roar', tackled Catholicism.[24]

The evidence at the moment does suggest that Burke had no paradigmatic influence on most leading Conservative politicians of the Victorian age. For example, Curzon, according to his most recent and best biographer, was not much interested in the ideas of Tory philosophers like Burke, and showed more engagement with men of action like Pitt and Canning.[25] Disraeli, who was interested in Tory political philosophy, was more than prepared to deify the Burke who 'placed his head upon the neck of the ancient serpent', Whiggery.[26] He lauded Burke in an election address as the worthiest of Buckinghamshire worthies.[27] There is little doubt, then, that Disraeli's official biographers were correct when they asserted that he was 'deeply penetrated with the spirit and sentiment of Burke's later writings'.[28] However, it is doubtful that Disraeli viewed Burke, splendid figure though he might have been, as a particularly *conservative* inspiration – on a par, for example, with Bolingbroke. As Disraeli, perhaps playfully, told Sir William Harcourt in 1873, Burke was indeed, for him, that 'arch-Whig trumpeter'.[29]

The Young England movement of the 1840s, partially inspired by Disraeli's novels, speeches, and factional manoeuvrings, illustrates the extent to which Burke's vision failed to penetrate deeply even those highly ideological, High Church, Tory circles which largely shared his sympathetic attitudes towards Irish Roman Catholics. Lord Blake, in his history of the Conservative Party, has written that the philosophy of Young England was based on Clarendon, Bolingbroke, Scott, Kenelm Digby and Disraeli, with no mention of Burke.[30] George Smythe, who, along with Lord John Manners and Disraeli, was one of the three principal leaders of the movement, cast his net quite widely over English history when he stood for Canterbury at the general election of 1847 on the principles of 'true Toryism'. Smythe praised a 'succession of heroic spirits', Falkland, Hobbes, Bolingbroke, Wyndham, Cobham, Shippen, Hynde Cotton, David Hume, Adam Smith, Pitt, Lord Grenville, Huskisson, and Canning, with Burke again standing out by his absence from among these 'noblest pilgrims in the world'.[31] A chief organ of the Young England move-

24 *Blackwood's Edinburgh Magazine*, December 1844, pp. 745–762.
25 David Gilmour, *Curzon* (London, 1994), p. 28.
26 From *Sybil*. W.F. Monypenny and G. E. Buckle, *Life of Benjamin Disraeli* (rev. ed., New York, 1929), I, p. 668.
27 Ibid., II, p. 841.
28 Ibid., I, p. 311.
29 Ibid., I, p. 695.
30 Robert Blake, *The Conservative Party from Peel to Churchill* (New York, 1970), p. 55.
31 Richard Faber, *Young England* (London, 1987), pp. 158–59.

ment, the monthly *Oxford and Cambridge Review*, full of applause for Disraeli's 'correct' views on English history and denunciations of the Protestant Reformation and the Glorious Revolution, is also remarkable for its silence on Burke.[32] Perhaps Burke's vision of English history, replete with positive images of the Old Whigs, 1688, and William III, and hence so different from the Disraelian vision, was too well known to elicit much enthusiasm from Young England.

The greatest Conservative political thinker of the nineteenth century, Lord Salisbury, seems also to have kept Burke's purported conservatism at arm's length. Like all English Conservative statesmen, Salisbury, in his willingness to preside over slow though steady change and progress, was a Burkean – as historians like A.L. Kennedy and E.D. Steele have often pointed out.[33] Salisbury, however, while often mentioning him in passing in his voluminous journalism, never tackled Burke's historical or philosophical contributions at quite the level that he addressed those of the Younger Pitt, Castlereagh or Wellington. Neither Lady Gwendolen Cecil, in her four-volume official biography of her father, nor Robert Taylor, in his more recent biography of Lord Salisbury, mentions Burke in their index. Two recent commentators, Michael Pinto-Duschinsky, who has analysed Salisbury's political thought, and Peter Marsh, who has related that political thought to Salisbury's methodology of statecraft, have either failed to emphasise or have explicitly questioned Burke's rôle in Salisbury's intellectual and practical makeup.[34] Then, too, despite his youthful championing of the Maoris of New Zealand, the mature Salisbury may have inhabited realms far from the racial generosity of the mature Burke. His reference to the Irish in his famous speech of 15 May 1886, during the Home Rule Crisis, as being as incapable of self-government as the Hottentots, and, if Henry Lucy is to be credited, his jeering at the skin colour of an Indian MP in 1895, jarred even in a nineteenth-century context.[35]

32 See especially *Oxford and Cambridge Review*, July 1845, pp. 1–3, 57, and September 1845, pp. 228–29.

33 For A.L. Kennedy see *Salisbury, 1830–1903* (London, 1953), pp. 196–97. For Steele see *Salisbury: The Man and his Policies*, ed. Lord Blake and Hugh Cecil (New York, 1987), p. 141.

34 Michael Pinto-Duschinsky, *Political Thought of Lord Salisbury* (London, 1967). Peter Marsh, *Discipline of Popular Government* (Sussex, 1978), pp. 10–11.

35 Marsh, *Discipline of Popular Government*, p. 92. Henry W. Lucy, *Memoirs of Eight Parliaments, 1868–1906* (New York, 1908), p. 114. Salisbury's son, Lord Hugh Cecil, however, fully integrated Burke into the Tory pantheon in his *Conservatism* (London, 1912), pp. 40, 61–62. Perhaps Andrew Roberts' forthcoming life of Salisbury will deal more fully with Burke's influence on the prime minister.

III

The *Quarterly Review*, flagship of the Murray literary empire, was the leading (and loneliest) champion of Burke among prominent post-1832 conservative publications. This factor was due chiefly to John Wilson Croker (1780–1857), the *Review's* political commentator, close friend of Peel and Wellington, former MP, and, arguably, the most important Tory publicist of the first six decades of the nineteenth century. Croker made no apologies and engaged in no qualifications in his enthusiasm for Burke. In the *Quarterly*, in 1835, while commenting on the newly-minted Tamworth Manifesto, Croker proclaimed himself in all things a disciple of Burke. Ten years later, in the same publication, he thought Burke 'the greatest authority that ever wrote on political ethics'.[36] Privately, Croker told Lord Aberdeen that Burke was 'our great master'.[37] Yet, while Croker unquestionably saw himself as carrying the undiluted Burkean torch into the mid-nineteenth century, it might well be that he shared a political fate quite similar to that of his 'dear master'; their mature opinions were increasingly at variance with those of the wider Conservative Party. The Irish Protestant Croker (like the Irish Protestant Burke) supported Catholic emancipation and this led to a bitter, if temporary, political break with the then anti-Catholic Peel in 1827. In the 1840s, Croker strenuously urged the state endowment of the Roman Catholic church in Ireland, a factor which hardly endeared him to an increasingly Protestant-orientated Conservative Party. Although his opinions on foreign and imperial questions were not necessarily published in the *Quarterly*, Croker's increasing, if private, anti-imperial views had a decided Burkean tinge to them. In 1838, with rebellion rife in Canada and trouble apparent on the North-West frontier of the Indian empire, Peel 'heard from Croker himself ... that there was not the slightest advantage in retaining either Canada or India'. Peel concluded of his close friend that 'in all colonial politics he seems to be a Radical'.[38] In 1854, Croker thought Britain was in the wrong regarding the Crimean War, worried about the sufferings of the parents of British soldiers, and suspected that the French were bribing the conservative press to adopt an anti-Russian bellicosity.[39] Croker's attitudes on all sorts of issues, then, were as difficult to graft upon the Conservative Party as Burke's had been. When Croker bemoaned, in

36 *Quarterly Review*, February 1835, p. 269; September 1845, p. 565.
37 British Library, Aberdeen Papers, Add. MSS. 43196, Croker to Aberdeen, 4 June 1851.
38 McLennan Library, McGill University, Montreal, Hardinge Papers, 2/17, Peel to Hardinge, 9 December 1838.
39 Perkins Library, Duke University, Croker Papers: Croker to Lyndhurst, 20 October 1854; Croker to Hardwicke, 17 November 1854.

1854, shortly before his retirement from the *Quarterly*, that Burke's views were 'going out of fashion', with their 'effectual fire' paled, one wonders if he coupled that sentiment with the decline of his own once striking influence in the counsels of the Conservative Party?[40]

Looking at the nineteenth-century Tory or Conservative Party as a whole, it is difficult to determine any clear or direct Burkean influence either on its press or on its leading statesmen. In part, Burke may never have appeared completely convincing as a Tory. When a prominent contributor for the new conservative journal of the 1880s, the *National Review*, called Burke 'a Whig of the Whigs',[41] he may have underlined a basic problem that almost all Tories had with Burke's legacy. Then, from the 1830s to the 1860s, and arguably even into the 1870s, the Conservative Party was battered from without and weakened from within by religious disputes involving varieties of Anglicanism, whether originating at Oxford or Exeter Hall. It was these religious questions which often defined politics for Young England or the young Lord Robert Cecil, or which bedevilled Disraeli's attempts at Conservative unity. On such matters, the Burkean tradition had little to say, largely moulded as it was in a political world broadly insulated from both High Church and Evangelical enthusiasms. Then, when Ireland became *the* prime issue dividing Conservatives and Liberals after 1880, the Burkean tradition might well have proved antithetical to a united Conservative Party. Gladstone surely thought so.

Of all major Victorian politicians, Gladstone was possibly as much influenced by Burke as any. He read Burke at Eton and, as a young Conservative in the 1830s, frequently cited him in *The State in its Relations with the Church*.[42] The Burkean imagery was still present for the now Liberal Gladstone during the initial crisis of Home Rule. Brooding on Ireland, he read Burke on his famous Norwegian cruise in August 1885 and meditated upon Burke's 'magazine of wisdom' in December 1885, when he (or his son) first tentatively raised the Home Rule banner.[43] Gladstone, however, was not an unalloyed admirer of Edmund Burke. In 1891, he told his amanuensis, John Morley,

---

40 Croker to Murray, 13 April 1854, *Croker Papers*, ed. Louis J. Jennings (London, 1884), vol. III, p. 311.

41 *National Review*, December 1883, p. 525.

42 Richard J Helmstadter, 'Conscience and Politics', in Bruce L. Kinzer, ed., *Gladstonian Turn of Mind* (Toronto, 1985), pp. 3, 17–20.

43 A. Warren, 'The Return of Ulysses', *Parliamentary History*, vol. 9, pt. 1 (1990), p. 194. A.B. Cooke and John Vincent, *The Governing Passion* (New York, 1974), pp. 313–16. H.C.G. Matthew, *Gladstone, 1875–98* (Oxford, 1995), p. 295. Burke's most distinguished biographer, in fact, thinks Burke's influence over Liberals in the nineteenth century greater than over Conservatives. Conor Cruise O'Brien, *The Great Melody* (London and Chicago, 1992), p. 111.

that he considered Burke 'a tripartite man: America, France, Ireland – right
as to two, wrong in one'. Morley then reminded the Grand Old Man that
Burke was also correct on India and home affairs, to which the response was
'Yes, yes – quite true. Those ought to be added to my three.'[44] That Gladstone
thought Burke correct on all save French matters was characteristic of late-
nineteenth-century Liberalism. The Conservatives would no doubt, if asked,
have reversed the Gladstonian formula, placing Burke as wrong on all save
French affairs. Yet, by the 1890s, the French Revolution, with its Vendées
and Terrors, was far enough away from the Conservative consciousness to
question (or ignore) any Burkean rôle as an icon of the Conservative Party.
Would the Conservative party of the twentieth century, faced with even greater
exterminations, be more receptive to a Burkean message?

---

44 John Morley, *Life of William Ewart Gladstone* (New York, 1903), vol. III, p. 469.

The Influence of Burke's Writings in Post-Revolutionary France

Yves Chiron

The *Reflections on the Revolution in France* was undoubtedly the text which brought Burke to the attention of the French public. By the time the work was published in England, on 1 November 1790, one of Burke's correspondents in France, Pierre-Gaétan Dupont, had already undertaken to translate it. This translation was published in Paris less than a month later, on 29 November, and was an immediate success. On 30 November Dupont was able to tell Burke that 2,500 copies had been sold – a significant figure at that time, especially considering that the French edition was 544 pages in length. The book went through numerous reprints. Within three months, 10,000 copies had been sold in Paris and, in addition, 6,000 copies of 'pirated' editions were printed in Strasbourg and Lyons.

Before looking at the reception given to Burke's book in France – the first extended counter-revolutionary text in Europe – we should note that other writings by Burke had already been translated into French. As a result, his name was not entirely unfamiliar in educated circles. His criticism of British policy in America was known through the publication in 1775 of *Discours d'Edmond Bourke* [*sic*], *Membre du Parlement d'Angleterre, sur les moyens de conciliation avec les colonies*. Before the translation of the *Reflections*, there had also appeared in French three short pieces in which Burke formulated his first negative judgments on the French Revolution. They were *Discours de M. Burke sur la situation actuelle de la France, Extrait du discours prononcé dans la Chambre des Communes d'Angleterre le 9 février 1790* and *Lettre de M. Burke, membre du Parlement d'Angleterre, aux Français*.

These last three texts contain many of the themes which resurface in the *Reflections* and which had a strong influence on French counter-revolutionary thinkers in the nineteenth century. For example, members of the National Assembly were censured in them for aspiring to create a new régime *ex nihilo*. They had set out to draft a constitution by sweeping away most of their existing institutions. In Burke's words, the French nation was 'advancing laboriously over rubble towards a ghost bearing the sign *Constitution*. But it had one to hand, a good Constitution, when its Estates-General was assembled in three distinct Orders. If it had had public virtue or simply prudence, it would have used its monarch's disposition and made these Estates permanent under the authority of a king whose only wish was to know what the abuses were in order to put an end to them.'[1]

Another criticism taken up by Burke in his *Reflections* and by many counter-revolutionary writers from the nineteenth century onwards, concerned the Declaration of the Rights of Man and of the Citizen, which was adopted by the National Assembly in August 1789. Burke denounced the 'abstract' principles and the universalist pretensions of this Declaration, and he posited against these rights of men the 'rights of the English', which were rooted in practice and forged by history. He wrote that the consequences of the 1789 Declaration were 'to inculcate in the nation's mentality a system of destruction, by giving the people the power to axe all civil and religious authorities and by handing over to them the sceptre of opinion'.[2]

I. BURKE AND RIVAROL

Antoine de Rivarol (1753–1801), who had made his reputation under the *ancien régime* as a brilliant literary critic, became, in 1789, one of the most determined adversaries of the French Revolution, emigrating at the end of 1790 and working thereafter as an agent for the émigré princes in Brussels. Between July 1789 and November 1790 he was the principal editor of the *Journal politique national*, a royalist paper published by Abbé Sabatier.[3] Under the heading 'Résumés', he wrote a commentary on contemporary political events in the form of a chronicle. His particular talent as a writer lay in his carefully crafted, oblique criticisms rather than in direct attacks. He was far from being a superficial thinker, though, and his critique of the French Revolution was similar in many respects to that being developed by Burke at the same time.

Burke's correspondents kept him very well informed about French political life in 1789 and 1790. One in particular was J.B. Decrétot, a deputy for the Third Estate, who, from a very early stage, sent several letters to Burke's son, Richard, describing the first meetings of the Estates-General and its transformation into the National Assembly. Decrétot also used to send the printed texts of speeches made by the deputies in the Chamber. However, Burke was not at that time acquainted with Rivarol's articles in the *Journal politique national*, and the political analyses of these two men developed in parallel.

1   *Discours de M. Burke sur la situation actuelle de la France* (Paris, 1790), p. 10.
2   Ibid., p. 11.
3   Rivarol, *Journal politique national et autres textes* (Paris, 1964).

It would be possible to establish a very informative table of quotations to indicate how close the judgments of Burke and Rivarol were on the French Revolution. There are similar analogies and even similar modes of expression. 'Nature, once it is well known, becomes our reason', writes Rivarol in protest against the constructivist and abstract reasoning of the deputies, who were drawing up a constitution for France in 1789.[4] It is not difficult to find in Burke the same argument about the relationship between nature and history. When Rivarol affirms that he is speaking 'in the name of mankind and of centuries of experience',[5] he reminds us of Burke's words: 'In history a great volume is unrolled for our instruction, drawing the materials of future wisdom from the past errors and infirmities of mankind.'[6]

It was precisely through the lessons of history that both writers reached the same conclusion about the likely outcome of the revolutionary ferment. Rivarol later recalled: 'In 1790, people asked me how the revolution would end. My reply was very straightforward: "Either the king will have an army, or the army will have a king." I added: "One of our soldiers will be lucky because revolutions always end with the sword: Sulla, Caesar, Cromwell".'[7] Rivarol was anticipating Napoleon Bonaparte and the coup of 18 Brumaire, which put an end to the French Revolution. At exactly the same time, Burke was making this prophecy: 'It is known, that armies have hitherto yielded a very precarious and uncertain obedience to any senate, or popular authority ... In the weakness of one kind of authority, and in the fluctuation of all, the officers of an army will remain for some time mutinous and full of faction, until some popular general, who understands the art of conciliating the soldiery, and who possesses the true spirit of command, shall draw the eyes of all men upon himself. Armies will obey him on his personal account.'[8]

It would be easy to give many other examples illustrating the similarities between Burke and Rivarol. Indeed, Burke, in a long open letter to Rivarol's brother, recognised this intellectual closeness and delivered a fine eulogy on the man who was the first French counter-revolutionary. The letter was written on 1 June 1791 (after the publication of the *Reflections*), when Burke had just read the 'Résumés' sent to him by Rivarol's brother: 'I have seen your brother's admirable annals too late to profit by them; they may rank with those of Tacitus. I agree that there is a close resemblance in our way of thinking; this is a confession which may appear to you to be as presumptuous as it is sincere. Had I seen these papers before writing on the same subject, I

4 Rivarol, *Journal politique national*, p. 133.
5 Rivarol, *Les plus belles pages* (Paris, 1989) p. 30.
6 *Reflections*, 247.
7 Rivarol, *Les plus belles pages*, p. 36.
8 *Reflections*, 342.

should have enhanced my own work with several quotations from this brilliant work rather than venture to express less adequately the thoughts which we share.'[9]

II. BURKE AND DE MAISTRE

Rivarol and Burke reached similar conclusions independently; but this was not true of some of the great counter-revolutionary authors at the end of the 1790s and during the following decades. Here Burke exerted a real intellectual influence. The case of Joseph de Maistre (1753–1821) provides the best illustration of this.

De Maistre came from the Kingdom of Savoy and, according to Jean Tulard, began his career as 'a young magistrate fascinated by the Enlightenment'. A freemason who did not consider himself an opponent of the monarchy, he was an interested observer of the early days of the revolution, and soon became one of its most implacable adversaries. 'The suppression of the *parlements*, the Declaration of the Rights of Man, his reading of Burke and the invasion of Savoy in 1792 caused him to swing round in the direction of the counter-revolution.'[10] He fled into exile in Switzerland, but in 1803 he was sent by the King of Sardinia as an envoy to St Petersburg, where he stayed for fourteen years. On his recall to Turin he became chief magistrate and minister of state, maintaining all the time an output of works advocating absolutism in the state and Church and opposing the spread of liberal political philosophy.

We know the exact moment when Joseph de Maistre discovered the *Reflections*. It was at the beginning of 1791, two months after the appearance of the the first French translation.[11] On 21 January that year de Maistre wrote about the book to his friend Joseph-Henry Costa: 'I was delighted, and I can hardly find words to convey to you the extent to which it reinforced my anti-democratic, anti-Gallican ideas. My aversion for everything that is

9   *Lettre de M. Burke sur les affaires de France et des Pays-Bas; adressée à M. le Vicomte de Rivarol* (Paris, 1791). See also *Correspondence*, VI, 265–70. Rivarol was flattered by this tribute and wrote: 'We were the first in France to criticise the revolution before the taking of the Bastille; Burke acknowledged this himself in an excellent letter addressed to my brother, which has been published and of which we are very proud.' *Les plus belles pages*, pp. 29–30.

10 B. Valade, 'Les théocrates', in ed. J. Tulard, *La Contre-révolution. Origines, histoire et postérité* (Paris, 1990), p. 288. See also, H. de Maistre, *Joseph de Maistre* (Paris, 1990), pp. 148–49.

11 From the 'Catalogue de la Bibliothèque de Joseph de Maistre' prepared by Jean-Louis Darcel, *Etudes maistriennes*, n.1 (1975), pp. 1–91. We know that de Maistre read the work in its fifth French edition published in Paris in 1791.

being done in France is turning to loathing.'[12] On several occasions in his work, de Maistre paid tribute to Burke and recognised the intellectual debt that he owed him. For example, with regard to one of the central themes of Burke's philosophy, the impact of nature in history, Joseph de Maistre wrote: 'Mr Burke has said with a profundity that one cannot cease to admire that *art is man's nature.* These words contain more truth and wisdom than the works of twenty philosophers with which I am acquainted.'[13]

Edmund Burke had been one the earliest authors to challenge the theories of Jean-Jacques Rousseau, whom he considered to be 'the great professor and founder of *the philosophy of vanity*'.[14] Joseph de Maistre frequently denounces Rousseau as one of the principal ideological instigators of the French Revolution. Like Burke, de Maistre also looks to experience as the source of wisdom, and he shares Burke's detestation of abstract theory in politics. De Maistre also derives from Burke, as well as from other British historians and jurists, his 'conception of law as the written sanction of custom, itself an expression of natural morality'.[15]

There are, at the same time, significant differences between Burke's thought and de Maistre's. The providential interpretation of the revolution, that it was divine punishment – 'châtiment divin' – is not found in the former, nor is the theocratic perspective which is characteristic of the author of *Les Soirées de Saint-Pétersbourg* and *Du Pape.* It has been said, with some justification: 'The French counter-revolution does not share Burke's sense of liberty, his attachment to representative institutions, his concept of prescription, nor, above all, the obvious value ascribed to English history as a model to follow.'[16] We can, however, find, in many of de Maistre's works, considerable treatment of the British constitution, which the author calls 'the most wonderful balance of powers the world has ever seen'.

III. COUNTER-REVOLUTIONARIES AND LIBERALS

Burke's influence on French political thought in the nineteenth century was spread among different intellectual groups.

Following Rivarol and de Maistre, counter-revolutionaries continued to be influenced by his writing. Among these was Louis de Bonald (1754–1840),

---

12 Quoted by Jean-Louis Darcel, introduction to Joseph de Maistre, *De l'Etat de nature, Etudes maistriennes,* n.2 (1976), p. 12.
13 De Maistre, *De l'Etat de nature,* op. cit., p. 75.
14 *Letter to a Member of the National Assembly, in Works,* II, 536.
15 De Maistre, *De l'Etat de nature,* op. cit., p. 117.
16 François Furet, 'Burke ou la fin d'une seule histoire en Europe', in *Le Débat,* no. 39, p. 65.

who, like de Maistre, was an important representative of the theocratic movement. Bonald came from noble stock and had been appointed mayor of
Millau before the revolution. In 1790 he agreed to be elected President of the
Assembly in that *département*, but he resigned on 31 January 1791 in protest at
the passing of the Civil Constitution of the Clergy by the National Assembly.
A few months later he left France for exile in Germany. He has a claim to
being considered the leader of the theocratic movement, which advocated the
submission of temporal power to the spiritual authority. For Bonald, social
and political issues were, first and foremost, religious questions.

Returning to France in 1797, Bonald wrote for a number of journals and
published several philosophical and political works. In 1815 he was elected to
the Chambre des Députés and, after being re-elected three times, he was appointed to the Chambre des Pairs by Louis XVIII. He exerted considerable
influence in politics, where he was one of the most visible representatives of
the ultra-Right, and his thought influenced authors who followed the theocratic school: Lamennais, Buchez, Bautain and Blanc de Saint-Bonnet.

In his search for a definition of nature, but also in the primacy he gave to
experience and history over reason and abstraction, Bonald followed Burke's
example. Alfred Cobban stresses this point in his work *Edmund Burke and the
Revolt against the Eighteenth Century*: 'The idea that political values must be
judged in their relation with the historical community seems to us the fundamental lesson of Burke's political theory.'[17] In this sense, Bonald is emi-
nently Burkean. The title of his principal work, *Théorie du pouvoir politique
et religieux dans la société civile, démontrée par le raisonnement et par l'histoire*
(1796), published in exile in Germany, is well in keeping with this respect
for the lessons of history. In this work he contrasts favourably the 'natural
constitution' of societies which arises out of human nature with the attempts
by men to establish an artificial, or 'exterior' form of government based on
theory. 'This conflict between man and nature', he continues, 'is the sole
cause of the contentions which appear in the heart of religious and political
societies.'[18]

But Bonald's thought diverges from Burke's to a greater extent than does
de Maistre's. Furthermore, Bonald does not have Burke's oratorical panache.
His arguments are rather ponderous, and they stress spiritual over temporal
power to a degree which would have been unacceptable to Burke.

While the theocratic and counter-revolutionary tradition moved further
and further away from Burke's pragmatism, there appeared, in the second

17   Alfred Cobban, *Edmund Burke and the Revolt against the Eighteenth Century* (London,
     1960), p. 258.
18   Bonald, *Théorie du pouvoir ...* (Paris, 1966), pp. 19–20.

part of the nineteenth century, a liberal interpretation of Burke's writings. It was one that did not centre upon the *Reflections*, of course, but was based on his previous commitment to liberty in Ireland, India and America. Philippe Raynaud writes: 'Nothing is more revealing of the difficulties of Burke's position than the way in which his works have been received by French political factions: the counter-revolutionaries took up many of his arguments but they had to eliminate the liberal elements from his philosophy; the liberals were able to accept his condemnation of the despotic or anarchic tendencies of the revolution, but they could not follow him in rejecting the revolution completely, since 1789 represented for them the dawn of liberty in France.'[19]

So, while liberals were attracted to Burke's campaigns, their fascination was mixed with reservations and disagreement. As early as 1789, among the moderate and reforming deputies of the Constituent Assembly, some of the King's supporters, called *monarchiens*, had been propounding views which were similar to Burke's in certain respects but also very different in others. Jacques de Cazalès (1758–1805) adopted Burke's position in denying that the Assembly had any authority to draft a constitution and the same was the case with François de Montlosier, the author of the *Essai sur l'art de constituer les peuples* (1791). But while both revealed themselves to be admirers of English institutions in the tradition of Montesquieu, they were also opening the way to the liberal movement which would flourish in the nineteenth century.[20] In the coming decades, this liberal body distanced itself increasingly from the counter-revolutionaries and came to oppose Burke's analysis of the revolution on several issues. In particular, one of the fundamental aspects of Burke's thought is his rejection of 'constructivism' (though the word itself was coined later). This involved on his part a threefold rejection: of rationalism (the 'mechanical philosophy'); of voluntarism (the will is not 'the measure of good and evil'); and of individualism.[21] It was mainly with regard to the third of these that French nineteenth-century liberals differed from Burke.

The Orléanist Charles de Rémusat was probably the liberal thinker who expressed his disagreement with Burke's political philosophy most strongly and substantially, although he still considered Burke's legacy one of great importance.

In 1853, when he had become one of the leaders of the liberal right-wing in the Second Empire, Rémusat devoted two long articles to Burke in the *Revue des Deux-Mondes*.[22] In them he outlined the life and thought of a man

---

19 P. Raynaud, preface to *Réflexions sur la Révolution de France* (Paris, 1989), p. xcv.

20 Cf. Jacques de Saint-Victor, *La Chute des aristocrates. 1787–92, la naissance de la droite* (Paris, 1992), pp. 298–302.

21 Cf. Stéphane Rials, 'La Contre-révolution: le procès du constitutionnalisme volontariste', in *Révolution et contre-révolution au XIX siècle* (Paris, 1987), pp. 13–21.

22 Charles de Rémusat, 'Burke, sa vie et ses écrits', in *Revue des Deux-Mondes* 1853, pp. 209–61 and 435–90.

whose struggle on behalf of Irish Catholics and American settlers he so admired. Yet he did not fail to show his disagreement with Burke on the subject of liberty and Burke's interpretation of the revolution. Rémusat, the liberal, blamed him principally for having failed to understand the uniqueness of France's situation under the *ancien régime*. Rémusat explained that the English, particularly since Magna Carta in 1215, had had liberties and rights which it was their duty to protect forever; but France had still to consolidate these liberties and rights. The French had had 'to remake [their] history so that liberty might be historic; liberty in France is a newcomer which had to be born through action ... There lies the weakness of Burke's argument.'

One of the permanent features of liberal thought right up to the present time has been the distinction between the *necessary* revolution of 1789, which heralded a régime of liberties and a system founded on the sovereignty of the nation, and the *uncontrolled slide* in 1793 which led the revolution to sink into the Terror. That distinction does not appear in Burke's thinking. One of the most famous pages in his *Reflections* is his description of the assault on the palace of Versailles on 5 and 6 October 1789 by a rabble manipulated by the Parisian revolutionary clubs. Soldiers were massacred, Louis XVI and the royal family were taken away by force to Paris and imprisoned in the Louvre. For Burke, the Terror began on that date, not in 1793. These events, he writes, bear witness to 'a revolution in sentiments, manners and moral opinions'.[23]

It should be noted, though, that several historians writing today agree with Burke's interpretation of the events of October 1789. For instance, Frédéric Bluche's opinion is that 'the point of no return was finally reached with the happenings of 5 and 6 October 1789, when there was no protest at the massacre of the guards at Versailles, and when Louis XVI became the powerless hostage of revolutionary Paris'.[24]

IV. FROM MICHELET TO TAINE

In the nineteenth century, the *Reflections* was certainly not ignored by French historians. Under the Restoration several authors of historical essays endeavoured to follow Burke's example and to show that France had no need of a written constitution. Two examples are, C.P. Ducanel in *La constitution non écrite du royaume de France et les preuves qu'elle n'a jamais cessé d'exister un seul instant, d'être en vigueur depuis Clovis jusqu'à ce jour* (Paris, 1814) and F.T.

---

23   *Reflections*, p. 175.
24   Frédéric Bluche, *Septembre 1792, logiques d'un massacre* (Paris, 1986), pp. 246–47.
25   Jules Michelet, *Histoire de la Révolution française* (Bibliothèque de la Pléiade, Paris, t. I), p. 440.

Delbare in *Les constitutions révolutionnaires en opposition avec la volonté de la nation* (Paris, 1815).

These pieces of historical research, completely neglected today, were rapidly eclipsed by various competing schools of history: liberal (Thiers and Mignet), socialist (Buchez and Roux, Louis Blanc), and romantic (Lamartine). These different views of the French Revolution were all far removed in spirit from Edmund Burke's analyses. The most virulent attack on Burke appeared in Jules Michelet's *Histoire de la Révolution française* which was first published in 1847. For Michelet, the *Reflections* was 'a foul, angry book, as violent as those by Marat, and in view of the consequences, murderous in its own way!' Far from considering Burke as a worthy intellectual opponent, Michelet treated his book merely as a muddled pamphlet: 'I searched for a doctrine with a naiveté that makes me feel ashamed now. I found only insult and contradiction.'[25]

However, with the appearance, in 1875, of Hippolyte Taine's *Les Origines de la France contemporaine*, many of Burke's analyses were rehabilitated. The preface of *Les Origines* itself has Burkean overtones, such as when Taine states that 'the sudden invention of a new Constitution that is appropriate and durable, is an undertaking beyond the power of the human mind ... If it exists, it is a matter of *discovering* it, not putting it to the vote. Besides, our preferences would be futile; nature and history have already chosen for us; we have to fit in with them.'[26] Taine's descriptions of the 'revolutionary days' and his portraits of certain leading revolutionaries also contain comments closely reminiscent of Burke. The connection is not surprising. Taine was familiar with English literature and history, and he was able to read Burke in the original. Even if Taine's thinking is enriched by other sources, the overwhelming influence of Burke is very clear. In *Les Origines* he quotes Burke on several occasions and calls him the 'profoundest theoretician of political liberty'.[27]

This judgment by Taine is an appropriate point to conclude the discussion of Burke's legacy in nineteenth-century France. The next century was to produce views that were equally contradictory, but it is worth observing that Burke would no doubt have accepted willingly both the counter-revolutionary and the liberal epithets that have been described above. After all, he was a liberal not of the post-revolutionary, but of a pre-revolutionary, world.[28]

---

26 H. Taine, *Les Origines de la France contemporaine* (Robert Laffont, collection 'Bouquins'), t. I, 1986, p. 4.
27 Ibid., p. 399.
28 For examples of these contrasting views of Burke's thought, see P. Manet, *Les Libéraux* (Paris, 1986) and S. Rials, *Révolution et Contre-Révolution* ... See also Y. Chiron, *Edmund Burke et la Révolution française* (Paris, 1987), and 'Edmund Burke' in *La Contre-Révolution. Origine, histoire et postérité*, pp. 85–97.

'Setting People on Thinking': Burke's Legacy in the Debate on Irish Affairs

Conor Cruise O'Brien

I

For much of the nineteenth century, thoughtful members of the upper and middle classes in Britain regarded the writings of Edmund Burke as a treasure-house of political wisdom. Liberals and conservatives were agreed on that, though not entirely on where Burke's wisdom had most revealed itself. The former valued most his writings on America and India, with their emphasis on respect for the principle of consent of the governed; the latter were naturally more impressed by his writings on the revolution in France. Liberals may have felt that he had gone too far in his polemic against the French Revolution: conservatives had little enthusiasm, even in retrospect, for his understanding of the American one.

There was, nevertheless, a general feeling among educated people that Burke had been broadly right about both revolutions. Certainly, he had shown a kind of prophetic power in realising, earlier and more clearly than his contemporaries, that these events were of world-historical importance, and his great posthumous reputation rested primarily on his writings about them, casting a long shadow over British and European political thought in the century up to 1914.[1]

Against this background, and up to the 1880s, Burke's writings on Ireland – abundant, deeply considered and deeply felt though they are – did not seem particularly important to the English. This was because Ireland itself didn't seem important. But from 1880, for a period of just over a decade, the 'Irish Question' came to dominate and convulse the politics of the United Kingdom. This was the result of an uneven and intermittent interaction between forces making for different kinds of social and political change in Ireland and in the rest of the then United Kingdom of Great Britain and Ireland.

---

1 Burke's political wisdom was exaggerated up to the First World War, but it has been underestimated since. Possibly these two points are connected: if the generation that brought the world to disaster in 1914 had venerated Burke for his political wisdom, then the post-war generation may have decided, without reading him, that Burke must have been a fool or a fraud. They would have done better to read him.

94

In Ireland itself, the social changes were largely a consequence of the demographic impact of the Great Famine of 1845–48. In this period, about a million people died and about a million emigrated to North America, mainly to the United States. A pattern of emigration was established, and the population of Ireland continued to fall after those years. In the United States the Irish community grew accordingly, earning power and influence, and many – probably most – of the people in that community maintained strong ties with their relatives in Ireland, who were overwhelmingly of Catholic tenant-farmer stock.

This situation fuelled feelings of hostility, primarily towards the Irish landlords (mainly Protestant) but also towards England, the Protestant power which had conquered the Catholic Irish and established the alien landlord system. Among the more politicised there was a fixed belief that the Irish Famine had been man-made – the result of policies calculated to exterminate a people, something we might now call genocide. Linked to this belief, but more deep-seated, was a feeling of shame over the passivity of the famine victims, who had gone to their deaths 'like lambs to the slaughter'.

While the attempt of some twentieth-century political activists to equate the nineteenth-century Irish famine to the Holocaust of the European Jews nearly a hundred years later is a spurious piece of rhetoric, there is a genuine and close similarity between the post-famine attitudes of Irish Catholic people in Ireland and America, and post-Holocaust attitudes among Jews, especially in Israel and America. In both cases there was a new and grim determination which could be expressed in two words: 'Never again!'

As far as nineteenth-century Ireland was concerned, the moment of truth for the 'Never again!' people came at the end of the 1870s, when a new famine seemed to be looming. The response to this threat was brilliantly innovative and became unprecedented in its success. This was the movement known as the 'New Departure', of which the primary political organ was the Land League.

In Ireland, the Land League, founded by Michael Davitt, organised the tenant farmers to refuse rent and resist eviction. In America, the Irish emigrants, at the call of John Devoy and others, gave financial and propaganda support to the Land League on a scale never before available to any Irish movement. At Westminster and in Ireland, Charles Stewart Parnell emerged as the political leader of the whole movement. His slogan, 'Keep a firm grip on your homesteads', summed up the immediate object of the movement – and it worked. Wherever the Land League chose to concentrate its efforts, it succeeded in ostracising and intimidating the landlords and their agents, to the accompaniment of enormous publicity. (The British government's conspicuously ridiculous showdown over this tactic in 1880, in the case of the County Mayo land agent Captain Boycott, gave the word *boycott* to the world.)

By 1881, it had become apparent to William Ewart Gladstone, the Prime Minister, that the Irish land system had become unworkable. He determined to introduce a radical piece of legislation, which became the Land Act in the same year. It revolutionised the Irish system of land tenure and conceded most of the tenants' demands. This was a signal victory for 'Never again!'

II

Under the impact of the general turmoil caused by these events, Matthew Arnold, poet, essayist and political commentator, decided to collate and present to the public a number of Edmund Burke's letters, tracts and speeches on Irish affairs. Arnold had had the idea of compiling such a collection at a time when British policies towards Ireland were being reassessed, and he hoped that a study of Burke would have a benign effect on that process.[2] In Burke's words, which Arnold made his own in his preface, he hoped that Burke would 'set [people] on thinking'. In retrospect, this hope was only *partially* fulfilled in Arnold's view. The greatest statesman of the Victorian age, Gladstone, did indeed have his mind 'set on thinking' by Burke's writings, and the main result of that thinking – the Home Rule Bill of 1886 – was to fill Matthew Arnold with just the revulsion and dismay that it inspired in most Englishmen of the time who had never read a word of Burke.

The influence of Burke's mind over Gladstone's at the time when Gladstone was moving towards his great decision on Home Rule may be seen in John Morley's *Life of Gladstone*. In late 1885 and early 1886, Gladstone was reading Burke 'nearly every day' and wrote in his diary:

> December 18 [1885] – read Burke; what a magazine of wisdom on Ireland and America.
> January 9 – made many extracts from Burke – *sometimes almost divine*.

'We may easily imagine,' says Morley, who was a biographer of Burke as well, 'how the heat from that profound and glowing furnace still further inflamed strong purposes and exalted resolution in Mr Gladstone.'[3]

---

2   The editor of the definitive edition of Arnold's prose works, R.H. Super, tells us: 'The idea of bringing out a selection of Burke's principal writings on Ireland was presumably Arnold's, not his publisher's. Proofs of the text began to reach him about 20 April 1881. The Preface was not sent off until about 10 May. The volume was published about 4 June.' *Prose Works of Matthew Arnold: English Literature and Irish Politics* (Ann Arbor, 1973), p. 416.

3   Morley, *Life of Gladstone* (London, 1903), vol. III, p. 280.

One of Gladstone's former Cabinet colleagues, the Duke of Argyll, a conservative Whig who knew his Burke and also knew his Gladstone, was dismayed to learn that the Prime Minister was reading Burke and warned him that 'your *perfervidum ingenium Scoti* [enthusiastic Scottish genius] does not need being touched with a live coal from that Irish altar'.

It is hard to resist the conclusion that the Duke had a clearer idea – or sounder intuition – of the forces at work in Burke's writing than Arnold did, though *both* ended up taking a position against Home Rule. Arnold and Gladstone, on the other hand, set out to read Burke from much the same point of view, but came to conflicting conclusions. Both believed that most Englishmen were unaware of how badly the Irish – specifically the Irish Catholics – had been treated in the past, and that a more sympathetic approach to their plight was now called for. But *how much* more sympathetic? It would appear that Arnold, at the time he prepared his collection for publication, did not realise the lengths to which Gladstone was preparing to go on the Land Settlement – let alone on Home Rule.

Burke's 'wisdom', like that of the ancient oracles, is ambiguous. There are contradictions between the emotional thrust of his writings on Ireland and certain, specific, programmatic utterances. At first, Gladstone and Arnold went along with the general thrust, and did not diverge, in any obvious way, over specifics. Both agreed with Burke that the connection between Britain and Ireland needed to be strengthened, not weakened. However, Gladstone came to hold that the connection would be strengthened by making concessions to Home Rule – limited self-government within the empire, as demanded by a large majority of the overwhelmingly Catholic Irish electorate. Arnold believed, passionately towards the end of his life, that Home Rule would bring about the total separation of Britain and Ireland. This was not a dispute that could be resolved by drawing upon anything specific that Burke had said. The circumstances had changed drastically in the years since Burke's death, and no true Burkean could make light of such changes. In the *Reflections on the Revolution in France*, Burke had written: 'Circumstances (which with some gentlemen pass for nothing) give in reality to every political principle its distinguishing colour, and discriminating effect. The circumstances are what render every civil and political scheme beneficial or noxious to mankind.'[4]

Specific solutions, then, were not on offer. Yet it can be argued that Gladstone's bold enterprise was more in tune with the spirit of Burke's writings on Ireland than was Arnold's anxious and cautious sympathy.[5] By the

---

4 *Reflections*, 90.
5 The development of Arnold's attitude towards Irish affairs is subtly and sensitively explored in an important essay, 'Matthew Arnold's Fight for Ireland', by Owen

mid-1880s, Gladstone's attitude differed from that of Arnold in acknowledging the weight of the demands of a large majority of the Irish people, even though these demands appeared exorbitant to many in the United Kingdom and to a compact and determined minority in Ireland itself.

Had he been born a hundred years later, Burke would probably have supported Gladstone's position, backed as it was not only by the poor tenant-farmers, but by most middle-class Catholics and most influential members of the Catholic hierarchy. This, however, is speculation. In practice, Gladstone accepted the emotional impact of Burke's writings and interpreted it as favourable to Home Rule. This was possible because the bulk of those writings constitutes a great and memorable tract against the Protestant ascendancy over Catholics. By the late-nineteenth century, the rigid caste lines which Burke had known in Ireland, especially in his youth, no longer had the backing of the laws; but Protestant ascendancy remained a social and economic fact, and the main – almost the sole – opponents of Home Rule in Ireland were the Protestants. An appeal to the high authority of Burke among the British ruling class was a good way of undermining Irish Protestant opposition. The Irish Protestant record, as expounded by the man who was then regarded as the greatest of British political thinkers – and himself a Protestant of sorts – was tellingly used against the Irish Protestants of the late-nineteenth century. Thus, whatever Burke thought and intended, the influence of his Irish writings, in the late-nineteenth century and after, favoured those who were seeking to adjust, or at least attenuate, the British connection and to undermine the position of the staunchest defenders of the Union in its existing form.

Matthew Arnold died on 14 April 1888, almost two years after the introduction of the first Home Rule Bill. Perhaps realising that he had fallen into something of a trap over Burke and Ireland, Arnold turned, in his last years, to a significantly different body of Burke's writings: those on the revolution in France. This was the Burke of the Tories, who could now lead the fight against Home Rule. Owen Dudley Edwards writes:

> Increasingly Burke had been his great mentor on Irish questions, and in 1881 he had faithfully edited Burke's *Letters, Speeches and Tracts on Irish Affairs*, the great storehouse of his own logic that Ireland must be given a sense of British concern for her welfare and an equal participation in the benefits of empire. Now he would turn to Burke again, to the Burke who broke remorselessly with old friends and party ties

Dudley Edwards, in Robert Giddings (ed.), *Matthew Arnold between Two Worlds* (Vision Press, 1986). In the matter of Anglo-Irish relations, Arnold's influence was of little direct political significance. Culturally, it was important in opening the way for a sympathetic hearing of the Irish literary revival of the 1890s.

against the anarchy of the French Revolution and its British supporters and sympathisers. Was it not just such anarchy that he saw in Ireland? And was it not just such treason to mankind to permit it to flourish? Burke had not seen an Ireland in arms, but he had seen the dangers that his Ireland might fall into the hands of designing enemies of civilisation and history, of truth and culture. That time had now arrived.[6]

So Edmund Burke, in two different aspects of his thought and writing, had now been enlisted on both sides of the great Home Rule controversy. 'Setting people on thinking' is indeed a hazardous and unpredictable enterprise.

III

It is an enterprise all the more hazardous given our uncertainty about Burke's own relation to the condition of the Irish Catholics.

Burke is something of a ventriloquist; we are not always sure from what direction his voice is coming. For example, he speaks of himself as an Englishman more than once in his writings on Ireland. He was not, in fact, English, either as the term was used in his own time, or earlier. He was born in Ireland of Irish parents, and his ancestry, as far as it is known, is entirely Irish and of native, settler stock. His English contemporaries did not take him to be English. John Wilkes said that Burke's oratory 'stank of whiskey and potatoes' – an ethnic eureka, if ever there was one. Later, a more subtle critic, the great feminist Mary Wollstonecraft, took exception to his usurpation of the pronoun *we* to mean the English. Burke sat for English constituents in the mainly English Parliament of Westminster, and no doubt he was concerned to stress that in matters of statecraft he was speaking for the English generally, and not for his 'little platoon', the Irish. (He would have had a better title to the description 'British' had he chosen to use it, but it does not appear that he ever did.)

The matter cannot be separated from the ambiguities of Burke's religious affiliation. He is writing about the Irish Catholics, a people to whom – according to law, professed denomination and social convention – he did not belong. He was baptised into the Church of Ireland (in communion with the Church of England) and remained a member of that Church to the end of his life, so far as is known.[7] According to the law, Edmund Burke was a member of that Irish Protestant Ascendancy which he so detested.

6   Owen Dudley Edwards, 'Matthew Arnold's Fight for Ireland', op. cit., p. 192.
7   See my discussion of this point in *The Great Melody* (London, 1992), pp. 590–91.

Hostile contemporaries were sceptical about Burke's Protestantism, and not without reason. His early years in public life in England were dogged by rumours that he was a crypto-Catholic, and throughout his life cartoonists depicted him in the garb of a Jesuit. His connections with the Irish Catholic people were, in fact, about as close as they could be without his actually being a Catholic.

Burke's mother, Mary Nagle, was and always remained a Catholic. The Nagles were a family of Catholic gentry in the Blackwater valley; one of them, Richard Nagle, had been Attorney-General to James II, and they all suffered, in varying degrees, from the ruin of the Jacobite cause. Burke's earliest schooling was at a Catholic and Gaelic speaking 'hedge-school' near his Nagle relatives, and he stayed closely attached to his mother's side of the family all his life.

About Edmund Burke's father, Richard, Thomas Copeland has written that 'almost nothing is certain'. It seems probable, however, that Richard Burke had been a Catholic, who conformed to the Established Church in order to be allowed to practise the law. This was quite a common strategy at the time, and one denounced by some bishops of the Church of Ireland. Certainly, a Richard Burke did conform to the Established Church in 1722, seven years before Edmund Burke was born and about the time Edmund Burke's father must have started his professional career. It is not certain that the Richard Burke who conformed was Edmund's father, but there is a strong family tradition that it was. The eminent Irish genealogist Basil O'Connell refers to this tradition as 'the univocal tradition of the statesman's Nagle collaterals' – of whom O'Connell is one.[8] I have no hesitation in accepting the family tradition on this point: there was no reason to make it up, and the transaction was nothing to boast about.

Against that probable background, consider the following passage from a letter of Edmund Burke to his own son Richard, concerning the Oath of Conformity, which was required of Catholics before they could enter the professions:

> Let three millions of people but abandon all that they and their ancestors have been taught to believe sacred, and to forswear it publicly in terms the most degrading, scurrilous, and indecent for men of integrity and virtue, and to abuse the whole of their former lives, and to slander the education they have received, and nothing more is required of them.[9]

8 See *Journal of the Cork Historical and Archaeological Society*, vol. LX (July–December 1955).
9 *Works*, VI, 68.

Later writers were to see Burke as a liberal Protestant, moved by a generous compassion for the Catholic underclass. W.B. Yeats, in a fit of idealising Protestant Anglo-Irishry, cited Burke among their heroes and stressed the gratuitous and disinterested nature of his exertions on behalf of Ireland: 'People of Burke and of Grattan/That gave though free to refuse.'[10]

It wasn't really like that. It was more like the case of a Jew whose father had chosen assimilation, through conformity to the Established Church, and who felt torn as a result. The family position of Karl Marx was remarkably similar to that of Burke. Marx's father, the son of a rabbi, conformed to the Lutheran Church, so Karl was supposed to be a Lutheran. Such situations do themselves 'set people on thinking', but they don't necessarily set them on thinking in the same ways or in the same direction. Marx and Burke solved their problem in opposing ways; but it was essentially the same problem.

Burke felt an abiding loyalty to the people from whom he came, and from whom he might seem to have defected. It was a loyalty which cost him dear, and it is tinged with horror: a horror which can, on rare occasions, take on a Swiftian intensity. There is a remarkable passage in the *Speech at Bristol, Previous to the Election* (1780), in which Burke's horror of the Penal Laws and their consequences can hardly be separated from a horror of the people degraded by those laws:

> In this situation men not only shrink from the frowns of a stern mag-
> istrate: but they are obliged to fly from their very species. The seeds of
> destruction are sown in civil intercourse, in social habitudes. The blood
> of wholesome kindred is infected. Their tables and beds are surrounded
> with snares. All the means given by Providence to make life safe and
> comfortable are perverted into instruments of terror and torment. This
> species of universal subserviency, that makes the very servant who waits
> behind your chair the arbiter of your life and fortune, has such a ten-
> dency to degrade and abase mankind, and to deprive them of that as-
> sured and liberal state of mind, which alone can make us what we ought
> to be, that I vow to God I would sooner bring myself to put a man to
> immediate death for opinions I disliked, and so to get rid of the man
> and his opinions at once, than to fret him with a feverish being, tainted
> with the jail-distemper of a contagious servitude, to keep him above
> ground an animated mass of putrefaction, corrupted himself, and cor-
> rupting all about him.[11]

10 W.B. Yeats, '*The Tower*', III, 12.
11 *Works*, II, 148.

We do not know what the good burghers of Bristol, assembled in the Guildhall, can have made of all that. Certainly these words could not have contributed towards getting Burke re-elected as Member for Bristol, even if that had still been a possibility. (In the event he had to find another seat.) But there is no passage in all Burke's writings on Ireland which conveys so clearly the feeling of what it is like to live under such laws; and more especially the feeling of what it was like to escape living under them, by the skin of your teeth – or, rather, your father's teeth.

IV

Matthew Arnold, as we have seen, hoped to influence a great contemporary debate about Ireland by invoking Burke; and Burke's writings, operating on the mind of William Ewart Gladstone, did indeed influence that contemporary debate, though in a way Arnold found very disconcerting.

Despite this unpredictability, it may be tempting to try to relate those writings to our own debate about Ireland today – such as that is. On the whole, it is a temptation that ought to be resisted. A hundred years ago it was natural for English gentlemen to appeal to Burke as an authority accepted both by Liberals and Conservatives. Today, no prime minister with a serious political decision to make would sit for hours, as Gladstone did, reading Burke and taking notes. Conservatives do, occasionally, quote or misquote Burke, to lend a touch of class to an otherwise dreary speech, but that's about it. I doubt whether either Garret FitzGerald or Margaret Thatcher – the architects of the Anglo-Irish Agreement – had read much Burke and I do not know what effect he might have had on them if they had read him, although I do feel that he would have fortified them in feeling that they were doing the right thing. (I say this with mild dismay. My admiration for Burke borders on idolatry, but I have very deep reservations about the Anglo-Irish Agreement.)

Essentially, the Anglo-Irish Agreement is a deal between Irish Catholics and the British at the expense of Irish Protestants in their 'Ulster' bastion.[12] Those who hope to move, under cover of that Agreement, gradually in the

12   The conclusion of this Agreement was accompanied by a great deal of verbiage about 'reconciling the two traditions' in Northern Ireland, but all that was cant, and of the hollowest description. The reality has been the Dublin–London deal. The general thrust of Burke's writings on Ireland is in the direction of some such deal. More to the point, at least emotionally, is the fact that the impression of the Protestant Ascendancy that we get from those pages is such as to isolate the impoverished and frustrated heirs of that Ascendancy in the Northern Ireland of today. This is all the more so when the heirs in question celebrate the memory of that Ascendancy every July and August, with reverberating nostalgia.

direction of a United Ireland would not find much warrant in Burke, as-suming they wanted any. It was Burke's enemies, the United Irelanders, who thought and hoped in terms of an Irish nation, without distinction of religion, separate from Britain. Burke thought, and wrote, of the Irish Catholics as a na-tion. That much, at least, is profoundly relevant today. The Irish Catholics are indeed a nation. The Ulster Protestants know they don't belong to that na-tion and don't want to be dominated by it (though, of course, they enjoyed dominating it as long as they could). In their hearts, the Irish Catholics, while continuing to pay lip-service to 'United Ireland' ideals, do not regard the Ulster Protestants as belonging to the same nation as them either. What the Catholics want is to have their land back, and this is what the Protestants want to stop them having. We are, in fact, witnessing a kind of smouldering holy war over ancestral land, carried on under a cloud of confused and mis-leading slogans.

There is nothing in any of this to surprise Edmund Burke. The holy war was already hundreds of years old in his own day. Since then, and with some help from him, the balance has shifted in favour of the Catholics. He would have had to welcome the shift in the balance, but he would also have had a word of advice which Irish Catholics might take to heart in the aftermath: 'Surely the state of Ireland ought for ever to teach parties moderation in their victories.'[13]

However, it is not for such speculative, contemporary relevance that Burke's writings on Ireland are worth reading: it is because Burke stretches the mind and imagination of his readers in unexpected and sometimes startling ways. Matthew Arnold's experience with Burke, when applied to practical politics, was almost comically disconcerting, like an exploding cigar. Yet at a deeper level, and as a poet, Arnold was absolutely right in his action: 'setting people on thinking' is what it is all about. Burke will always enrich the thinking of his careful readers in relation to whatever matter concerns them most. It does not have to be Ireland, and it is probably better if it is not, since the prob-lems of Ireland inevitably attract vain quests for definite answers, with their consequent intellectual, moral and political entanglements.

So read Burke on Ireland, and then think about something else.*

---

13 Burke to Charles James Fox, 8 October 1777. *Correspondence*, III, 387.

* This essay is taken from the author's introduction to the Cresset Library edition of *Letters, Speeches and Tracts on Irish Affairs* (1988) and is reproduced here with the kind permission of the author.

The Political Economy of Edmund Burke

Norman Barry

I

At first glance there seems to be something of a paradox about Burke's writings, especially where economic matters are concerned. There is an apparent contradiction between the method that underpins his politics and the type of reasoning which inspires his economics. As is well known, Burke's politics resists abstract reasoning detached from experience and his political recommendations depend upon subtle explorations of the nuances of history. All this is to the detriment of any supposed universal propositions. His political economy, however, is very much in the classical tradition, which employs a style of reasoning that proceeds by remorseless logic apparently indifferent to time, place and the intricacies of circumstance.

Furthermore, his most acclaimed political writings seem to be suffused by a certain sentimentality – a romantic yearning for an idealised past which almost defies the exigencies of the moment. It would be foolish to ignore his colourful language in praise of the French monarchy, and especially of Marie Antoinette, in his *Reflections on the Revolution in France*.[1] Did he not write disparagingly (in the same passage) of 'sophisters, economists and calculators' as *dramatis personae* in the French tragedy? And does not his oft-repeated paean for the political virtues of a natural aristocracy based upon landed property conflict sharply with the openness and mobility of market society – a form of economic order which is adept at generating new forms of property, few of which can be guaranteed to produce the disinterested ruling class he strove so hard to sustain?

Much of this apparent contradiction can be put down to Burke's penchant for the dramatic, his preference for the verbal flourish of the littérateur over the cold logic of the economist. For when he wanted to use economics as an aid to political theory, he was as cognisant of its pitiless conclusions as anyone in the classical tradition. Indeed, Adam Smith is famously reputed to have said that Burke 'was the only man who, without communication, thought on

---

1 'I thought ten thousand swords must have leaped from their scabbards to avenge even a look that threatened her with insult ... ' *Reflections*, 170.

[economic] topics as he did'.[2] In fact, it does not require a thorough knowledge of Burke's thought to realise that there is no deep contradiction between his politics and his economics, nor any need to 'periodise' his writing into stages in which economics gradually assumes pre-eminence over politics (or *vice versa*). Although his most complete, and almost self-contained, work on political economy, *Thoughts and Details on Scarcity* (1795), was written towards the end of his life and does conclusively express the depressing implications that economics has for politics, it is quite consistent with his earlier opinions on the subject, dating back to the 1760s.

The obvious lack of sentimentality in his political economy is not at all disharmonious with his politics. After all, the latter is suffused with the belief that there are serious limits to political action, and that the rationalists have erred grievously in their wild over-estimation of the possibilities of achieving human improvement through direct government intervention in the natural process of social evolution. The supposed nature of economics as a 'value free' science would also be, for Burke, something of an illusion; for the laws of the market are not only perfectly consistent with conventional and traditional morality, but any attempt to breach them is doomed to fail as it involves a violation of the moral, natural law. The economists Burke attacks are ignorant of proper economics; they are the rationalists who arrogantly attempt to defy what are the laws of God.

Burke was fundamentally a free market economist who accepted the theory of human nature on which that doctrine is grounded, and he endorsed the dictates of policy that flow from that understanding. These dictates assert that human (and consequently social) well-being is best achieved by permitting individuals to follow their natural inclinations in striving to better themselves. It is a process which makes possible the harnessing of an ultimately benign self-interest to benefit unknown people. As he argued in his *Speech on the Economical Reform* (1780), 'commerce ... flourishes most when it is left to itself'.[3]

In other writings he was to go even further and, in a manner almost reminiscent of Mandeville's notoriously amoral *Fable of the Bees* (1705), he explicitly recommends the deliberate cultivation of self-interest, even greed: 'But, if the farmer is excessively avaricious? – why, so much the better – the more he desires to increase his gains, the more interested is he in the good condition of those upon whose labour his gains must principally depend.'[4] In fact, Burke took Adam Smith's (rather sanitised) view of the social effects of

---

2 Quoted in C.B. Macpherson, *Burke* (Oxford, 1980), p. 20.
3 *Works*, II, 109.
4 Ibid., V, 89.

self-interest, that there is ultimately a harmony between the diverse endeavours of participants in an economic process that is governed by the signals of the price system and subject to the constraints of traditional rules of justice.

Burke actually moves beyond the classical economists with his nascent appreciation of the rôle of 'middlemen', 'jobbers' and 'speculators' in a market system.[5] The Smith-Ricardo tradition dealt almost exclusively with labour, capital and land as the factors of production, and had been obsessively concerned to explain the returns each earned, that is, respectively, wages, interest and rent: Burke had an embryonic theory of profit as the reward for the exploitation of gaps in the market by astute individuals. Of course, at the time that he was writing, the Industrial Revolution was in its infancy, so he could not have even anticipated the great entrepreneurial achievements that were to occur. His comments describe not so much the innovators of productive techniques but the value created by any market traders (speculators) whose activities help to co-ordinate the actions of the direct producers. He even hinted that monopoly, if achieved by genuine market trading, was not that reprehensible;[6] he probably thought that it was temporary and forever vulnerable to competition and the flux of economic life. What he really opposed was state-sanctioned monopolies, and his long campaign against the East India Company was partly inspired by his loathing for the monopoly powers it had acquired through politics. A state monopoly could never be validated as an example of prescriptive right, no matter how long it had been established.

Of course, as Burke was well aware, speculators and other allegedly non-productive market traders aroused great envy. Their profits appeared to come not from any physical input but from their capacity to anticipate correctly future demand, and from their skilful use of the money and credit system (though, as we shall see below, Burke was careful to distinguish between genuine market speculation and speculation on government debt). The prejudice against entrepreneurship continues to this day: witness the attacks on the 'paper manipulators' during the 1980s. But Burke had no such moralistic and physicalist view of economics; for him money itself was productive. He had no objection to what he called 'the love of lucre'; and the minor criticisms he makes of that love when it is carried to 'a ridiculous, sometimes to a vicious, excess' derive from his aesthetic sensibilities rather than from any theoretical objections.[7]

There is, furthermore, a consistency between his basic economics and his admiration for property as an essential bulwark against state power in a civil society. He had, perhaps, an excessive faith in the value of landed property,

5   Ibid., 96.
6   Ibid., 98–99.
7   *Works*, V, 313.

but his appreciation of the social value of other forms of property is very important. Indeed, his praise for the landed aristocracy was qualified by his belief that the opportunities for the acquisition of property by new entrants to the market should not be diminished. His objection to British policy in Ireland was based precisely on the fact that, until much-needed reforms were made towards the end of the eighteenth century, the native Irish were inhibited by unjust laws from acquiring property. The social value of property was that it gave people an interest in their society and a stake in its long-term future. Without the opportunity to acquire land, the ultimate harmony between self-interest and social utility could not be realised. As he said in his *Tracts Relative to the Laws against Popery in Ireland*: 'Confine a man to momentary possession, and you at once cut off that laudable avarice which every wise state has cherished as one of the first principles of its greatness.'[8]

Burke is notorious for his hostility to the state intervening in the market to satisfy welfare demands, but his arguments here were not based on any kind of emotional prejudice or class interest. It is true that his partly sentimental and partly utilitarian affection for the aristocracy influenced much of his political thought, but many of his critical comments on the rôle of government in society were derived from his thorough grounding in classical economics. His arguments depended largely on his appreciation of the constraints that the laws of scarcity place on the continuous pleas for government to maximise social welfare – pleas that were becoming increasingly strident in his lifetime. His views on these matters anticipate a famous comment made by Lord Robbins in 1931. Economics, Robbins said, is about the 'necessities to which human action is subject'.[9] Thus, however morally valid welfare claims may be, they are always qualified by the constraints imposed by scarcity and the infinity of human wants that confront all policy-makers. In any case, Burke repeatedly claimed that the laws of economics were consistent with morality and the will of God.

II

Burke's most succinct discussion of economic theory is his *Thoughts and Details on Scarcity*, and it is instructive to set this work in its historical context. It was written in response to action taken by local magistrates to alleviate suffering caused by a recent bad harvest. In the famous Speenhamland case, the magistrates had used outdoor relief in subsidising the wages of labourers. This had gone beyond previous interventions under the Elizabethan Poor Law,

8   Ibid., VI, 43.
9   Lionel Robbins, *The Nature and Significance of Economic Science* (London, 1931), p. 5.

which were exclusively directed at the indigent poor, widows and orphans and the elderly and infirm. The system of outdoor relief, which was fixed to the price of bread, was later subjected to severe criticism by Ricardo, but Burke anticipated much of the argument.

The economic system, according to Burke, is governed by laws which are nearly as compelling as those of the physical world. The most governors can do is to recognise the force of those laws and adjust policies to the dictates of nature. This means that government should stay out of the market because the natural laws of supply and demand will ensure that resources will be allocated in the most socially efficient ways: 'The moment that government appears at market, all the principles of market will be subverted.'[10] Burke was also an early advocate of free trade, though he would probably have limited this to the British empire – an example of his occasional willingness to qualify pure economic theory by political considerations.[11]

A distinction may be made between government interference in the market in the cause of efficiency and the rôle that is often recommended for government in redistributing the wealth created by an unimpeded market process. Certainly, modern social welfare theory contends, with some plausibility, that scientific economics does not necessarily exclude the latter rôle. Although a welfare system will have some effect on productivity in that it might produce a disincentive to work in certain circumstances, the moral case for welfare might well override the allocative prescriptions of pure theory. In the modern world, most governments are eager to sacrifice economic efficiency for some improvement in *social* welfare.

Burke did not make this distinction clearly and some of his arguments against public welfare were couched in the form of rigid scientific theorems, as if all welfare improvements were literally impossible. However, there is a good reason for his position. In his day there was very little surplus from the economic process that was readily available for redistribution. It was also the case that the particular form of welfare pioneered by the magistrates at Speenhamland was disruptive of the resource allocation of the market: it was simply a bounty to the employers of labour. Therefore Burke's strictures do have a particular purchase here. His objections to other forms of state action for the relief of suffering may not be so plausible.

In the circumstances of his own time, Burke is quite open about the question of direct public interference with the labour market. He says that: 'Labour is a commodity like every other, and [its price] rises or falls according to the

10   *Works*, V, 98.
11   See Francis Canavan, *The Political Economy of Edmund Burke* (New York, 1995), pp. 192–94.

demand.'[12] It must be treated unsentimentally and be subjected to 'all the laws and principles of trade, and not to regulations foreign to them'.[13] However, this does not mean that the employer and employee (in his example, farmer and labourer) are in conflict. Their interests are ultimately reconcilable through the market. The farmer needs healthy and well-fed labourers and the latter need employment. The employer provides the capital without which commerce could not function. If the state were to intervene, it would most likely direct capital to activities which were unsustainable according to the laws of supply and demand. And although the market may not always reflect accurately the true value of the labourer's work, Burke's appeal is not to state intervention but to 'eternal justice'.

There is no difference in view between Burke and Adam Smith on this issue of the self-correcting and automatic functioning of the price system; but perhaps Burke is even more decisive than Smith in his insistence that the laws of commerce are inexorable, and that the likely victims of any attempted interference are the very people who are the objects of the reformers' compassion. There is something almost deterministic in Burke's description of the market process: 'the wheel turns round, and the evil complained of falls with aggravated weight on the complainant'.[14]

It is demand that determines the value of labour, not 'need', however compelling the case for wage subsidies might be to ill-informed moralists. Thus, the factor that is crucial in the determination of wages is the size of the labour force, and while Burke had none of the fears about population that so agitated Malthus, he was very much aware of the fact that the prosperity of the labourers was closely bound up with their numbers. He lived at a time of relative economic tranquillity, and his basic optimism about the market in Europe was reinforced by his knowledge of the economic state of France before the revolution. He had few of the fears about the future of the capitalist system that other classical economists often displayed.

Through similar reasoning Burke was fiercely opposed to egalitarianism; a loathing that was no doubt accentuated by his dire warnings derived from his knowledge of the schemes of the radicals of the French Revolution. His criticism here was a combination of both economic and moral considerations. A forced redistribution would be pointless; there are simply not enough resources to go round to satisfy the demands of the utopian dreamers. When the egalitarians prevail in politics, prosperity does not circulate throughout the mass of society, as it does when markets are left undisturbed, but 'they pull down

12 *Works*, V, 85.
13 Ibid., 89.
14 Ibid., 90.

what is above'.[15] And despite his Christian theology, for Burke the market
price was the just price. Rather like the Roman Catholic economists of the
School of Salamanca, Burke saw the just price as that which is not distorted
by monopoly or other extra-market privileges.[16]

But the most important moral reason for Burke's rejection of any form of
levelling is his belief that civil society depended on a class of property holders.
It is property that tempers and constrains political power, and once property
and power are in the hands of the state liberty is under serious threat. Thus,
although his preference is for the preservation of landed property, this in no
way leads him to attenuate the value of wealth acquired by the familiar market
methods. In addition to these quasi-utilitarian justifications for property there
is also the claim, expressed forcefully in the *Reflections*, that the expropriation
of property which has been validated by prescription is a violation of Burke's
rather convoluted conception of natural law.

III

Independent of Burke's anti-egalitarian strictures or his objections to any attempt to disturb the market's determination of all prices, the question remains:
'What is a conservative, free market theorist to do about those who cannot
make their own way in the market, who are the victims of sudden changes in
the economy or whose labour market value is below subsistence?' Burke has
aroused great criticism here for seeming to absolve the state from any formal
responsibility for their well-being. He says that 'to provide for us in our necessities is not in the power of government'.[17] But the fact that Burke had
good, pragmatic reasons for not enjoining the state to perform a welfare rôle
(he commented that once the magistrates start to feed the people, the demand
will be unlimited – an example of 'moral hazard' that concerns today's sceptics
of social welfare[18]) does not mean that we are all absolved from that responsibility. The duty to relieve suffering may be one of 'imperfect obligation',
ranking below the duties to keep promises, respect property and so on, but
charity is a feature of Christian morality. Thus, ultimately: 'Whenever it hap-

15   Ibid.
16   It is doubtful whether the theory of the 'just price' (which is different from the market
     price) was ever a feature of Catholic economic thought. For sixteenth-century Catholic
     thought in Spain, see M. Grice-Hutchinson, *The School of Salamanca* (Oxford, 1952).
17   *Works*, V, 83.
18   'Moral hazard' occurs when aid to a deprived group encourages the size of the group
     to grow. It is a big problem in welfare theory and politics today. See N. Barry, *Welfare*
     (Milton Keynes, 1990), ch. 7. It was solved in a harsh way by the 'less eligibility' test
     of the 1834 Poor Law Amendment Act. This act was passed largely as a response to
     the Speenhamland policy.

pens that a man can claim nothing according to the rules of commerce and the principles of justice, he … comes within the jurisdiction of mercy.'[19]

It was perhaps easy for Burke to say this at a time of relative prosperity but, given that he was no doctrinaire believer in *laissez-faire*, it is not obvious that his answer would be the same in the face of a real calamity, such as a famine. He does have some clear guidelines for governmental action,[20] which indicate that it should be very limited, but he also admits to exceptions, the extent of which will, presumably, be decided according to circumstance. No doubt, if he did he have to justify extraordinary government action in the face of an 'exception', he would endeavour to make its ameliorative rôle as consistent as possible with laws of necessity.

Even in the *Reflections*, a work that occasionally shows most vividly those elements of sentimentality and romanticism that permeate Burke's political philosophy, the sound realism of his economics breaks out. It nicely complements his politics. The most interesting issue is perhaps the financing of the French national debt.[21] The *ancien régime* had bequeathed to the revolutionaries a significant debt and, to avoid repudiation (which would have had an adverse effect on their future ability to raise taxes), they decided to issue to the debt-holders a paper asset, the *assignat*. These assets were backed by property: but this property was acquired by simple seizure of Church lands and goods (which were later to be sold, gradually). Apparently this was permissible because nobody 'owned' them. Thus, the debt-holders did not enjoy a direct exchange of debt for land but were compelled to accept what were in effect promissory notes that would only be redeemed later. In fact, the *assignat* became a currency and, like all paper currencies, it was subject to inflation.

People were compelled to accept *assignats* for goods in the market, but as the currency declined in value they lost confidence in the free exchange system. As in all inflations, the poor suffered the most. The whole experiment produced massive speculation and, for Burke, this had malign social significance as well as adverse economic consequences. For the speculators in the national debt had quite different interests from traditional property holders, who held their assets in the form of land – a source of permanence and stability. In France, as a direct result of the revolution, money and land were separated so that a transient class of wealthy people was created, who derived their fortunes from their skill in exploiting the highly volatile market in paper assets. The new monied class was never accepted by the aristocracy, and this exclusion was a constant source of resentment, which further undermined

19   *Works*, V, 92.
20   Ibid., 107–8.
21   *Reflections*, 223–26.

social stability. Things were different in Britain, where there was much less differentiation between the two types of wealth, land and money, and where they complemented each other. The landed class provided stability and permanence while the commercial class provided necessary entrepreneurship and economic innovation.

The French Revolution also produced another class of disaffected people, the intellectuals, who had no understanding of the permanent things. In fact, driven as they were by abstract ideas, they had nothing but contempt for the aristocracy and the Church, and little understanding of proper economics.

Ultimately, of course, Burke's major complaint was against the confiscation of landed property, which removed the primary bulwark against unbridled political power. The whole episode turned Burke against national debt financing (Hume and Smith were always opposed to it) precisely because it led to a harmful form of speculation. He had earlier not been very concerned about the national debt (unless it was raised to finance unjust wars) since, in his view, the willingness to lend to the government was a sign that people had confidence in their institutions.

The political implications of the French experience were horrific for Burke. The attack on the landed class and on the Church almost destroyed those essential intermediary institutions of society. It was these social arrangements which bound the people to government by way of a complex network of reciprocal moral obligations, and this was a much more satisfactory source of legitimacy than the unbridled will of the people. The latter produced alienation: the people became atomised individuals, relieved of the subtle duties imposed by traditional institutions, rules and practices. But the comforts of these intimate arrangements were also denied them and, since there was nothing substantial between individuals and the state, the people were vulnerable to despotism. As Burke never tired of pointing out, the radical individualism with which the French Revolution began eventually produced a massive system of centralisation.

But it might well be asked whether this is not precisely the nightmare that extreme *laissez-faire* economics produces? Are not the participants in a market society those same atomised individuals of the French Revolution? Isn't their allegiance only to the profit system? Isn't their fidelity to laws and institutions provisional on them maintaining the market, with its opportunities for personal gain? Surely property accumulated through trade, and possibly ephemeral success in the market, cannot satisfy the tasks of providing that permanence and stability which Burke so stressed? Is not the market system itself, characterised as it is by restlessness, change and uncertainty, a constant threat to civil society?

It is questions such as these that have led critics to doubt the consistency between Burke's politics and his economics. Perhaps the familiar charges have greater relevance to today's *laissez-faire* theorists, who celebrate more anonymous and impersonal markets than existed in Burke's time. The rapidity with which these markets move and the threat that certain transactors, such as corporate raiders, pose to established communities, seem not to fit with Burke's belief in continuity and in slow and gradual evolution. After all, Burke was writing about the economics of a primarily agricultural community in which land was all-important. In such a context there does seem to be a symmetry between his economic and his political prescriptions. His theory of property as a 'trust' is particularly important here: land and valuable goods are held not just for consumption by the present owner, to be disposed according to the whim of the market, but are to be preserved for the benefit of future generations. This surely implies that Burke thought the value of certain things was not solely determined by the market.

All these charges of inconsistency, and even of self-contradiction, have some plausibility. Burke was the least ideological and dogmatic of political thinkers, so it is not surprising that his thought should reveal indeterminacies and even paradoxes. However, there is an underlying pattern to his thought and his political economy blends nicely with it. The point of his economics is that it advises statesmen of the limits of political action. The social world is 'law-governed' in that resources are allocated according to principles that can be *known* – that scarcity is an unalterable fact of the human condition and that our wants are more or less infinite. Thus, although statecraft may in a sense take precedence over political economy in our understanding of the conditions of social order, it is always exercised within constraints, about which political economy informs us.

From this perspective the differences between pre-capitalist and capitalist society are not relevant, for every society has eventually to take cognisance of political economy. We are not free to choose any economic order we want, at least not without having to experience the demonstrable consequences of our choices. The fact that in his *Thoughts and Details on Scarcity* Burke wrote mainly about agricultural economics should not blind us to the truth that the modern industrial economy was already underway in his time or, more importantly, to the valid argument that economic laws, in a general sense, apply at all times and places whatever the variety of forms of economic institutions. Burke was fully aware of the importance of commerce and entrepreneurship, despite his reverence for landed property. Indeed, the virulent complaints he made about speculation were not intended to attack the principle, but were only aimed at the perverse form of speculation produced by misguided government intervention.

His sense of the importance of property, and his argument that it should be over-represented in governmental institutions, was not a function of sentimentality and sheer prejudice but a consequence of his realisation that unbridled democracy is not conducive to the interests of the majority. As he wrote in 1790: 'The will of the many, and their interest, must very often differ.'[22] Modern public choice theory tells us that coalitions of minority interests are almost always formed in a vote-maximising democracy, and they defeat the genuine public interest, leaving everybody worse off.[23] No doubt public choice theorists would not welcome Burke's method for generating the public interest through the disinterested actions of a 'natural aristocracy', but they are still addressing problems first highlighted by him.

Although it is possible to read his political economy without the metaphysical trappings that tend to accompany it, there is a symmetry in the political and economic aspects of Burke's thought. They are both structured around the idea of a divinely-ordered (and fundamentally benign) universe. Even more decisively than Adam Smith, Burke saw some divine purpose behind the self-correcting mechanism of the market and that mechanism's consistency with a non-rationalistic natural law. It is an attitude, or philosophical predisposition, which warns us to be modest in our hopes for human improvement: 'It is not in breaking the laws of commerce, which are the laws of nature, and consequently the laws of God, that we are to place our hope of softening ... divine displeasure.'[24] The twentieth century would have produced fewer catastrophes if his modest advice had been heeded.

22 Ibid., 141.
23 See G. Tullock, *The Vote Motive* (London, 1976).
24 *Works*, V, 100.

Edmund Burke's Philosophy of Rights

Joseph Pappin III

Burke's philosophy of the rights of men offers a powerful rejoinder to that of liberal individualism. It is built upon a political method that is critical of abstract reasoning based on principles divorced from historical circumstances and highly critical of the associated concepts of the social contract, the state of nature, absolute rights and the democratic theory of political representation. Burke did not set out to sacrifice rights to circumstances, but, through his understanding of the natural relationship between man and society, he managed an effective reconciliation of the two and showed how rights can promote the purpose and cohesion of society.

'Liberal individualism' in this context calls to mind what Michael Sandel, in his recent work *Democracy's Discontent*, terms 'Kantian liberalism'. Sandel defines this brand of liberalism as 'the claim that we are separate, individual persons, each with our own aims, interests, and conceptions of the good life'. Thereby, rights are separate from and prior to any conception of the good, and the effect of this outlook has been to turn society into a 'procedural republic'. It is precisely this separation of 'rights' from the 'good', or the 'common good', and the emphasis on the autonomy of individuals that makes liberalism a threat to the social bond and spirit of community that underpinned Burke's position on rights and duties.

Under the reign of liberal individualism people discover a plethora of rights which endanger the very cohesion and existence of society. They are encouraged to proclaim economic rights to such things as income maintenance and job security, social rights to health care and education, to name but a few. Each of these rights lays a claim against everybody else – in the form of society – who must find a way of meeting these claims. Furthermore, such rights almost by necessity come into conflict with one another. One man's right to a minimum wage may lead to job displacement in companies which cannot afford to employ x number of employees at a certain base level of income. The claim to 'reproductive rights' as reflected in the 'pro-choice' movement secures the expectant mother's right to abort her unborn child, precluding any freedom of choice in the future for that aborted human being. If hunting is banned in the name of 'animal rights', then the proliferation of certain animals may endanger the livelihood of farmers.

It is a strange inversion of the social order to grant individual rights legal standing above and against a society which is called upon to protect those very rights. It is a theory built upon a mythical state of nature, where ultimate freedom exists and in which individuals are not naturally social but are prepared to contract away just the freedom necessary for security in an artificial system. It is precisely this tradition of individual rights that Burke opposed and that he traced back to the political philosophy of John Locke.

I

Burke's first criticism of the notion of rights he was attacking is its assumption that individuals have claims or privileges antecedent to all society, which they cede to a popular sovereign in return for security. This picture of people born free in a state of nature, contracting away their freedom voluntarily, and entitled to reclaim it at their pleasure, has, for Burke, the consequence of stripping the individual of all natural relations with those around him. Furthermore, it necessarily turns other people, who possess the same rights, into obstacles to one's own will and freedom. The only solution to this morass of conflicting desires is to call upon the power of the state, which becomes an instrument of individual wants and establishes a pretended freedom in which appetites can easily come to dominate both the individual and the state. The 'rights of men' dangerously underscore the priority of the individual over society and yet, at the same time, give the state responsibilities to satisfy those rights which would invariably fetter the individual and entail a substantive concession on his part even to live within that state.

When Burke speaks negatively of the 'rights of men', it is to this abstract notion that he is referring. He denies that any political theory can be based on this idea of the individual, standing in total independence and outside all civil and social relations. He also rejects the implications of the right to self-government – the right of individuals to determine for themselves, even without precedent or context, their political allegiance and to change it each day, *de novo*, if they so wish.

The logical consequence of such 'rights of men' is that individuals have the right to act as they will, not as they ought, and it earns a forthright rebuke from Burke in the first of his *Letters on a Regicide Peace* (1796): 'As to the right of men to act anywhere according to their pleasure, without any moral tie, no such right exists. Men are never in a state of *total* independence of each other. It is not the condition of our nature.' The whole theory is defective in assuming a state of nature existing above society and all that train of duties and obligations which contain and restrain our daily activities. It lies in a condition of 'abstract perfection', which, for Burke, is its 'practical defect'.

He writes in the *Reflections*: 'Government is not made in virtue of natural rights, which may and do exist in total independence of it; and exist in much greater clearness, and in a much greater degree of abstract perfection: but their abstract perfection is their practical defect. By having a right to everything they want everything.'[1]

Burke refers to these rights elsewhere as 'metaphysic', because they exist only in ideal form, detached from all circumstances. He does not in every instance deny the existence of such natural or original rights, but he does deny their direct applicability to society and politics: 'These metaphysic rights entering into a common life, like rays of light which pierce into a dense medium, are, by the laws of nature, refracted from their straight line. Indeed, in the gross and complicated mass of human passions and concerns, the primitive rights of men undergo such a variety of refractions and reflections, that it becomes absurd to talk of them as if they continued in the simplicity of their original direction.'[2] Abstract rights of men may exist independent of all practical application, but when, as aspirations, they are applied to real circumstances they undermine the very relations they are intended to strengthen.

In effect, Burke is rejecting any pre-social state of nature in which the individual is found in possession of pristine, original rights that he may hold virtually in defiance of society. Indeed, as human beings are by nature social, how is it that they can be found in a pre-social state of nature anyway? For Burke, the starting point of any political thought must be the 'civil social man', and the first mistake of the 'rights of men' philosophers is that they have 'totally forgotten [man's] nature'. He asks, 'How can any man claim, under the conventions of civil society, rights which do not so much as suppose its existence? Rights which are absolutely repugnant to it?'[3]

Those thinkers, such as John Locke, who believe that in the 'state of nature' human beings exist in a state of perfect freedom, typically conceive of society as a contract entered into by the free consent of individuals. Burke sees society as a contract, but of a different sort:

> Society is indeed a contract. Subordinate contracts for objects of mere occasional interest may be dissolved at pleasure – but the state ought not to be considered as nothing better than a partnership agreement in a trade of pepper and coffee, calico or tobacco, or some other such low concern, to be taken up for a little temporary interest, and to be dissolved by the fancy of the parties. It is to be looked on with other reverence; because it is not a partnership in things subservient only to the gross

1   *Works*, V, 216. *Reflections*, 150–51.
2   *Reflections*, 152.
3   Ibid., 156, 150.

animal existence of a temporary and perishable nature. It is a partnership in all science; a partnership in all art; a partnership in every virtue, and in all perfection. As the ends of such a partnership cannot be obtained in many generations, it becomes a partnership not only between those who are living, but between those who are living, those who are dead, and those who are to be born. Each contract of each particular state is but a clause in the great primeval contract of eternal society, linking the lower with the higher natures, connecting the visible and invisible world, according to a fixed compact sanctioned by the inviolable oath which holds all physical and moral natures, each in their appointed place.[4]

By this definition we find ourselves bound in society far from any choice or consent on our part. Insofar as there is any consent it is virtual, or implied, not actual. Our choice is tacit in that we do not remove ourselves from civil society, but rather we choose to remain within it, enjoying its advantages and fulfilling the duties and obligations which are ours by virtue of our place in society. That place exists within a divinely created order: 'I may assume, that the awful Author of our being is the Author of our place in the order of existence; and that having disposed and marshalled us by a divine tactic, not according to our will, but according to his, he has, in and by that disposition, virtually subjected us to act the part which belongs to the place assigned us. We have obligations to mankind at large, which are not in consequence of any special voluntary pact. They arise from the relation of man to man, and the relation of man to God, which relations are not matters of choice.'[5]

God has given us a social nature. That nature bears the stamp of a natural law that does not ordain a brute-like, savage existence, noble or otherwise, but finds individuals naturally within society. Civil society is the natural artifice of human beings and a divine gift, and, as such, it is clear that it has a purpose beneficial to each member. Burke makes the point in the *Reflections*: 'He who gave our nature to be perfected by our virtue, willed also the necessary means of its perfection – He willed therefore the state – He willed its connection with the source and original archetype of all perfection.'[6] The fundamental principles of Burke's political philosophy, then, are not to be found so much in the origins of society, like Locke's, but in its end and purpose. Its primary end serves a moral purpose of helping to perfect human nature in knowledge, virtue, custom and habit.

4   Ibid., 194–95.
5   *Works*, III, 79.
6   *Reflections*, 196.

This is an instance in which Burke appropriates political philosophical terminology from his own time and gives it a classical meaning. Thus, he asserts roundly that: 'The state of civil society ... is a state of nature; and much more truly so than a savage and incoherent mode of life. For man is by nature reasonable; and he is never perfectly in his natural state, but when he is placed where reason may be best cultivated, and most predominates. Art is man's nature. We are as much, at least, in a state of nature in formed manhood, as in immature and helpless infancy.'[7] Those who insist that Burke denigrates reason in favour of natural feeling and sentiment need to reflect on this passage. Society is a product of human contrivance and it provides the context for the full development of human reason. Civil society *is* man's natural state.

Within the movement towards popular sovereignty and majority rule signalled by false 'rights of men' theories, Burke recognises the ascendancy of the will over reason, law, and even natural feelings and sentiments. The will endangers those inclinations which give evidence of a respect and reverence for an ordered, hierarchical society. Instead, according to Burke, the people must become 'conscious that they exercise, and exercise perhaps in a higher link of the order of delegation, the power, which to be legitimate must be according to that eternal, immutable law, in which will and reason are the same'.[8] In other words, Burke emphasises our duties and obligations in society against the dominance of will. Burke does not deny outright that the origins of civil society were ever voluntary, or even that they were born of violence and lawlessness. In fact he acknowledges that in numerous instances this was undoubtedly the case. In any event, the continuance of civil society 'is under a permanent standing covenant, coexisting with the society; and it attaches upon every individual of that society, without any formal act of his own. This is warranted by the general practice, arising out of the general sense of mankind.'[9]

The alternative, Lockean approach leads to unlicensed appetites, in Burke's view, which, through the emergence of a tyrannical majority or unrestrained general will, end in democratic despotism. The emergence of the doctrines of the 'rights of men' and of the social contract removes the restraint supplied by the natural law as it is historically reflected in the common law. More than being born free, for Burke we are destined to be ruled by law. In a speech during the impeachment of Warren Hastings he declared: 'We may bite our chains if we will, but we shall be made to know ourselves, and be taught that man is born to be governed by law; and he that will substitute *will* in the place of it is an enemy to God.'[10]

---

7   *Works*, III, 86.
8   *Reflections*, 191–92.
9   *Works*, III, 78.
10 Ibid., VII, 101.

II

What does Burke offer in place of the abstract 'rights of men' and an unnatural state of nature? After all, though he refuses to equate rights with will, he
does use the language of rights. He speaks of the 'chartered rights of men',
and true 'rights of mankind', which include 'benefits' secured for men by society. He believes that, for the sake of these benefits, an individual must divest
himself 'of the first fundamental right of uncovenanted man, that is, to judge
for himself, and to assert his own cause. He abdicates all right to be his own
governor. He inclusively, in a great measure, abandons the right of self-defence,
the first law of nature ... That he may secure some liberty, he makes a surrender in trust of the whole of it.'[11]

However, to proceed from this position to argue that that act of sacrifice
can form the continuing basis of a contract with society, revocable if certain
conditions and expectations are not met, is not only flawed, but lacks the historical perspective of our rights and liberties as being, in Burke's words, an
'entailed inheritance'. Instead, Burke argues, our rights are those actual, concrete liberties and benefits which have been secured over time, reflect the traditions of a nation and are recognised and expressed in charters and covenants
that give them a status and respect which makes them practically inalienable
save for just cause. Time, history and tradition provide an important sanction and safeguard for these rights: 'You will observe,' writes Burke in the
Reflections, 'that from Magna Charta to the Declaration of Right, it has been
the uniform policy of our constitution to claim and assert our liberties, as an
entailed inheritance derived to us from our forefathers, and to be transmitted to
our posterity; as an estate specially belonging to the people of this kingdom
without any reference whatever to any other more general or prior right.'[12]

In Britain, among the safeguards of these rights Burke identifies a hereditary crown and the unwritten constitution. The British 'look upon the legal
hereditary succession of their crown as among their rights, not as among
their wrongs; as a benefit, not as a grievance; as a security for their liberty, not
as a badge of servitude'.[13] Rights are historically achieved liberties, secured over
time, enjoying the nourishment, sustenance and enrichment of established
institutions which mediate and protect them. Covenants and charters become
part of the constitutional fabric of a country and exist as a barricade against
all attempts at subverting our historically achieved liberties. Collectively, and
over time, they constitute a contract quite different from the sort envisaged
by Locke. Burke argues, in the *Appeal from the New to the Old Whigs* (1791),

11   *Reflections*, 150.
12   Ibid., 119.
13   Ibid., 111.

that 'the constitution of a country being once settled upon some compact, tacit or expressed, there is no power existing of force to alter it, without the breach of the covenant, or the consent of all the parties. Such is the nature of a contract.' The British constitution, then, serves to secure and protect the chartered rights of mankind, which Burke contends to be the true rights of men.

These rights are true in that they are both legitimised by God's will and rooted in the practices of society. In his *Speech on Fox's East India Bill* (1783), Burke says: 'The rights of men, that is to say, the natural rights of mankind, are indeed sacred things; and if any public measure is proved mischievously to affect them, the objection ought to be fatal to that measure, even if no charter at all could be set up against it.' How are these rights 'sacred things'? The covenanted state of men is not limited to the charters, constitution and common law of Britain. There is also a higher law and eternal order of things to which all people are bound. Burke calls them 'the faith, the covenant, the solemn, original, indispensable oath, in which I am bound by the eternal frame and constitution of things, to the whole human race'. The individual is naturally bound in relationships to one another and to God, who is the 'awful Author of our being', and 'of our place in the order of existence'.[14] We are free to ignore these obligations, but at a loss of virtue and diminution of our own selves. The 'indispensable' oath is original in being written in the very heart and nature of human beings and for the same reason renders null and void any public measure raised against the natural rights of mankind.

Burke continues in his *Speech on Fox's East India Bill*:

> If these natural rights are further affirmed and declared by express covenants, if they are clearly defined and secured against chicane, against power, and authority, by written instruments and positive engagements, they are in a still better condition: they partake not only of the sanctity of the object so secured, but of that solemn public faith itself, which secures an object of such importance. Indeed, this formal recognition, by the sovereign power, of an original right in the subject, can never be subverted, but by rooting up the holding, radical principles of government, and even of society itself. The charters, which we call by distinction *great*, are public instruments of this nature; I mean the charters of King John and King Henry the Third. The things secured by these instruments may, without any deceitful ambiguity, be very fitly called the *chartered rights of men*.[15]

We have, therefore, a divinely created order in which human beings hold a place, linking in their very natures both the invisible and visible order of

14 *Works*, III, 79.
15 Ibid., II, 176.

things, and extended and expressed in historical manifestations and particularities of a civil society, entailing these rights as actual benefits and advantages rather than abstractions independent of circumstances.

In contrast to Locke, who considered individuals in a state of nature as 'all equal and independent', enjoying 'perfect freedom to order their actions and dispose of their possessions as they think fit',[16] Burke believes that 'the state of civil society ... is a state of nature'.[17] He denies that there are any natural rights that can truthfully be used as the basis of a claim to the total independence of individuals, even in a state of nature. Any such rights he calls 'pretended rights' and asserts that they 'are all extremes; and in proportion as they are metaphysically true, they are morally and politically false'.[18] They are 'metaphysically true' merely in the sense of being logically consistent, but they have no moral or political application because they are unreal ontologically. Burke is using the term metaphysical in a pejorative sense – that of sheer, logical abstraction, equal to itself but nothing more than pretension. Rights, by their very nature, must have an application in the realms of morality and politics, they must presume human beings in relation with each other. But these pretended rights do not; they are, therefore, 'politically false'.

So Burke refuses to settle social and political questions by an appeal to original rights existing in a pre-civil state of nature. Natural rights are, or should be, a product of prudential judgments, consistent with natural law. In this sense, natural rights are not so much denied as presupposed in civil society, and they are expressed and particularised in a legal and conventional form, even as the positive law is a concrete realisation of the natural law. That man's most fundamental rights are those natural rights expressed in conventional forms should not be puzzling, for 'art is man's nature', and the artifice of convention is an extension of man's social nature. Our human nature must be expressed socially, and, by the pattern of its own telic structure, through the artifice of civilisation. It is this pattern and structure which serves to perfect human nature.

III

The most notable passage defining the authentic and true rights of men was penned by Burke in the *Reflections*:

> Far am I from denying in theory, full as far is my heart from withholding in practice (if I were of power to give or withhold) the *real*

16 See, Locke, *Second Treatise on Civil Government*, ch. 2.
17 *Works*, III, 86.
18 *Reflections*, 153.

rights of men. In denying their false claims of right, I do not mean to injure those which are real, and are such as their pretended rights would totally destroy. If civil society be made for the advantage of man, all the advantages for which it is made become his right. It is an institution of beneficence; and law itself is only beneficence acting by a rule. Men have a right to live by that rule; they have a right to justice, as between their fellows ... They have a right to the fruits of their industry; and to the means of making their industry fruitful. They have a right to the acquisitions of their parents; to the nourishment and improvement of their offspring; to instruction in life, and to consolation in death. Whatever each man can separately do, without trespassing upon others, he has a right to do for himself; and he has a right to a fair portion of all which society, with all its combinations of skill and force, can do in his favour. In this partnership all men have equal rights, but not to equal things ... and as to the share of power, authority, and direction which each individual ought to have in the management of the state, that I must deny to be amongst the direct original rights of man in civil society; for I have in my contemplation the civil social man, and no other. It is a thing to be settled by convention.[19]

It is important to note that this list of rights describes our reciprocal duties and responsibilities towards others as much as, if not more than, the privileges and benefits we might wish to obtain for ourselves. In fact, Burke fashions here the social context in which society helps each of its members to realise and perfect himself in a state of mutual obligations, duties and responsibilities, discharged and secured for one another. It requires an ordered, lawful, restrained society, disciplined by manners and customs, to gain the rewards of industry, to educate the young, or to enjoy the rule of law and the advantages of social affection and consolation amidst life's many uncertainties and hardships.

Burke's list also recognises that in the middle of social obligations we are still individuals, and that great scope should be given to our personal freedoms and liberties so that, insofar as we do not trespass on others, we have the right to do for ourselves what is favourable to our own existence, even at the risk of a certain loss of virtue. Nonetheless, this is a 'partnership', and the condition of the exercise of our rights lies in the recognition and honouring of the 'moral ties' and social bond that bind our lives together in association with one another.

We cannot properly understand Burke's philosophy of rights unless we consider this relational account of rights. While we may have entered civil society by a voluntary pact, whether or not we have, and whether or not by

---

19 *Reflections*, 149–50.

violence or coercion, the fact of our existence in civil society entails our presumed consent to a litany of sometimes burdensome duties towards others.
These moral duties are maintained by an implied consent, as Burke explains
in the *Appeal from the New to the Old Whigs*: 'Parents may not be consenting
to their moral relation; but, consenting or not, they are bound to a long train
of burdensome duties towards those with whom they have never made a convention of any sort. Children are not consenting to their relation, but their
relation, without their actual consent, binds them to its duties; or rather it
implies their consent.' Moreover, Burke declares that, 'The place that determines our duty to our country is a social, civil relation.' It is just and right that
we meet these duties and, if our nature is perfected through such acts, and
if justice is concerned with what is due to another, and binding upon us, then,
in full partnership and solidarity with our fellow men, we must have the
liberty and means to meet these obligations.

   Burke holds firmly that civil society has an end, and, moreover, that the
end is 'a conservation and secure enjoyment of our natural rights' which, he
argues in his *Tracts Relative to the Laws against Popery in Ireland*, 'is the great
and ultimate purpose of civil society; and that therefore all forms whatsoever of government are only good as they are subservient to that purpose to
which they are entirely subordinate'.[20] As civil society is made for the 'secure
enjoyment of our natural rights', which Burke refers to as the 'advantage
of man', then those advantages secured become our right. In opposition
to Burke, the so-called 'full rights of men' would be for 'each to govern
himself'. For Burke, as he states in his *Speech on the Representation of the
Commons in Parliament* (1782), those 'who plead an absolute right cannot be
satisfied with anything short of personal representation, because all *natural*
rights must be the rights of individuals; as by nature there is no such thing
as politic or corporate personality; all these ideas are mere fictions of law,
they are creatures of voluntary institution; men as men are individuals and
nothing else'. Those who champion such an understanding of natural rights
'lay it down that every man ought to govern himself, and that where he cannot go himself he must send his representative; that all other government is
usurpation; and is so far from having a claim to our obedience, it is not only
our right, but our duty, to resist it. Nine-tenths of the reformers argue thus,
that is, on the natural right.'[21] Burke does use the language of rights and he
does apply a philosophy of rights to his political thought, but he denies the
validity of any concept of rights which strips the individual of all moral relations and ties, and conceives of individuals as naturally free and anterior to
society.

20   *Works*, VI, 29.
21   Ibid., 145.

The foundations of government are 'laid not in imaginary rights of men ... but in political convenience, and in human nature; either as that nature is universal, or as it is modified by local habits and social aptitudes'.[22] Burke sees in the pretended 'rights of men' the ascendancy of the will-to-power over reason, human nature, natural feeling and sentiment, which form the fabric of civil society and political community. Furthermore, those who would overturn traditional chartered rights and liberties for arithmetical equality of rights and freedoms have not considered what recourse they will have when such governments themselves become tyrannical, driven to the levelling of differences by an unbounded general will. Burke well construes the consequences for political authority of an abstract rule of rights mathematically extended and applied within society: 'When tyranny is extreme, and abuses of government intolerable, men resort to the rights of nature to shake it off. When they have done so, the very same principle of necessity of human affairs to establish some other authority, which shall preserve the order of this new institution, must be obeyed, until they grow intolerable; and you shall not be suffered to plead original liberty against such an institution.'[23]

Burke not only recognised the dangers of the tyranny of the majority, but his understanding of rights highlights the central fallacy of his opponents to which such practice would lead. 'By these theorists the right of the people is almost always sophistically confounded with their power,' he warns in the *Reflections*, ' ... but till power and right are the same, the whole body of them has no right inconsistent with virtue, and the first of all virtues, prudence. Men have no right to what is not reasonable, and to what is not for their benefit.'[24] In effect, we have no right to that which is not just, or to that which does not perfect our nature through virtue, to that which is not reasonable, or not for our benefit.

At issue for Burke is the title to political authority. His political philosophy is grounded in the natural law, from which our rights emanate and to which they must conform. True it is that governments exist to provide for us advantages and benefits, to help meet our most basic needs and wants, and, as Burke contends, 'Men have a right that these wants should be provided' by political wisdom. 'Among these wants is to be reckoned the want, out of civil society, of a sufficient restraint upon their passions ... In this sense the restraints on men, as well as their liberties, are to be reckoned among their rights.'[25] When citizens consider their various rights, such as those to free speech or a free press, who among them considers restraints upon their passions

22 *Works*, III, 109.
23 *Works*, VI, 99–100.
24 *Reflections*, 153–54.
25 *Reflections*, 151.

also to be a right? Such restraint, provided by the limits of government, of our laws and of our customs, serves a moral purpose and conforms to our nature as rational, social beings. Burke warns that unrestrained passions 'forge our fetters' and become a disease to social and political order. It is easy to congratulate ourselves on the possession of our liberties and freedoms, but their abuse and excess violate our rights to an ordered society and existence and prevent us from obtaining the advantages and benefits of a truly civil society.

What is required for a richer understanding of Burke's philosophy of rights is to keep before us his claim that society is 'a partnership in every virtue, and in all perfection'.[26] Our moral ties and relations make of us the members of this partnership, and as there are no rights inconsistent with virtue, and as virtue serves to perfect human nature, then rights are best viewed not as an assertion of self-rule or a claim to original 'total independence', but as governed by an end or purpose which is, as Francis Canavan writes, 'the full intellectual and moral development of human nature'.[27] This is not the perfection of human nature in the abstract, nor an elevation of the community or state at the expense of any one human person, but the perfection of the living human person in partnership with others, in a spirit of solidarity and reciprocity. As Aristotle argued in his *Politics*, 'it is reciprocal equivalence that keeps a state in being'.[28] The spirit of mutuality, reciprocity, solidarity, and civic responsibility, in which human beings seek their fulfilment in association and partnership with one another, characterises Burke's philosophy of rights, and this moral spirit is nurtured by society, protected by the state. So, it is not surprising to hear Burke declare that the 'nation is a moral essence, not a geographical arrangement, or a denomination of the nomenclator'. Because of this, 'the votes of a majority of the people, whatever their infamous flatterers may teach in order to corrupt their minds, cannot alter the moral any more than they can alter the physical essence of things'.[29]

CONCLUSION

Returning to liberal individualism, or Sandel's 'Kantian liberalism', the government of the 'procedural republic' does not hold that it should provide a 'vision of the good life'. Instead, that system holds, according to Sandel, that government 'should provide a framework of rights that respects persons as

26   *Reflections*, 194.
27   Francis Canavan, *Edmund Burke: Prescription and Providence* (Carolina Academic Press, 1987), p. 117.
28   Aristotle, *Politics*, bk. II, ch. 2.
29   *Works*, V, 220 and III, 76–77.

free and independent selves, capable of choosing their own values and ends'. Choices are not governed by standards of natural law, but the law of our own self-preference. This is reflected in Jean-Paul Sartre's existential philosophy of values, which holds that values are a result of individual, human choice, or Nietzsche's philosophy in which values reside in the 'Will to Power' of the single individual. For Sartre, our values reflect an 'upsurge of freedom' governed by no created nature, glorifying the sheer freedom of 'being-for-itself'.

Without a transcendent standard delimiting good and evil, discovered, not created, by human reason and acted on by our own free wills within the social context of our own place in the world, Sartrean and Nietzschean nihilism constitute the logical alternative. Strangely, neither Sartre nor Nietzsche acknowledges the existence of natural rights, because they chafe against any conception of an essence-bound existence, governed by a substantial nature. But for Burke, rights demand the priority of a natural law and of a human nature, and of a purposeful existence within a God-created universe as the context for all rights. There are no rights that violate the purpose for which something exists. There is no right to enslave an entire people against their will and without any political representation. While the necessities of political order may require only the gradual enfranchisement of a people, the unfettered suppression of a people's political freedom – a freedom which is grounded in a nature whose proper perfection in virtuous behaviour requires such a freedom – is a violation of natural law and an unjustifiable circumscription of their rights.

A Burkean philosophy of rights requires a social context, in pursuit of a common good, in solidarity with one's fellow human beings, to secure the good and virtuous life, realising ends which belong to oneself according to one's own human nature and not through any arbitrary, capricious self-choice. Only through a return to this Burkean philosophy of rights can we recover the authentic 'rights of mankind' expounded by Burke, governed by the natural law and by a transcendent Creator who is the Eternal Law.

Research support for this essay was provided by the Earhart Foundation, Ann Arbor, Michigan, USA.

An Empire of Peoples: Burke, Government and National Character

Bruce Frohnen

There are many volumes of Burke's selected works containing passages from his writings on India, Ireland and America.[1] However, there have been very few extensive studies of whether any consistent theory of empire lies behind these writings.[2] It will be argued below that such a theory does exist, that it rests on Burke's view of the importance of governing different peoples in different ways, and that Burke applied this view to his writings on the British constitution as well as to the wider empire. The imperial constitution, he argued, like the British constitution, was based on principles of limited government and separation of powers and on a universal, immutable natural law which required that governors protect the varying interests of the people they governed. In other words, the British were bound by morality and tradition to govern their possessions in accordance with the needs of their inhabitants. The alternative, Burke warned, was that the British would become tyrants abroad and, at home, threats to their own constitution and the liberties it protected.

Burke did not have access to the vocabulary with which to define a 'people' or even a 'country' precisely.[3] He differentiated sharply among groups

---

1 See, for example, Peter J. Stanlis (ed.), *Edmund Burke: Selected Writings and Speeches* (Gloucester, Massachusetts, 1968); W.J. Bate (ed.), *Selected Writings of Edmund Burke* (Westport, Connecticut, 1960); E.J. Payne (ed.), *Burke's Select Works* (Oxford, 1892); R.J. Hoffman and P. Levack (eds.), *Burke's Politics* (New York, 1949); A.M.D. Hughes (ed.), *Edmund Burke: Selections* (Oxford, 1921).

2 One significant exception is Francis Canavan, *The Political Economy of Edmund Burke* (New York, 1994). That Burke thought a coherent theory of empire important is shown by his having traced 'all the calamities of this country to the single source of our not having had steadily before our eyes a general, comprehensive, well-connected, and well-proportioned view of the whole of our dominions, and a just sense of their true bearings and relations.' *Speech on the Nabob of Arcot's Debts*, in *Works*, III, 125.

3 Burke, for example, refers to the 'countries of Staten and Long Island' in his *Letter to the Sheriffs of Bristol on the Affairs of America*, in *Works*, II, 18. For a more complete discussion of Anglo-American use of the terms 'people' and 'country' see my *The New Communitarians and the Crisis of Modern Liberalism* (Lawrence, Kansas, 1996), pp. 217–18 and notes.

according to their ancestry and circumstances: the colonial 'children' of England had developed a separate character over the 150 years since their ancestors had landed in the New World; the inhabitants of British possessions in India had their own, widely different but ancient and respectable civilisation; Ireland's people shared a civil establishment with the British – one in which Burke, himself of Irish stock, was a prominent figure – though many Irish suffered greatly at British hands because of their supposedly hostile religion.

This diversity created great strains in ruling the empire. Burke was driven to defend Indian civilisation against what he saw as the corruption and tyranny of the East India Company's rule. He argued for religious toleration in Ireland in the interest of civil comity. Concerning America, he urged conciliation in dealing with a largely English people's demand for English liberty. However, in these diverse situations Burke also found congruities and unifying factors which enabled him to construct a concept of an empire which, constitutionally, would embrace them all.

I

Burke believed that societies are fragile and must be allowed to develop through a natural interaction between pre-existing institutions, beliefs and practices and changing circumstances. He regarded prudence as the first of political virtues because it guided the statesman in maintaining the coherence of society through changing times. Not all societies were worth conserving in his eyes – the revolutionary system in France, for example, was hostile to moral order and had to be destroyed – but any society capable of maintaining a moral order deserved acceptance, and one that fell within the British empire should have its fabric preserved by the colonists.[4]

Francis Canavan regards Burke's views on Britain's duties towards her possessions as based on a theory of trusteeship. Indeed, Canavan sees trusteeship at the root of much of Burke's political philosophy. He argues that Burke's view of the relationship between the British imperial rulers and their subjects parallels that of the British aristocracy and commoners: 'Government

4   See, for example, Peter J. Stanlis, *Edmund Burke and the Natural Law* (Ann Arbor, 1958). Stanlis provides the classic natural law reading of Burke's work. Gerald W. Chapman, in *Edmund Burke: the Practical Imagination* (Cambridge, Massachusetts, 1967), relegates natural law reasoning to a secondary rôle behind political prudence, but sees the same general principles at the root of Burke's views on disparate societies. I treat this issue at length in my *Virtue and the Promise of Conservatism: The Legacy of Burke and Tocqueville* (Lawrence, Kansas, 1994), chapters 2 and 3.

by the landed aristocracy is for the benefit, not of the aristocrats, but of the people at large, whose trustees the aristocrats are.' In both cases, those with power and property are duty bound to use them for the benefit of the unenfranchised and propertyless classes.[5]

As evidence for Burke's attachment to colonial trusteeship, Canavan cites Burke's indictment of Warren Hastings: 'When a British governor is sent abroad, he is sent to pursue the good of the people as much as possible in the spirit of the laws of [England], which in all respects intend their conservation, their happiness, and their prosperity.' Canavan adds that 'the East India Company and its officials were bound not only by laws of England, but by the charters through which they received powers from the Moghul empire in India. By accepting those powers "they bound themselves (and bound inclusively all their servants) to perform all the duties belonging to that new office, and to be held by all the ties belonging to that new relation".'[6] (Interestingly, Canavan argues that trusteeship was of limited use in Ireland because the rulers had insufficient affection for and interest with the local inhabitants.[7])

However, Burke did not want British governors, or even the British Parliament, to exercise *all* the powers of a trustee, for the inhabitants of imperial possessions, unlike the common people of Britain, had their own historically separate institutions and interests.[8] Colonisation did not entitle the British to appropriate property rights beyond those allowed for by relevant indigenous charters or required for the maintenance of effective government.

In the same way, the British constitution (and any government rightly constituted) limited the power of governors. Tradition, as much as statute, established the legitimacy of the claims of non-governmental institutions to autonomy. Burke's support of the landed aristocracy and the Church of England arose in large part from his concern that the political branches should not intrude excessively into civil society. Likewise, he argued that the institutions of Britain's territorial possessions ought to be allowed sufficient autonomy to maintain the coherence of their own societies. Burke's argu-

---

5   Canavan, op. cit., p. 40.
6   Ibid., pp. 40–41.
7   Ibid., p. 41. James Conniff makes much the same point in 'Burke and India: the Failure of the Theory of Trusteeship', in *Political Research Quarterly*, 46 (1993), pp. 291–309. Conniff argues that lack of democratic representation was the key flaw in the trusteeship of Britain over India. Yet his closing paragraph, in which he acknowledges the need for a commonality of interest and affection for beneficial relations, points to a problem deeper than the mechanics of politics, and one to which Burke himself looked as the key to empire.
8   The trusteeship explanation has limited utility in regard to Britain as well. Numerous classes and callings had their own rights, liberties, powers and responsibilities. The aristocracy was far from all-powerful.

ments here were opposed to 'geographical morality' – the term he applied with opprobrium to those who asserted that they had to assume arbitrary powers to rule people who lacked British customs. Rather, his vision was based on a natural law that demanded benevolent government, and a British constitution that sought to guarantee peoples against tyranny by recognising the legitimacy of countervailing institutions.

II. INDIA: ARGUING FOR SYMPATHY TOWARDS A FOREIGN PEOPLE

Burke spent fourteen years and the bulk of his political capital defending Indian society against the government of the East India Company and, in particular, its Governor-General, Warren Hastings. His reasons for doing this are clear: he felt that a venerable civilisation was being ruined by young profiteers and a system of organised corruption which was reaching back to infect Britain itself.

The sharp cultural and religious differences between Indian and British society meant that Burke had a difficult task to convince his countrymen that Indians were sufficiently like the British to merit concern and respect. He laboured to find a way 'by which India might be approximated to our understandings, and if possible to our feelings; in order to awaken something of sympathy for the unfortunate natives'.[9] This was a difficult task made all the harder by the insular nature of Indian civilisation; but if he had been asked why it was so important that the British should make the effort to understand India, especially when it would restrain them from looting a rich subcontinent, he would have replied simply that it was morally right to do so. Indian civilisation was flawed, but it had stood the test of time and, with its moral, benevolent, pacific and law-abiding population, it deserved respect and protection: 'God forbid we should pass judgment upon people who framed their laws and institutions prior to our insect origin of yesterday. With all the faults of their nature, and errors of their institutions, their institutions, which act so powerfully on their natures, have two material characteristics which entitle them to respect – first, great force and stability; and next, excellent moral and civil effects.'[10]

When Warren Hastings claimed, in defending himself against the threat of impeachment, that he had been forced to assume arbitrary power to govern effectively since the Indian people did not understand or value British liberties, Burke countered that 'all power is limited by law, and ought to be

9   *Works*, II, 183.
10   *Works*, VII, 46–47.

guided by discretion and not by arbitrary will ... All discretion must be referred to the conservation and benefit of those over whom power is exercised; and therefore must be guided by rules of sound political morality.'[11] The Governor-General's political duty was also a moral one: it was to protect the interests of the governed. Gerald Chapman has pointed out how Burke's view here is rooted in the assumptions of a natural law that embraces all societies and, in effect, makes members of other religions less 'foreign'. All religions, Burke believed, taught a common, basic morality – that is, to treat others with respect. As Chapman puts it: 'this cosmic and existential responsibility binds every man to every man (and to God) and imposes commensurate duty upon every power conventionalised by society in functions, rights and privileges.'[12] Hastings, having failed in his political duty, had broken the laws of morality.

Indeed, Burke turned Hastings' defence on its head, arguing that the fewer historical rights a subject people possessed, the more carefully they needed to be governed. 'Ruling over a people guarded by no distinct or well-ascertained privileges, whose language, manners and radical prejudices render not only redress, but all complaint on their part, a matter of extreme difficulty, – such an administration, it is evident, never can be made subservient to the interests of Great Britain, or even tolerable to the natives, but by the strictest rigour in exacting obedience to the commands of the authority lawfully set over it.'[13]

The very lack of historical rights made the government of India a dangerous matter. Only careful supervision by the authorities in Britain would see to the needs of both the mother country and her possession. Instead, that government had been placed in the hands of the East India Company, which had soon overstepped its proper bounds. Though he never made the point so explicitly, Burke seems to have been in agreement here with the sentiments of his friend Adam Smith, who wrote in the *Wealth of Nations* that 'the government of an exclusive company of merchants is, perhaps, the worst of all governments for any country whatever'. But the East India Company itself was a long-established institution with considerable political influence and it was not to be trifled with. Originally a trading concern, the Company had set up a government based on bribery that ruled every aspect of Indians' lives for its own benefit. Its government had become as corrupt as its business dealings, and its officers showed themselves incorrigibly tyrannical in India.

11   *Works*, VIII, 2–3. Note, also, Burke's discourse in his *Speech on Mr Fox's East India Bill*, in *Works*, II, 173–248, where Burke, at times, sounds almost as if he would rather Britain were not governing India at all. Because she found herself involved there, Britain had a duty to govern well, and clearly, for Burke, this meant with a light hand.

12   G. Chapman, op. cit., p. 272.

13   *Works*, VII, 173–74.

The result was frequently large-scale destruction and outright slaughter, and therefore its unsupervised power had to be removed for the sake of both India and Britain.[14]

By granting such powers to a trading company through parliamentary charter, Parliament had failed in its high responsibility to regulate affairs in India, and Burke lamented that the resulting combination of political and economic power had given the Company, in effect, 'unbounded licence to plunder'. Local inhabitants found themselves regulated in every aspect of their lives that was profitable to the Company, and protected in none. A new establishment was required, recognising local traditions and prerogatives and based more on trade than force – in fact, a system of government following India's former Muslim rulers in accepting existing Indian religions and customs and granting greater autonomy to native officials. Only a more distant, lenient and generous empire could preserve its moral integrity and, ultimately, prevent its own destruction. This was the motive behind Burke's promotion of Fox's India Bills in 1783, which were intended to subject India's governors to right-minded oversight and limitations based on the deepest principles of government. Burke called this legislation – not just rhetorically – a 'Magna Charta of Hindostan'.[15]

14 See *Works*, VII, 23–27. Burke's descriptions of calamities in India are noted for their poetic tone (and licence). The following example, from the *Speech on the Nabob of Arcot's Debts*, concerns the Indian tribal leader Hyder Ali's acts of vengeance against the East India Company. The revenge, of course, was visited upon the poor of the area. Ali gathered his armies, 'and compounding all the materials of fury, havoc, and desolation, into one black cloud, he hung for a while on the declivities of the mountains. Whilst the authors of all these evils were idly and stupidly gazing on this menacing meteor, which blackened all their horizon, it suddenly burst, and poured down the whole of its contents upon the plains of the Carnatic. – Then ensued a scene of woe, the like of which no eye had seen, no heart conceived, and which no tongue can adequately tell. All the horrors of war before known or heard of, were mercy to that new havoc. A storm of universal fire blasted every field, consumed every house, destroyed every temple. The miserable inhabitants flying from their flaming villages, in part were slaughtered; others, without regard to sex, to age, to the respect of rank, or sacredness of function, fathers torn from children, husbands from wives, enveloped in a whirlwind of cavalry, and amidst the goading spears of drivers, and the trampling of pursuing horses, were swept into captivity, in an unknown and hostile land. Those who were able to evade this tempest, fled to the walled cities. But escaping from fire, sword, and exile, they fell into the jaws of famine.' *Works*, III, 160. The British cared only that the land had been rendered unprofitable.

15 *Works*, VII, 28 and, II, 179.

III. IRELAND: OF ALTARS AND HABITATIONS

As an Irishman with many Catholic connections, Burke had great sympathy for the problems of his countrymen. The Irish Catholics suffered under laws specifically intended to destroy Catholic traditions and even the most respectable of Catholic families. These laws, introduced under William and Mary, eliminated primogeniture for Irish Catholics and encouraged children to convert to gain control of their parents' property. They also restricted educational opportunities for Catholics and banned them from owning weapons. As bad as the laws themselves was the reliance placed upon informers for their enforcement. The mutual trust on which any society should be based was broken down by the constant temptation to turn one's neighbour over to the authorities in the hope of gaining a large portion of his property.[16]

Burke objected particularly to the laws' purpose of punishing an entire people. Even bad laws must often be accepted for the sake of civil peace, but 'a law against the majority of the people is in substance a law against the people itself; its extent determines its invalidity ... It is not particular injustice, but general oppression; and can no longer be considered as a private hardship, which might be borne, but spreads and grows up into the unfortunate importance of a national calamity.'[17] The Popery Laws, in other words, were immoral.

Britain had given many legal and political institutions to Ireland in the centuries of domination, but she saw Catholicism there as a direct threat to her dominance. Only Burke's fellow establishment Irish – that one fifth of the population which belonged to the Irish Church and was in communion with the Church of England – had full civil and political rights. These people controlled the country's Parliament and had a duty to make laws consistent with the needs of the whole Irish people, as (in Burke's words) 'the essence of law ... requires that it be made as much as possible for the benefit of the whole'.[18] Instead, they had joined the British in enforcing laws that were hostile to the bulk of their own people.

Furthermore, Burke was troubled by the fact that many Irish Protestants considered religious ties close and endearing but felt 'their country to be no bond at all'. Such people wept for the oppressed French Huguenots while remorselessly oppressing Irish Catholics: yet it is a violation of nature and moral law when one harms those with whom one has grown up, shared daily life, and to whom one therefore owes one's primary loyalty.

---

16 See *Tracts Relative to the Laws against Popery in Ireland,* in *Works,* VI, 5–48.
17 *Works,* VI, 20.
18 Ibid., 23.

To lose all feeling for those who have grown up by our sides, in our eyes, of the benefit of whose cares and labours we have partaken from our birth, and meretriciously to hunt abroad after foreign affections, is such a disarrangement of the whole system of our duties, that I do not know whether benevolence so displaced is not almost the same thing as destroyed, or what effect bigotry could have produced that is more fatal to society.[19]

One should be an Irishman and a citizen of the empire before a Protestant or a Catholic, particularly as the creeds of Anglicanism and Catholicism were so close. It was absurd that differences in ritualistic detail or church discipline should have been allowed to disturb the peace and goodwill of either country or empire.

Burke's underlying concern was that, since all government rests on the benign convergence of interest and affection, the empire itself was an institution grounded on consent. He valued the empire, but he valued more the peace, prosperity and stability of its various peoples. These peoples were truly sovereign in the sense that laws had to reflect their interests to be just, and to enjoy their actual or implied consent. Should the Irish no longer express that consent, they should be allowed to withdraw from the empire.[20] The only alternative was chaos. 'I think,' Burke warned, 'the real danger of every state is, to render its subjects justly discontented.'[21]

The Popery Laws provided such justification. Attempting to legislate people out of their religion was unjust, and it was also tyrannical and futile in the same way that the French revolutionaries' later attempt to destroy religion would prove futile. The Irish people had been born into Catholicism, with its reverence for a priestly class and its other particular institutions, beliefs and practices.[22] They had maintained this attachment in the face of severe penalties, not least because the habits of thought and action had been ingrained in their nature over the centuries and had become central to their identity as a people. It was against their nature to become Protestants and unnatural to force them to convert.

Burke urged the British to face Irish discontent with compromise and generosity. He counselled a light hand, not because he thought that one opinion

19   Ibid., 27.
20   Ibid., 20–21.
21   Ibid., 46.
22   'Religion … is not believed because the laws have established it; but it is established because the leading part of the community have previously believed it to be true … The power of the government can with no appearance of reason go further coercively than to bind and hold down those who have once consented to their opinions.' Ibid., 32–33.

or culture was no better than another, but because he was convinced that
governments and empires can exist only with the consent and affection of the
subject people. Better to let a people remove themselves from the empire than
to allow habits of rule by force and terror to infect a free country like Britain.
Arbitrary rule in Ireland – or India, or America – would impoverish the empire and corrupt the mother country.

IV. AMERICA: A DIFFERENT KIND OF ENGLISHMAN

The complex and sometimes apparently contradictory nature of the empire
appeared most sharply in the Anglo-American relationship, where tensions
and conflicts between people of increasingly different character and circumstance were, ironically, aggravated by the common roots and the very principles of liberty that those peoples shared. Burke explained this situation in his
Speech on Conciliation with America (1775):

> My hold of the colonies is in the close affection which grows from
> common names, from kindred blood, from similar privileges, and equal
> protection ... Let the colonies always keep the idea of their civil rights
> associated with your government; – they will cling and grapple to you;
> and no force under heaven will be of power to tear them from their
> allegiance ... As long as you have the wisdom to keep the sovereign au-
> thority of this country as the ... sacred temple consecrated to our com-
> mon faith, wherever the chosen race and sons of England worship
> freedom, they will turn their faces towards you.[23]

The Anglo-American relationship was held together by bonds of affection
growing from common and quite recent origins; but no one could reasonably
expect the English in America, in effect the sons of England, to cling to the
mother country if they came to see her as a tyrant, and this possibility was
increased by the fact that, since their foundations, the American colonies had
changed much, and their people had developed a distinct character.[24] Serious

23   *Works*, I, 508. 'Do you imagine, then, that it is the Land Tax Act which raises your
     revenue? That it is the annual vote in the Committee of Supply which gives you your
     army? Or that it is the Mutiny Bill which inspires it with bravery and discipline? No!
     Surely, no! It is the love of the people; it is their attachment to their government, from
     the sense of the deep stake they have in such a glorious institution, which gives you
     your army and your navy, and infuses into both that liberal obedience, without which
     your army would be a base rabble and your navy nothing but rotten timber.' Ibid., 509.
24   Burke referred to Americans variously as 'our brethren', 'our rebellious children' and
     'offspring'.

misunderstandings had arisen as a consequence, all the more so because the Americans remained strongly attached to English liberties:

> I do not mean to commend either the spirit in this excess, or the moral causes which produce it ... Perhaps we might wish the colonists to be persuaded that their liberty is more secure when held in trust for them by us (as their guardians during a perpetual minority) than with any part of it in their own hands. The question is, not whether their spirit deserves praise or blame, but – what, in the name of God, shall we do with it?[25]

Burke did not endorse the violent manifestations of the Americans' insistence on liberty; but he refused to condemn an English people who only asked to retain their inherited liberties. Likewise, he accepted the implications of the American rejection of Parliament's claims to act as their trustees – that is, that British rule lacked consent and was, therefore, improper. The statesman's duty, given a national characteristic like the American love of liberty, was to treat with the colonies so as to maintain mutually beneficial relations. Precisely because the British were not trustees for America, they ought not to try changing the character of Americans, let alone punish them in an attempt to stamp out their love of liberty. As Burke observed: 'I do not know the method of drawing up an indictment against an whole people.'[26]

Burke drew on his early researches and his reading of Montesquieu to explain the freedom-loving character of the Americans and, in particular, their resistance to taxation without local representation. The colonists were not just 'descendants of Englishmen', but they had 'emigrated from [England] when this part of [the English] character was most predominant'. The seventeenth century was the high point of English struggles for liberty, which were bound up with the question of taxation because 'the great contests for freedom in this country were from the earliest times chiefly upon the question of taxing'.[27] The House of Commons itself grew out of disputes with the king over the people's desire for a voice in levying taxes. This character was encouraged by Britain's benign neglect, which helped to establish American traditions of ordered liberty. The colonists were allowed to form popular assemblies. These assemblies, operating for decades, gave the people habits of self-government and self-taxation, and the acceptance of these developments by Britain was taken by Americans to be a recognition of the right to enjoy them.[28]

25 *Works*, I, 469.
26 Ibid., 476
27 Ibid., 464.
28 Ibid., 465. See also *Letter to the Sheriffs of Bristol*, in *Works*, II, 32–33.

But diverging circumstances could not be ignored. The Puritan religions of the northern colonies inculcated a particular love of liberty among the inhabitants there. Differing from one another in many details, Dissenters and Puritans shared a history of struggle and persecution.[29] Ironically, Burke argued that southern colonists owed their love of liberty to the institution of slavery. Slavery had led free colonists to pride themselves on, and cling tightly to, their own freedoms.

Perhaps most troubling to the British, Americans developed a deep study of law which made them extremely jealous of their liberties, or, in Burke's own words, rendered them: 'acute, inquisitive, dexterous, prompt in attack, ready in defence, full of resources. In other countries, the people, more simple, and of a less mercurial cast, judge of an ill principle in government only by an actual grievance; here they anticipate the evil, and judge of the pressure of the grievance by the badness of the principle. They augur misgovernment at a distance, and snuff the approach of tyranny in every tainted breeze.'[30]

What should the British do with colonists who were jealous of liberties the mother country had bequeathed but no longer seemed to defend? The answer was to let legalistic 'rights' arguments die by giving Americans the substance of their demands, thereby reawakening habitual attachments to Britain. Peace and comity required that both sides forego distinctions of rights and powers, and only British conciliation could produce such forbearance.

> Leave the Americans as they anciently stood, and these distinctions, born of our unhappy contest, will die along with it ... But, if, intemperately, unwisely, fatally, you sophisticate and poison the very source of government, by urging subtle deductions, and consequences odious to those you govern, from the unlimited and illimitable nature of supreme sovereignty, you will teach them by these means to call that sovereignty itself in question.[31]

Talk of sovereign powers would spur the colonists to talk of natural rights. The resulting argument could only produce irreconcilable positions, particularly because Britain's claim, however right in abstract, flew in the face of America's nature and experience. Britain must seek peace 'by restoring the *former unsuspecting confidence of the colonies in the mother country*'. As in all other cases, 'the general character and situation of a people must determine

---

29   'And even that stream of foreigners, which has been constantly flowing into these colonies, has, for the greatest part, been composed of dissenters from the establishments of their several countries.' *Works*, I, 466.
30   *Works*, I, 468.
31   Ibid., 432–33.

what sort of government is fitted for them'.[32] Americans were spirited and so must be allowed more, not less, free rein than other subjects. Neither dominance nor force was required, and the goal had to be a return to affectionate, trusting relations.

American demands were not, in Burke's view, unreasonable, and the colonists had not yet called for perfect, abstract freedom. Instead, they sought a return to the 'happy and liberal condition', short of full freedom, that they were accustomed to enjoy.[33] A return to this time-sanctioned arrangement, defined by customary practices and chartered rights, would restore the affections on which all governments rely and ensure that America could be retained as part of the empire, secure in her liberties. It seemed that this was the only path to a successful reconciliation of the principle of liberty with the realities of circumstances and the demands of obedience. It was therefore a moral path, and an appeal above sectional interest to the law of nature.

V. BURKE'S CONSTITUTION OF EMPIRE

These three imperial conflicts, with which Burke dealt extensively, came at different times and presented him with diverse circumstances. But Burke tackled each with the same method and goals. Convinced that empires can (and should) last only on the basis of mutual interest and consent, he worked for imperial policies that would win the acquiescence of the inhabitants of British possessions.

Burke's call for conciliation and moderation was not simply a pragmatic response. It flowed directly from an understanding of empire that, like his view of the British constitution, was rooted in natural law. It was federal. Its chief legislature, the Parliament at Westminster, was to act only where subordinate bodies refused or were unable to fulfil their responsibilities. Whether colonial legislatures or Indian rajahs, indigenous institutions were to be accorded respect and power in the interest of fitting and limited government:

> The Parliament of Great Britain sits at the head of her extensive empire in two capacities: one as the local legislature of this island, providing for all things at home ... The other, and I think her nobler capacity, is what I call her *imperial character*; in which, as from the throne of heaven, she superintends all the several inferior legislatures, and guides and controls them all, without annihilating any. As all these provincial leg-

32 Ibid., 454, and 480.
33 Ibid., 404.

islatures are only coordinate to each other, they ought all to be subordinate to her; else they can neither preserve mutual peace, nor hope for mutual justice, nor effectually afford mutual assistance. It is necessary to coerce the negligent, to restrain the violent, and to aid the weak and deficient, by the overruling plenitude of her power. She is never to intrude into the place of the others, whilst they are equal to the common ends of their institution. But in order to enable Parliament to answer all these ends of provident and beneficent superintendence, her powers must be boundless. The gentlemen who think the powers of Parliament limited, may please themselves to talk of requisitions. But suppose the requisitions are not obeyed? What! Shall there be no reserved power in the empire, to supply a deficiency which may weaken, divide and dissipate the whole?[34]

Parliament, then, acted in two capacities: first, as the legislature of Britain; second, as a kind of super-legislature for the empire. In both these capacities Parliament's power was restrained within a constitution. In Britain, Parliament had to respect and follow the particular traditions and legal rights that had developed over time as the people had sought to conserve their society in the face of changing circumstances. In the empire, Parliament was bound by the traditions, laws and needs of the various peoples she governed. In both instances the final, crucial restraint came from an immutable natural law: government had to conform to the interests of the governed.

To serve its purpose in times of trouble the British Parliament's powers had, theoretically, to be boundless to enjoin imperial subjects to pull their weight and pay their fair share towards preserving the empire. But in practice Parliament's powers were limited by their proper object: maintaining a peaceful and prosperous empire. Only powers necessary to coordinate the legislatures of her possessions to the proper ends of peace, justice and mutual assistance should be used. To the extent that the exercise of these powers would tend to further contrary ends, it was unjustifiable. Arbitrary, high-handed actions tended to produce unrest – that is, the opposition of sovereign people. They were to be avoided in favour of conciliation whenever that was possible.

The American situation provides an excellent example of Burke's constitutional thinking. In discussing the appropriate British attitude towards taxation in America, Burke presented a hypothetical situation based in part on recent experience. Should Britain be at war and call on the colonies to contribute funds for its support, one or two might hold back, depending on others to protect them and pay their share. This could lead to the empire's bank-

---

34 Ibid., 434–35. (Emphasis in the original.)

ruptcy, or dissolution into warring camps, and so it was right and legal in such dangerous circumstances for Parliament to say: 'Tax yourselves for the common supply, or Parliament will do it for you.' But Burke went on to argue that 'this ought to be no ordinary power; nor ever used in the first instance. This is what I meant, when I have said at various times, that I consider the power of taxing in Parliament as an instrument of empire, and not as a means of supply.'[35] Direct taxation was to be resorted to only when the security of the empire was at stake.

Burke was well aware that to gain and retain an empire requires skill and goodwill as well as military might. No people can be kept enslaved forever: 'I am ... deeply sensible of the difficulty of reconciling the strong presiding power, that is so useful towards the conservation of a vast, disconnected, in-finitely diversified empire, with that liberty and safety of the provinces, which they must enjoy ... or they will not be provinces at all.'[36] They must either be driven into submission (which is unjust) or drawn into willing consent. Unfortunately, the task is made harder by the tendency to hubris on the part of the rulers: 'When any community is subordinately connected with another, the great danger of the connection is the extreme pride and self-complacency of the superior, which in all matters of controversy will probably decide in its own favour.'[37] Pride and complacency are the roots of arbitrary rule, tyranny and revolt.

How, then, is an empire to be maintained? With a light and liberal hand, and by recognising that other peoples have their own traditions, characters and ex-pectations. By appreciating that an empire is a combination of various peoples and that all governments – even imperial ones – rest, in the end, on consent.

For Burke, the institutional key to empire, as to liberty, was the mainte-nance of countervailing forces. Through a kind of federalism, the British em-pire would maintain local legislative governance subject to infrequently applied parliamentary supremacy. The more 'foreign' the possession, the less likely British governance was to prove beneficial and the less intrusive it should be. Burke sought to apply the same rule to all issues of imperial concern: as loy-alties grew out from our little platoons to more remote and so less familiar and loved persons, so governments had to recognise that their proper powers diminished as the group involved became more distant – both culturally and geographically. Burke argued that it was the imperial duty 'to conform our government to the character and circumstances of the several people who composed this [empire's] mighty and strangely diversified mass', and he was persuaded that 'government was a practical thing, made for the happiness of

35 Ibid., 435.
36 *Works*, II, 31.
37 Ibid., 21.

mankind, and not to furnish out a spectacle of uniformity, to gratify the schemes of visionary politicians'.[38]

Men are alike in that their characters are formed in large measure by circumstance – their families, churches and local traditions as well as their professions, physical surroundings and ancestry. They also share a common resistance to governmental fiat as a means of character modification. At the same time, there is a common pride in men which leads them to exert power in order to force uniformity on everyone. The pursuit of this object, as we have seen, whether it be the construction of a perfect political order or the defence of unlimited claims to sovereignty, produces tyranny because it is destructive of the moral order. The moral aspect of unity lies in respect and protection for local diversity.

These issues and concerns remain with us today. Led by the House of Representatives' Speaker, Newt Gingrich, the late American Congress sought to return to the American states powers that the central government had usurped over the preceding decades. Welfare policy, in particular, was to be 'devolved' in order to reinvigorate local governments and subject public policy to closer, more appropriate scrutiny. The primary policy justification was the conviction that local governments know better the circumstances of their areas and constituents than do the bureaucrats in Washington. Local officials know what particular rules will best promote self-reliance without imposing undue hardship. For example, they are in a position to calculate prudentially the work requirements necessary to receive welfare money or caps on the number of children for whom a woman can claim financial support.

It is curious at such a crossroads in American politics to see, across the Atlantic, a movement towards a 'United States of Europe'. Burke himself argued that Europe constituted a kind of community based on a common religion, Christianity, and a shared history. But this cultural commonality clearly has limits, and to the extent that government in Brussels would act directly upon the people – pre-empting national law – it would be seeking to homogenise diverse peoples. Any movement beyond trade and defence agreements contains the risk that particular circumstances and cultures will be forgotten or destroyed in pursuit of a rationalised, utopian vision of a unitary Europe. The result of such a move will be tyranny, as Burke would have predicted, because it must rest on contempt for local autonomy and tradition. Large populations spread over a vast expanse can share a common religion and history. But it is foolhardy and arrogant to act as if all men share enough common customs to make any one government fit for all. The thing that unites man is morality – his nature – not the uniformity of circumstance. Herein lies the great motivation towards empire, but also, potentially, its greatest evil.

38   Ibid., 29.

The Relevance of Edmund Burke

Sir Robert Rhodes James

I

When I first entered the House of Commons, as a Clerk in 1955, the last Churchill government had just ended, but the great man was still a member, and was to remain one for another nine years. His successor, Anthony Eden, was widely regarded as the outstanding parliamentarian of his time, as he was to prove at the height of the Suez crisis, when he was virtually the only minister who could command that turbulent House. There was Hugh Gaitskell, whose speech demolishing Rab Butler's 'pots and pans' autumn Budget in 1955 was one of the greatest demolition speeches I heard in the Commons – before Geoffrey Howe's in November 1990. There was Rab himself, master of the sly dig, but less than master of his colleagues. There was Nye Bevan, rather more a platform orator than a parliamentarian – but what an orator! There was the self-effacing but waspish Attlee, who could, and did, sting. Harold Wilson was establishing himself as one of the wittiest speakers in the House. His annual speech attacking the Budget always drew a packed and eager House, and usually a larger audience than the Chancellor himself. There was the rising Iain Macleod, developing into the best winding-up speaker on the Treasury Bench. There was Enoch Powell, whose speech on the Hola Camp atrocities, delivered after hours of waiting in the early hours of the morning, was unforgettable, and Harold Macmillan, whose one Budget speech, in 1956, was for the oratorical connoisseur as it announced, with much panache, the introduction of Premium Bonds.

In those days the press gave considerable coverage to the House of Commons, actually reporting speeches and commenting on them, instead of providing the miserable sketches – usually confined to the charade of Question Time – that we read now, along with snippets on the radio and television. But there are many perils in political nostalgia, especially for a politician, and, despite all this talent, I came across an elderly clerk who lamented to me: 'This place has never been the same since Mr Gladstone died.' No doubt there were old-timers in the 1840s, in a House that contained Palmerston, Peel, Shaftesbury, Cobden, Bright, Disraeli and Gladstone, who moaned yearningly about the great days when the Pitts, Fox, Sheridan and Burke held sway. As Burke himself wrote: 'To complain of the age we live in, to murmur at the present possessors of power, to lament the past, to conceive extravagant hopes of the future, are the common dispositions of the greatest part of mankind.'

In the case of Burke, however, the sad fact was that he rarely 'held sway' in the House of Commons itself. Some put his failure as a parliamentarian down to his Irish accent – indeed, his manifest Irishness – his somewhat harsh tone, and his awkward gestures in an age when oratory was more sophisticated and critically admired; others considered that Burke seldom actually debated a subject, but held forth with lofty discourses on topics that interested him, and often only him, at the time; he also frequently gave the clear impression that he thought little of the intellectual qualities of his audience and of most politicians. Suffering fools, if not gladly, then at least with some patience, is a key requirement for political success, and one in which Burke was seriously deficient. (Even Fox, who revered him, conceded that 'his temper was naturally hasty, and he was deficient in political tact'.) He did not take political disappointment well, which gradually gave to his speeches and writings an embittered vehemence. He became, in Fox's words, 'a most impracticable person, a most unmanageable colleague; [one who] would never support any measure, however convinced he might be in his heart of its utility, if it had been prepared by another'. There were occasions of open hostility when he rose in the House, and it was quite usual for members to make for the exits. His relations with his Bristol constituents were famously bad; every member of parliament in trouble with his electors reaches for Burke's imperious definition of the relationship between an MP and his constituency, conveniently forgetting – or not knowing – that Bristol won.

Nor could it be said, with the glittering exception of his sympathy and support for the American colonists, that he was notably consistent. It is certainly very difficult to attach to him any modern political label. Conservatives tend to regard him as one of their own, a staunch defender of the constitution, hater of the French Revolution and a man suspicious of innovations or meddling with established institutions; but those of a more radical hue may applaud his libertarian struggles for religious toleration (although not for infidels, 'outlaws of the constitution and the human race'), his American record, his support for Wilberforce's crusade against the slave trade, and his relentless pursuit of the Governor-General of Bengal, Warren Hastings, and the abuse of power by officials of the East India Company. Burke believed in party, but with the right for independence, and if this made him an infuriating colleague and opponent, it has also made him a fascinating subject for biographers, students of political philosophy, historians, and for generations of politicians.

In some respects Burke was like Churchill. He wrote and spoke so much, and on so many subjects, that he can be called as an authority on almost everything. A good example of this is the current debates in the Conservative Party about Europe. Baroness Thatcher presented an unforgettable address to the Edmund Burke Society in 1991, when she clutched Burke with great fervour as the first member of the anti-Maastricht brigade; but it would be quite easy to place him among the ranks of the Europhiles. And on the question of Bosnia, would we find Burke calling fiercely for war to defeat a new form of Jacobinism, or denouncing the evils and corruption of colonial rule?

But if fellow MPs found Burke the orator hard to take, and an explosive and unpredictable colleague, they read his speeches, pamphlets and books. They were joined by an increasing audience at home and abroad as it became clear that Burke had been right over America, and as the French Revolution began to follow the terrible course that he had predicted in his *Reflections*. This growing popularity, and these insights, were remarkable for a politician who never held office at the highest level. How do we explain them?

Burke was never what might today be called a career politician. When he settled in London he wanted to be a serious writer, and with the publication of *A Vindication of Natural Society* (1756) and *A Philosophical Enquiry into the Origin of our Ideas of the Sublime and Beautiful* (1757), his ambition seemed about to be realised. But then, after a time working for William Hamilton, Chief Secretary to the Lord Lieutenant of Ireland, he became private secretary to the Marquis of Rockingham: 'Newly, and almost as a stranger, I am come about these people,' he wrote. He accepted the pocket borough of Wendover in 1765 and thus, almost accidentally, entered politics.

This was not then, nor was it later, as unusual as it sounds. There are people even today who find themselves in Parliament unexpectedly. Obviously, it is not as common a phenomenon as it used to be, but I knew one colleague in the House who had not dreamed of standing for Parliament until he had a telephone call from the chairman of an Association asking if he was prepared to be their candidate. He decided he had no particular objection, and was duly elected, and often re-elected. In the Labour landslide of 1945, and the Conservative ones of 1931 and 1983, there were several amazed MPs who had stood, in effect, as paper candidates.

In Burke's case, his vigorous academic and journalistic training was now applied to the world of practical political problems, and the former undoubtedly shaped the nature and extent of his impact on the latter. The rôle of the intellectual actively engaged in politics has become increasingly rare, and is now regarded with even more suspicion than in his day. Politics, it is claimed, is not an intellectual pursuit but an incessant struggle for power, and a discipline of the 'here and now'. It is about policies and personalities – especially personalities – not about abstract notions or academic philosophies. It is this attitude that has played an important part in the growing gulf between academia and the political world, and it may not be as odd a coincidence as it seems that Oxford voted against conferring honorary degrees on both Burke and Thatcher.

The classic examples of the perils of political theorising, it has been claimed, are Marxist communism and socialism, which have brought nothing but disaster, and it is worth noting that the inspirers of socialist and communist thinking were not practical politicians. This may have had something to do with their systems' failure; if they had been buffeted by the hard realities of political life, they might have produced theories that had more to do with mankind as it actually is than as they wished it to be. But the politician or political observer who ignores the importance of ideas does so at his peril. Shaftesbury's exposure of the horrors of the worst aspects of the Industrial Revolution pointed to realities, not to dreams, but the activities of the Chartists and the Anti-Corn Law League played crucial rôles in the establishment of free trade in the second half of the nineteenth century almost as a religion rather than an economic policy.

The penalties for ignoring political thinkers may be great, too. British liberalism lost its ideological way, to be replaced by Labour, in the inter-war years this century, even though it had Keynes, Henderson and Beveridge as counsellors and polemicists. The few Conservative intellectuals in that dismal period made little impact, and some of them – notably Harold Macmillan and Noel Skelton (who coined the phrase 'property-owning democracy') – were regarded as dangerous semi-socialists. It took the traumatic defeat of 1945 to persuade a new generation of Conservatives, marshalled and inspired by Rab Butler, to ask some fundamental questions about the nature and history of Conservatism, and whether it had a serious political future.

Butler's own words are worth recording:

> I had derived from Bolingbroke an assurance that the majesty of the State might be used in the interests of the many, from Burke a belief in seeking patterns of improvement by balancing diverse interests, and from Disraeli an insistence that the two nations must become one ... What basically we were saying is that, untouched by morality and idealism, economics is an arid pursuit, just as politics is an unprofitable one.

It is interesting that Disraeli himself had drawn much from Bolingbroke and Burke, perhaps forgetting that Burke's first notable publication had been a parody of Bolingbroke that was so brilliant that some thought it had been written by Bolingbroke himself. But Burke's grasp of the importance of diversity, the multiplicity of centres of power, the importance of independent institutions such as the Church, the universities and the local magistracy, combined with an awareness of the imperfections and limitations of human nature, was central to Disraeli's thinking. Disraeli's mind was as good as

Burke's and there is a coherence to his political life that is often missed by historians, who tend to see the brilliant opportunist and calculating politician rather than the intellectual. It was one of Disraeli's great skills that he learnt to conceal his cleverness as his career developed.

Once he had reached Westminster, Burke made his mark as quickly as Disraeli was to do, and his first two speeches, defending the American colonists, caused a sensation and filled the town with wonder, as Johnson told Boswell. But, by contrast with Disraeli, this did not last. As he later remarked, with a certain satisfaction, 'I have always been in the minority.' A career politician does not care for being in the minority permanently, and this was Burke's course. In John Brooke's words: 'His political life is a series of negative crusades ... With many of the qualities required for leadership, he lacked the ability to sense the feelings of others, and always tried to impose his own.'

There is nothing wrong with this, but to contemporaries Burke was essentially what the Americans, in a singularly unlovely phrase, call 'a loner'. He preferred to be an independent gun barking on the wings of the political fray, rather than the leader of a formidable battery of central artillery, and often turned his fire on those who had thought they were his allies and companions. 'Can he wonder that he is represented as mad?' Johnson once remarked to Boswell of his great friend.

II

It is ironic that while Burke regarded himself as a Whig, one of the true heirs of the Glorious Revolution, he later came to be considered one of the oracles of Conservatism – a term unknown in his own time. This was essentially the result of his *Reflections on the Revolution in France*, one of the most powerful and enduring polemics in political literature. Usually, a speech or a book by a politician that attracts great attention at the time proves to be ephemeral. (Burke's great speech over nine days in the trial of Warren Hastings is as good an example as any.) Others, largely ignored at the time, achieve their importance later; one thinks of *Das Kapital*, and even *Mein Kampf*. But Burke's *Reflections* is highly unusual in the class of political literature written by an active politician.

It should be remembered that the book was published in 1790, after the fall of the Bastille and the promulgation of the new Constitution – which so attracted Tom Paine's admiration – and *before* the destruction of the monarchy and the Terror. Burke was writing against the background of widespread British satisfaction that a great European despotism had fallen, and that the principles of liberty, of which Burke himself had long been the most resolute of champions, had triumphed, and there was no shortage of voices to argue that England would profit greatly from the new French reforms. For Burke to be the one seriously dissenting voice in Parliament caused widespread surprise.

But by this stage in his life, the strands of Burke's thought and his practical experience of political mankind had come together. 'The nature of man is intricate; the objects of society are of the greatest possible complexity; and therefore no simple disposition or direction of power can be suitable either to man's nature, or to the quality of his affairs.'

The horrors that occurred in France in 1792 and 1793 caused a violent change of opinion in England, but the fact that Burke's warnings had been terribly vindicated was not the only factor that gave the *Reflections* such an immense and lasting effect. There were also the deep insights into political man that were intrinsic to the argument as a whole, and Norman Gash has expressed this accumulated wisdom perfectly:

> Fundamentally Burke's philosophy rested on three principles: history, society and continuity. Like all real Conservatives his ideas were conditioned by a certain view of humanity. Because he was conscious of the frailty, ignorance and evil in human nature, he believed that it needed the discipline of ordered society to liberate the best elements in mankind and restrain the worst. Society in this sense could only be an historical product, a thing of slow, natural growth; an organic entity, with unity and character, with a place for morals and religion. It was a framework for conduct, a defence against the excesses of individuals and the caprice of tyrants.

This fundamental message had its attractions even in 1790; it looked more compelling by 1793, and especially in its chilling depiction of the Jacobin future: 'In the groves of *their* academy, at the end of every vista, you see nothing but the gallows.' Burke passionately eschewed the extremes of libertarianism and despotism. His rejection of radical change in the British parliamentary system, unless to root out venality and corruption, at first made him look reactionary, but now appeared to be wisdom. His view that once established institutions are torn down the only likely result is the establishment of a new tyranny now had an immense impact, and effectively ended for the time being the wave of radicalism in which Wilkes and others, buttressed by the London mob, had invested such energy and hopes.

The *Reflections*, of course, provoked a violent counter-attack in Tom Paine's *Rights of Man* (1791–92), in which Paine justifiably denounced Burke's failure to understand the causes of grievance that had provoked the revolution, and derided Burke's appeal to the past and reverence for tradition, and his declaration that the Settlement of 1689 was binding on the British people forever. Paine certainly made a substantial point against Burke's weakest arguments in favour of the British political system, namely a situation in which Yorkshire, with a population of two million, had two MPs – the same number as Rutland – and Old Sarum, with three houses, had two members, while Manchester had none. And the new France had, at least, a written Constitution!

Of course, Burke had wildly exaggerated the virtues and charms of the *ancien régime*, and his almost purblind opposition to serious parliamentary reform provided Paine with an easy target; but Paine for his part wholly underestimated the tempests that the revolution had unleashed, and his revolutionary enthusiasms can be regarded as even more naïve than Burke's apprehensions. In several senses both were right, and both were wrong. Paine found it incomprehensible that one of the chief supporters of the Revolution in 1688 and the principal sympathiser with the American colonists should not endorse the French Revolution, which he himself put on a par with that of 1688; Burke was right to point out the substantial differences. Both books are classics of serious thought and invective; but Burke, who had so often appealed to the emotions of his readers and listeners, struck the deeper note.

The famous passage in the *Reflections* about Marie Antoinette has misled some into believing that the work was a defence of monarchy, whereas it was a warning of the perils of rootless rationalism and emotional anarchy and a defence of an ordered society based on the realities of highly fallible human nature. Burke's own liberal record absolved him from being considered simply reactionary, and it is this that gave Burke the philosopher his real political strength. If he had been simply a London pamphleteer, an Irish journalist, or an academic, little notice would have been taken of him; but the fact that he was an active politician – albeit an unsuccessful one in terms of office – made all the difference, both in the nature of the work and its public reception.

One might just add that, although it made Burke truly famous, the *Reflections* did not greatly change the perceptions of his colleagues about him, and we find Pitt the Younger returning to Auckland a letter of Burke's with the comment, 'I return Burke's letter, which is like other rhapsodies from the same pen, in which there is much to admire, and nothing to agree with.' The impression of the unstable, unreliable, excessively passionate 'Irish madman' proved to be very durable.

III

While I am uneasy about conferring upon Burke the accolade – or obloquy –
of being *the* oracle of British Conservatism, the *Reflections* struck deep chords
in me, when I first read it at the age of eighteen, and in my generation. Our
childhoods had been passed in the shadows of approaching war, then war itself, and the grim aftermath of half-peace. Looking at what had happened in
Germany, Italy and the Soviet Union after their revolutions, and having experienced social turmoil in our own country, we saw only too clearly how
valid Burke's warnings had been, and how relevant he was to our times.
What we craved was stability, not excitement or experimentation or utopias,
whether socialist or otherwise, and we became as suspicious of *enthusiasm* as
the great Tory, and scourge of the Whigs, Samuel Johnson had been.

I would not go so far as to say that Burke made me a Conservative, but
his words and message fell on very fertile ground, and not only intellectually.
Here was a man who seemed to court unpopularity almost perversely throughout his public life; like Churchill, he knew what being in the political
wilderness was like, and the great dangers of being proved right – the only
unforgivable crime in politics.

This is not to say that I have found him invariably right, of course. I do
not accept his veneration of the 1688 Revolution any more than his hope-
lessly idealistic and sentimental view of the French monarchy, or his lack of
understanding of the causes of the French Revolution. He could not possibly be described as a democrat. To write that 'to innovate is not to reform'
may be seen as wise by some, but not by me, although I entirely agree that
change for change's sake is not 'policy' and that political leaps in the dark
usually end in disaster. He was not at all an innovator, and although Disraeli
claimed him as one of his principal mentors, Burke would have been appalled
by what he would have considered Disraeli's dangerous radicalism, especially
on social and constitutional issues. (He would, however, have approved of
his, and Lord Randolph Churchill's judgment, that when reform was necessary to preserve the institutions of state, it must be accepted as an unpleas-
ant necessity: but he would not have embraced it, and certainly not inspired
it.)

I believe that Burke would have shared my unhappiness about the direction of politics during my last years in Parliament. Here, a 'philosophy' had
come to hold sway which claimed an intellectual basis, but which had none.
There was no sense of history, and historical authorities – such as Burke
himself – were paid ritual obeisances rather than read and understood. There
were some vague and impressionistic recollections and prejudices, but, apart
from these, the past was a closed book. Assessments of success and achievement rested entirely on financial and materialistic considerations, and this

would have repelled Burke. Nor, famously, did this philosophy accept the existence of such a thing as society; so it missed one of the fundamental points that Burke had made, which is that there is such a thing – and we all *know* it. The accompanying advocacy of experimental change and centralism would have dismayed him, and he would have considered that this type of political thought ignored each of his basic, and interlocking, tenets – history, society and continuity. He would, I am sure, have seen nothing conservative in any of it, and would perhaps have found cause to remind us of one of his most famous observations:

> Magnanimity in politics is not seldom the truest wisdom; and a great empire and little minds go ill together.

Edmund Burke and the Politicians

Michael Gove

Edmund Burke and his little platoons have been conscripted as often in battles between Tory factions as in the Conservatives' battle against other parties. Body-snatching is as much a part of ideological struggle as it was of Edinburgh medicine in the nineteenth century – and in both a Burke has been central. Burke's name and, a little more rarely, quotations from his work have been used by Conservative politicians to confer respectability and authority on the positions they have felt it necessary to adopt in their struggle for mastery.

The frequency with which Burke has been used has varied with the intensity of argument within the Conservative Party. At times of broad consensus within Tory ranks and across the party divide, his name has been less prominent. But old soldiers never really die, and although Burke's name faded from public debate in the years after 1945, it was heard again more frequently at those points in the seventies, eighties and nineties when the Tories became more attuned to ideology and, indeed, riven by it.

It may seem paradoxical that Burke, who abjured the 'hocus-pocus of abstraction' and argued that 'politics ought to be adjusted, not to human reasonings, but to human nature; of which reason is but a part, and by no means the greatest part', should find his words most resonant at a time when the 'stupid party' was engaged in intellectual dispute, but there are good reasons why Tories should seek Burke's posthumous blessing for their positioning. In division and uncertainty, the Conservative, like most human creatures, will crave the impression of continuity. It is no accident that the symbols of British citizenship are most cherished in Ulster where that identity is constantly questioned.

Whichever side in the Tory battle can claim authority for its ideas from the traditions of the tribe will have a better chance not only of winning but of securing assent for its triumph. Burke's words, like a medieval crown, can be used to lend legitimacy to the new masters. Moreover, the 'melody' of Burke's philosophy can render sweeter the harsher tones of disputants.

This essay will consider two works which borrow heavily from Burke and which were written in the aftermath of a change in the Tory party's leadership, when the direction of the party was in dispute.

I

From its defeat in 1945 until Edward Heath's defeat in its leadership election in 1975, the Conservative Party was ill-at-ease with any ideology that was identifiably conservative. Although the Tories were in office for seventeen of those years, they made little effort to challenge the collectivist consensus which emerged in the Second World War and was given its fullest expression by the 1945–51 Attlee administration.

The Tories nibbled at the edges of an ever-expanding state with some tax-cuts and denationalisation, but they never developed a sustained critique of collectivist assumptions. The mixed economy was a given, Mr Butskell its enlightened manager, the man in Whitehall knew best (although the Tories might feel he should occasionally give some attention to the men in White's). The hegemony of managerial collectivism provided little space in political debate for ideas, certainly within the Tory party. Macmillan and Home, with differing degrees of sincerity, practised patrician aloofness from any form of philosophy. Mr Heath preferred 'facts and figures', efficiency and systems to ideas. It was a rare Tory who would advance an ideological case, even for traditional Toryism, and Conservatives preferred to study the proceedings of the National Economic Development Council to Burke, let alone Lord Hugh Cecil, Salisbury, Oakeshott or Bolingbroke. There were exceptions, most notably Quintin Hogg and Enoch Powell, but both, although immensely talented in their own way, were considered too eccentric ever seriously to challenge for the leadership.

One of the consequences of this preference for the managerial to the philosophical was a hollowing-out of Tory self-confidence, where a surrender to the abstract rights of labour and a socialist vision of wealth creation were defended as a form of pragmatism. From Walter Monckton's appeasement of organised labour in Churchill's 'Indian Summer' government, to Edward Heath's defeat at the hands of the miners, the Conservatives had no coherent strategy for dealing with the trades unions, who, in their arrogance and influence, had robbed Parliament of its power to govern in the interests of the whole nation.

Burke saw through the empty formularies of Rousseauism and recognised that the abstractions of universal rights lead to a loss of real liberty. Until the late-seventies the Tories lacked anyone with similar acuity to see through the Labour-inspired social contracts with the trade unions which, in their own way, damaged traditional British liberties. There were purist free market critiques of trade union power advanced by thinkers outside the Conservative Party but, aside from the lonely figure of Enoch Powell, precious few within Tory ranks were prepared to mount a suitably bloody ideological attack on collectivist thinking.

There were flourishes of apparently genuine conservatism between 1945 and 1975, such as the presentation of Edward Heath as 'Selsdon Man'; but they were more image than substance. Selsdon Man was the coinage of Iain Macleod, designed to secure a few favourable newspaper headlines but not rooted in any genuine conversion to old Tory principles. It was a piece of counterfeit conservatism. In government, Mr Heath, without a proper conservative philosophy, soon found himself without office.

The election of Margaret Thatcher to the leadership of the Conservative Party saw Burke in the front-line again. Caricatured as a housewife promoted beyond her talents who saw the complexities of international economics in terms of the household budget, she presided over an intellectual renaissance in the Conservative Party. Although the official platform of the Conservatives in opposition was not given a detailed, radical overhaul, a more trenchant public face was presented and there was an engagement with hard thinking. Mrs Thatcher embraced the ideas of organisations such as the Centre for Policy Studies and the Institute for Economic Affairs as well as immersing herself in the ideas of a new generation of conservative thinkers and providing inspiration for High Tory polemicists such as Maurice Cowling and Roger Scruton.

But although she plundered freely from old and new texts on the Right, it was her opponents within the Conservative Party who enlisted Burke first. Forced to raise their game by her vigour, advocates of liberal, or consensual, Conservatism sought to make Burke their ally. The most prominent and impressive was Ian Gilmour. In *Inside Right*, its title indicating both intimacy with the Tory party and his position within it as a centrist, he attempted to defend his vision of Toryism against what he saw as the importation of a narrow neo-liberalism.

Gilmour, an elegant writer and accomplished historian of the eighteenth century, published *Inside Right* in 1977. Subtitled *A Study of Conservatism*, its heart is a series of essays on Tory thinkers from trimmer Halifax to Lord Hailsham, with Burke at the centre. The work, however, is less an historical survey than an attack on the direction the Conservative Party appeared to be taking under its new leader. Gilmour was a member of her first Cabinet, and he was careful in the book to praise her from time to time, but he was out of sympathy with her developing approach. His criticisms are directed at the distorting effects that too great a faith in the free market might have on the Tory party.

He was also concerned that the Thatcher leadership's determination to reverse the collectivist ratchet and roll back the frontiers of the state would prove stronger meat than the body politic could stomach, and he quoted with approval Burke's injunction that parties would do better 'to follow, not to force, the public inclination' in preference to 'noisy political action injected with ideology'. In contrast to the more militant tone which Mrs Thatcher brought to bear in the struggle with socialism, Gilmour preferred Burke's conciliatory credo, 'we compensate, we reconcile, we balance'.

Gilmour feared the influence of liberal economists such as the Austrian Friedrich von Hayek on Tory policy through the advocacy of free-marketeers such as Keith Joseph and Ralph Harris of the IEA. He sought to put clear blue water between traditional Toryism and the minimal state beliefs of Hayek and his followers. He argued that 'the Tory emphasis on authority and loyalty has always ruled out the night-watchman state', and he defended a state large enough to provide benefits by quoting from Burke in the *Reflections* to the effect that government was: 'a contrivance of human wisdom to provide for human wants. Men have a right that these wants be provided for by their wisdom.'

Gilmour summed up his position by arguing that the Tory party 'like the Church of England, seeks the Via Media'. Although not a frontal attack on Mrs Thatcher, it could not be construed as anything other than a sideswipe at her intention to move away from the middle-way policies of post-war Tory governments. His invocation of the 'night-watchman' state and his disparaging references to noisy political action and ideology appear designed to clothe his opponents in the tightest of ideological strait-jackets. Sensitive to the direction in which Mrs Thatcher wished to go, he sought to portray the ultimate destination as wholly uncongenial for a Tory.

But Mrs Thatcher was not travelling a road which would make Conservatives the intellectual serfs of Austrian professors. She was engaged in a process of renovation, clearing away the barnacles which forty years of creeping collectivism had allowed to gather on the British state. She wanted Britons to rediscover the spirit of Elizabethan buccaneering, Georgian self-confidence and Victorian self-improvement which had allowed the country to flourish. She wanted to reanimate the virtues apparent before inflation and state spending started to grow as quickly as the state's power and independence declined.

Her radical reactionary stance unsettled Conservatives who mistook inertia before the enemy advance for continuity. It was not, however, easy to present this stance comfortably in the tradition of Burke's thought. His scepticism and her zeal mark them out as individuals of different humours. Yet Mrs Thatcher was a necessary scourge of those who were genuinely opposed to Burke. She was also, in her reverence for the constitution and family life, his heir. And without her energetic assault on the Left, politics would have remained a matter of managerialism and bureaucracy with less attention paid to excavating Tory truths.

II

Throughout the early eighties Burke's name was used, although not as promi-
nently as Disraeli's, to signal coded dissent from Mrs Thatcher's policies in
government. Figures on the left of the Conservative Party, most elegantly
Chris Patten, said nothing directly critical of the government, but their broader
discourse was studded with warnings about the danger of straying too far from
pragmatic pieties.

Mrs Thatcher only occasionally used Burke to buttress her arguments.
She preferred poetry to philosophy as the leavening in her speeches, quoting
from Betjeman, Tennyson and, most generously, Kipling. However, in 1984,
secure after an election victory, Mrs Thatcher quoted Burke in her Carlton
lecture. As a reproof to internal critics unhappy with her activist stance, she
starkly cited the warning attributed to Burke: 'All that is needed for evil to
triumph is for good men to do nothing'.

Mrs Thatcher was specifically attacking the welter of pressure groups, like
the trade unions, which sought to influence the democratic process and
ratchet up government spending – with unhappy consequences for traditional
freedoms and the health of the political system. But she was also reminding
her party that Conservatism, as Burke would have understood it, depended
as much on vigorous partisanship and an assertive engagement with opponents as on a feel for how much the sinews of the state could bear.

Mrs Thatcher embodied Burke's belief that it was better 'to run the risk
of falling into faults in a course which leads us to act with effect and energy,
than to loiter out our days without blame, and without use'. But vigorous
though she might be in her own defence, Mrs Thatcher had to wait until after
she had fallen from office to find a champion who could fashion Burke's philosophy into an impressive weapon for her cause.

In his book *Modern Conservatism* (1992), David Willetts, the Conservative
MP for Havant, makes a spirited attempt to point up the common threads
which tie the Major leadership to Mrs Thatcher's and to discern their debts
to the past. Written, like Gilmour's book, two years after the defenestration
of a leader, it is a work more of defence than dissent.

Willetts sees Burke as a proto-Thatcherite free-marketeer who, in his
Thoughts and Details on Scarcity, made a liberal economic case against regulation of the grain supply which was closely in line with the ideas of Adam
Smith, the father of free market thinking. *Thoughts and Details on Scarcity*
reads as rigorously as any tract from the IEA. To his credit, Ian Gilmour
quotes liberally from it in *Inside Right*, if only to point up what he saw as the
occasional contradictions in a politician of great amplitude.

In the polemic, Burke asks 'when a man cannot live and maintain his family by the natural hire of his labour, ought it to be raised by authority?' and

concludes 'No'. He maintains that 'to provide for us in our necessities is not in the power of government ... the labouring people are only poor because they are numerous ... patience, labour sobriety, frugality and religion should be recommended to them. All the rest is downright fraud.' He also asserts in the same text that 'the laws of commerce ... are the laws of nature and consequently the laws of God'.

Gilmour argues that Burke's distrust of the abstract is undercut by his advocacy of liberal economics, but Willetts maintains that the desire to 'truck, barter and exchange' is among man's most natural inclinations and cites Adam Smith's belief that the urge to better oneself is the driving human impulse from which 'public and national, as well as private, opulence is originally derived'.

Willetts is not solely intent on reclaiming Burke for liberal economics. He attempts to show that Burke recognised that liberty – economic or political – could only be sustained by continuity in institutions, and he concludes on this point that Burke was a superior thinker to Disraeli, for example, because he appreciated that 'a successful, coherent Conservatism has to tie together free market economics and a sense of community'.

To that end, Willetts employs one of the most frequently quoted passages of Burke's which, with its commercial metaphor but genuflection to tradition, emphasises how dependent economic man is on the settled practices of the community he inhabits: 'We are afraid to put men to live and trade each on his own private stock of reason; because we suspect that the stock in each man is small, and that individuals would do better to avail themselves of the general bank and capital of nations and of ages.'

Willetts also quotes with approval another famous passage on the nature of man's sentiments and the rootedness in community from which other virtues spring: 'To be attached to the subdivision, to love the little platoon we belong to in society, is the first principle (the germ as it were) of public affections. It is the first link in the series by which we proceed towards a love to our country and to mankind.' He uses Burke's analysis of how patriotism and economic improvement both spring from a reverence for the local and the familiar to make the case for a 'communitarian' or 'civic' Conservatism, and in so doing he is recognising that the economic arguments of the 1980s had been won. Faith in planning, incomes policies and nationalisation was the province of a dwindling sect with ageing prophets. However, the Left had not retreated altogether but moved onto potentially more promising terrain. It was developing a critique of Conservatism as inadequate to deal with the social change brought by economic growth and insensitive to the needs of the community because it deified the individual.

Willetts was trying, while still celebrating the achievements of the 1980s, to show that Conservatism was more durable and flexible than its opponents liked to believe. In arguing that Mrs Thatcher was less *laissez-faire* and more pragmatic than her enemies thought her, and in maintaining that the communitarian strand in Tory thinking was always apparent, Willetts was serving a specific party, as well as a broader ideological, purpose. In stressing Mrs Thatcher's flexibility and her adaptation to Burkean 'circumstances', he sought to make the genuinely more pragmatic approach of John Major seem less of a departure from her example.

Willetts' polemic is skilfully argued and, although the work of a practising politician and not a detached observer, it is certainly truer to the balance of Burke's thinking than the interpretation favoured by Gilmour fifteen years before.

It is also shrewd in recognising that the changing circumstances of the nineties demanded a different rhetoric from Tories than that deployed in the eighties. Community is the product of prejudice, not planning, custom not commissions, and unless the Tories address social concerns effectively they risk yielding their natural heartland to their enemies.

By nature John Major prefers a conversational to a hortatory or didactic tone in his own rhetoric, but, influenced by Willetts, he has stitched Burke into his own speeches. In his 1993 Carlton lecture, he echoed the language of little platoons when he sought to link home and nation with his invocation of 'the unbroken chain of community linking ... the Union of the United Kingdom with the little union of families and local communities'.

As the Conservative Party adapts to the challenges of the next century, a new language will have to be developed and Burke will be plundered by those fighting for a turn at the helm. The use of his name, or his words, is no sure guide to where a politician stands on the Right, but the intelligent use of his thought is, at least, an indication of sensitivity to the need for a proper obeisance to the party's past in preparation for the future.

Burke after the Cold War: Bourgeois Triumphalist or Cassandra?

Mark Almond

> But, after all, for what purpose are we told of this reformation in their principles, and what is the policy of all this softening in ours, which is to be produced by their example? It is not to soften us to suffering innocence and virtue, but to mollify us to the crimes and to the society of robbers and ruffians.
>
> (*Letters on a Regicide Peace*, Letter IV)

Within a few years of the publication of *Reflections on the Revolution in France*, the savagery of the Terror and the rise of a 'popular general' had confirmed for all but the purblind admirers of Jacobinism Burke's standing as a prophetic critic of utopian ambitions in politics. During the relatively happy nineteenth century, his analysis of the utopian urge could be neglected as irrelevant, but after the Bolshevik seizure of power in Russia in 1917, Burke's themes regained their resonance. With the onset of the Cold War, following the West's brief delusion that, after the defeat of Nazism, cooperation with Stalin's genocidal régime could become permanent, Burke's influence as the author of a prescient critique of what he called 'theoretic dogma' was secure – at least on the conservative or classical liberal side of politics.[1] Even in the age of détente, the best that could be said was that the Soviet communists had lost their revolutionary urge and calmed down into men 'we can do business with'.

But does Burke have any useful insights for international policy today, after the end of the Cold War and the abandonment of communist doctrines by régimes from Berlin to Vladivostok? It is striking how, in *Reflections on the Revolutions in Europe*, his optimistic parody of Burke's *Reflections*, Lord Dahrendorf finds little of relevance in Burke's thinking and, apart from endorsement of Burkean 'trimming' to keep the ship of state afloat, rejects

---

1 For the revival of interest in Burke after the Bolshevik Revolution, see Conor Cruise O'Brien's introduction to *Reflections*, 56ff.

Burke's values as out-of-date where they are not too commonplace to be attributed to him alone.[2] If the threat of communism has disappeared, what
place is there for Burke?

I

That Burke would have abhorred Marxism-Leninism is self-evident. If he
would have been whole-heartedly delighted by communism's collapse as the
ruling ideology across the Soviet bloc, would he have relished the consequences of its end? At first sight the answer seems obvious. Burke, the defender of property and religion, not to mention the rights of the oppressed
around the globe, could hardly have failed to applaud the destruction of the
Berlin Wall. Certainly, the man who wrote the immortal passage about the
mob's irruption into Marie Antoinette's chamber in Versailles would never
have thought ten thousand swords must have leaped from their scabbards to
avenge even a look that threatened Nicolae and Elena Ceausescu, nor would
he have shed tears on the dictators' execution by their former comrades on
Christmas Day 1989. But Burke was not a man for naïve triumphalism any
more than he was a hide-bound pessimist.

Burke could distinguish between Thermidor and Restoration. The fate of
the Ceausescus at the hands of Iliescu and other former protégés would not
have deluded him into thinking that a new dawn had broken over Romania.
Two hundred years earlier, Robespierre's execution by other 'terrorists' did
not convince Burke to look favourably on the Directory: 'I hear another in-
ducement to fraternity with the present rulers. They have murdered one
Robespierre. This Robespierre, they tell us, was a cruel tyrant, and now that
he is put out of the way, all will go well in France … It is the old *bon-ton* of
robbers, who cast their common crimes on the wickedness of their departed
associates.'[3]

Just as Burke saw the true nature of the French Revolution before anyone
else, so he was alert to the twists and turns of Jacobin policy and self-interest. He was aware that the world loves normality, or at least its appearance,
and that years of upheaval simply deepen the desire for a return to a familiar state. Unlike the Foxites, who admired each deviation in French policy as
the dawn of happier times, Burke warned against taking at face value former
Jacobins' protestations of virtue reborn.

2   See Ralf Dahrendorf, *Reflections on the Revolution in Europe* (Chatto Counterblasts:
    London, 1990), p. 154. Burke would have felt even less sympathy with the post-
    Marxist Hegelian triumphalism of Francis Fukuyama's 'end of history' thesis.
3   *Works*, V, 397.

His great considerations on this theme are to be found in his *Letters on a Regicide Peace* (1796), which build on the thinking of the more famous *Reflections*. Several years on from 1989, naïve assumptions that 'people power' alone brought the end of the Communist Party's hegemony in the Soviet bloc need to be challenged. So does the view that any kind of privatisation will produce a market economy such as exists in the West or was envisaged by Burke or his great contemporary Adam Smith. Anyone contemplating the frequently unsettling peculiarities of post-communism could do much worse than refer to Burke. Instead of looking only to the *Reflections* as a possible guide, the *Letters on a Regicide Peace* offer Burke's assessment of the first apparently post-revolutionary transition in his own time.

If the Terror had confirmed Burke's warning about the nature of the French Revolution, Thermidor seemed to offer hope to those who had enthused over the fall of the Bastille and had not recognised the likely implications for the future of the bloodshed it involved. With the overthrow and execution of Robespierre, Saint-Just, *et al.*, wasn't France at last returning to normal? Even some of Burke's sharpest criticisms of the revolutionary régime's past methods, such as the confiscation of church lands and other property, seemed to be met by the new Constitution of France, adopted in August 1795, which modified the Rights of Man proclaimed in 1789, dropping the internationally-subversive word 'Fraternity' and instead announcing that: 'The rights of man in society are liberty, equality, security and property.'

Just as the House of Lords had considered making the anniversary of the storming of the Bastille a public holiday six years earlier, so the Constitution of the Year III was welcomed in Great Britain as a sign that France was making the transition to normality.[4] After three years of war against the revolutionary threat, many voices in Pitt's administration as well as among the indomitable appeasers of the Jacobins on the Foxite benches thought the time had come for peace with the surviving murderers of Louis XVI, of his Queen, and of scores of thousands of others.

At the height of the Terror, Burke had set out his conditions of peace with France in a letter to Emperor Woodford on 13 January 1794: 'When I see a fundamental change in its whole system, by the extinction of the Jacobin clubs, by the re-establishment of religion, and the restitution of property on its old foundations, and when I see a government, whatever it may be, founded upon that property, and regulated by it, I shall then think France in a negotiable condition.'[5]

---

4 Norman Hampson, *Will and Circumstance: Montesquieu, Rousseau and the French Revolution* (London, 1983), p. 150.
5 *Correspondence*, VII, 521.

Even after the execution of Louis XVI, Burke hoped that France would abandon Jacobinism. But he had no faith that the Jacobins would undergo a similar change of heart. Since 1989, the apparent introduction of capitalism by former communists has aroused little such scepticism. Burke understood the political efficacy of what the Germans call *Etiquettenschwindel* – the idea that changing labels changes substance. The restoration of the name Russia in place of the Soviet Union by a President who had presided over the demolition of the Ipatiev house in Sverdlovsk (naturally renamed 'Ekaterinburg') would no more have persuaded Burke that the past had been reborn than Orwell meant us to believe that the reversion of *Animal Farm* to *Manor Farm* wiped out the crimes of the pigs' régime after the expulsion of Mr Jones. In 1795 Burke noted that the 'indivisible Republic' had suddenly changed its name and all political sheep were expected to forget yesterday's French Republic and bleat the title of the new state: 'It changed its name of usurped power, and took the simple name of *France*. The word France is slipped in just as if the government stood exactly as before that revolution ... By sleight of hand the Jacobins are clean vanished, and it is France we have got under our cup.'[6] Two hundred years later, he would not have missed the same trick.

Although it took only seven years, rather than seven decades, for many Jacobins to renege on their revolutionary creed, Burke's indignation and suspicion about the sincerity of the Directors could apply in its moral force to today's renegade communists who now cross themselves as they enter their casinos and erect the Tsarist double-headed eagle on their monuments.

In 1795 Burke was outraged by the brazen impertinence of the Directors of the new order in France, expecting outsiders to take them at face value – and realistic enough to recognise that many would. He drew attention to their past actions and faith in the cause of Jacobinism, and to their unprecedented claim to trustworthiness, that they had never believed a word with which they had justified their previous bloodshed:

> The regicides, they say, have renounced the creed of the Rights of Man, and declared equality a chimera. This is still more strange than all the rest. They have apostatised from their apostasy. They are renegades from that impious faith, for which they subverted the ancient government ... And now, to reconcile themselves to the world, they declare this creed bought by so much blood to be an imposture and a chimera. I have no doubt that they always thought it to be so, when they were destroying everything at home and abroad for its establishment ... But this is the very first time that any men, or set of men, were

6   *Works*, V, 363–64.

hardy enough to attempt to lay the ground of confidence in them, by an acknowledgment of their own falsehood, fraud, hypocrisy, treachery, heterodox doctrine, persecution and cruelty. Everything we hear from them is new.[7]

From 'New Labour' in Britain to the boundaries of China, the airwaves are thick with declarations by former left-wingers demanding trust because they never believed what they professed yesterday. Nowadays, they imply that what they once believed and expected others to act upon should not bind them forever or even disqualify them from leadership. This is accepted because, since 1795, shallowness and changeability of principle have become virtues. Two centuries of the corrosive power that Burke decried has eaten into the modern soul. Consequently, whatever the benefits of the abolition of the totalitarian state since 1989, the continuance in office and the dominance of the economy by its former agents across much of the once-communist world should make us pause for thought about the nature of the changes of the past few years. But analysis of the winners and losers of the end of communism has hardly begun.

II

Burke, who crusaded against Jacobinism and advocated a 'long war' to grind down revolutionary infection in France, was taken up as a prophet of the Right in the Cold War, and much of his criticism of Jacobinism could be levelled against Leninists *a fortiori*. However, just as Orwell's anti-totalitarian fiction *Animal Farm* was right on target against Stalinism but has not lost its relevance with the abandonment of the Marxist faith by Stalin's heirs, so Burke's attack on the infinite malleability of the principles of the Jacobins after Thermidor has contemporary resonance for us, as battalions of former communist apparatchiks set themselves up in business as democrats and traders – our natural partners in the East. They have become the chief beneficiaries of the formal collapse of the communist system. Already in 1795 Burke recognised the peculiarity of post-revolutionary transition: yesterday's radicals become today's respectable politicians, but it is still they who set the terms of the debate.

Although Burke welcomed the benefits of what we now call capitalism and urged policies which would promote trade and sound money as the basis of prosperity, he saw the market system as the basis of civilised society rather

7   *Works*, V, 414–15.

than its goal. Burke was horrified by the French Revolution's implacable ideological drive and the brutality associated with it; but he was also distressed
by the socio-economic consequences of the revolutionaries' upturning of all
hierarchy and established values, including specie. Insofar as the French
Revolution opened up markets and was a bourgeois phenomenon, Burke was
suspicious of its moral impact, since religious faith and financial credit were
both sacrificed on the Jacobin altar. The combination of the attack on religion
and the sale of church property, the *biens-nationaux*, and the basing of a new
currency, the paper *assignat*, on such an unjust and insecure footing led him
to predict in the *Reflections* that France would become 'wholly governed by
the agitators in corporations, by societies in the towns formed of directors of
assignats, and trustees for the sale of church lands, attornies, agents, money-
jobbers, speculators, and adventurers.'[8] (Burke decried Henry VIII's 'tyranny'
in dissolving the monasteries for much the same reason.)

Inflation and speculation (in other men's property) were the key economic
characteristics of revolutionary France, according to Burke. Today, his criticism of the gaming mentality that is encouraged by a wholesale transference
of wealth by political *fiat* rings tellingly when we think of the growing influence of the mafia in Russia and other former Soviet republics. What eloquent
scorn Burke would have summoned up to respond to Western apologists for
nomenklatura-privatisation: 'The old gaming in funds was mischievous enough
undoubtedly; but it was so only to individuals. Even when it had its greatest
extent, in the Mississippi and the South Sea [Companies], it affected but
few, comparatively.' But the French had created a paper money and inflationary system combined with speculation which encompassed everyone:
'With you a man can neither earn nor buy his dinner, without a speculation.
What he receives in the morning will not have the same value at night. What
he is compelled to take as pay for an old debt, will not be received as the
same when he comes to pay a debt contracted by himself; nor will it be the
same when by prompt payment he would avoid contracting any debt at all.
Industry must wither away. Economy must be driven from your country.
Careful provision will have no existence. Who will labour without knowing the
amount of his pay? Who will study to increase what none can estimate? Who
will accumulate, when he does not know the value of what he saves? If you
abstract it from its uses in gaming, to accumulate your paper wealth would
be not the providence of a man, but the distempered instinct of a jackdaw.'[9]

The inflationary impact of the revolutionary régime's reliance upon the
biens-nationaux as the underpinning of the *assignats* reminds us of the naïve

8   *Reflections*, 313.
9   Ibid., 310–11.

faith many Western bankers show in contemporary Russian finances on the grounds of the country's buried mineral and energy wealth. Burke noted that the weakest and poorest were the worst affected by inflation: 'The truly melancholy part of the policy of systematically making a nation of gamesters is this; that though all are forced to play, few can understand the game; and fewer still are in a condition to avail themselves of the knowledge.' Burke sets out the cruel fate of the peasant under hyperinflation: 'The townsman can calculate from day to day: not so the inhabitant of the country. When the peasant first brings his corn to market, the magistrate in the towns obliges him to take the *assignat* at par; when he goes to the shop with this money, he finds it seven per cent the worse for crossing the way. This market he will not readily resort to again.' Burke foresaw how soon town and country would come to blows in France: 'The townspeople will be inflamed! They will force the country people to bring their corn. Resistance will begin.'[10] So far in Russia a placid and long-suffering national character has borne the depredations of inflation and the *de facto* confiscation of savings by a government élite which scorns to pay wages to miners and peasants alike despite repeated promises. But even in Russia there may yet be a second Pugachev rising to scourge the most crudely self-interested and bogus-Western élite since the reign of Catherine II.

Above all, though, Burke saw a sinister method in the inflationary madness of the Jacobins. He knew that the *assignat* favoured the bourgeoisie because their representatives controlled its issue. Investment in agriculture became counter-productive. Today in Russia hardly any investment takes place among Russians, and even the inflow of foreign funds is largely from Western governments or the IMF to the Russian régime or its nominally private representatives. The interpenetration of government and commerce in Russia is far from creating a market economy in the Western sense, though it has helped to produce a *jeunesse dorée*. The 'new Russians', children of Mr Brezhnev's élite, are utterly unconcerned about the well-being of the plebs. The Burke who defended millions of impoverished Indians against the exactions of Warren Hastings and his minions would not have been indifferent to the plunder of the former Soviet Union by its one-time guardians.

10 Ibid., 311 and see also 359. Ironically one of the few serious debates about the real nature of the transition in the East has taken place in the *New Left Review*, where an unrepentant Marxist decried the new Russia endorsed by the ex-communist John Lloyd. See Peter Gowan, 'Neo-Liberal Theory and Practice for Eastern Europe', in *NLR* 213 (September/October 1995), pp. 3–60, and Lloyd's defence of the new Russia in ibid. 216 (March/April 1996), pp. 119–40.

III

Burke saw in his own time that short-sighted economic interests allied with academic and journalistic babble could blind people to issues of principle and longer term self-interest. In the second of the *Letters on a Regicide Peace*, he wrote almost prophetically of the power of this combination to persuade people everywhere of illusions: 'The correspondence of the monied and the mercantile world, the literary intercourse of academies, but, above all, the press, of which they had in a manner entire possession, made a kind of electric communication everywhere.'[11] Modern television and radio provide that electric simultaneity of opinion which in the 1790s seemed to be transmitted spontaneously through the atmosphere.

Long before the fall of the Berlin Wall, there were capitalists who were indifferent or hostile to liberty – and not just Soviet agents of influence like Armand Hammer. By the mid-1990s it had become the norm in the *Financial Times* or *Wall Street Journal* to regard the so-called 'reform communists' as preferable to the anti-communist Right across the former Soviet bloc. Thus, the *Financial Times* could write favourably of a 'public sector purge' of non-communists after the electoral victory of the reformed communists in Hungary in 1994, seeing the reappointed ex-communists as 'well-qualified' – unlike the people whom they had replaced, who, of course, had been denied access to the particular qualifications possessed by Hungary's communist élite for several decades.[12]

The attractions to Western businessmen and journalists of dealing with non-ideological experts in the East is, in fact, a highly ideological development, and one which Burke would have deplored as he denounced the anxiety of Foxites and others to make a regicide peace. Then, Burke recognised that Thermidor represented another burst of Terror, one approved of by all and sundry even if they had praised its victims until the day before, but hardly a sign that the ex-Terrorists were about to renounce power to a legitimate source of authority, either royal or popular. Furthermore, such dealings have little to do with profoundly important Burkean themes like the rule of law, the rights of property and the sobriety and diligence of the merchants in creating a successful economy. Instead, the unifying cult of a mechanistic view of the market conflicts strongly with Burke's emphasis on community and national identity.

Burke's distaste for the militant nationalism exploited by the French revolutionaries did not imply a rejection of all nationalism or patriotism. Quite the contrary. He regarded traditional identity and its defence as valuable norms. He rejected the synthetic creation of harmonised political and administrative identities:

11 *Works*, V, 259.
12 'Hungary in public sector purge', *Financial Times*, 26 October 1994.

No man ever was attached by a sense of pride, partiality, or real affection, to a description of square measurement. He never will glory in belonging to the Chequer, No. 71, or to any other badge-ticket. We begin our public affections in our families. No cold relation is a zealous citizen. We pass on to our neighbourhoods, and our habitual provincial connections. These are inns and resting-places. Such divisions of our country as have been formed by habit, and not by a sudden jerk of authority, were so many little images of the great country in which the heart found something which it could fill. The love to the whole is not extinguished by this subordinate partiality ... The citizens are interested from old prejudices and unreasoned habits, and not on account of the geometric properties of its figure.[13]

The Western political élite – both in the United States and across the European Union – has been deeply unsympathetic, or even downright hostile, to anti-communists who have seen the restoration of national independence or national culture as key themes in their politics. The collapse of the multi-national communist states such as the Soviet Union and Yugoslavia seem to defy the trend towards supranational integration promoted by Washington and Brussels.

After 1989, there was a common mistaken assumption that a resurgent, illiberal Right, rather than a renewed Left, was the greatest challenge to the establishment of a Western-orientated new order, even though former communists, whether as born-again nationalists or hardly-reformed variants of their past selves, were far more likely to hold power or return to it across broad swathes of Eurasia.[14] Fear of the chimera of a nationalist backlash led former advocates of liberty in the East, as well as former fellow-travellers, to endorse the communist comeback.[15] Indeed, so common are endorsements of the old nomenklatura's recovery of political power to complement its continuing hold on economic power that it no longer seems anomalous that the *Financial Times* could optimistically headline the victory of the Bulgarian

---

13 *Reflections*, 315.
14 Anne Applebaum, 'The Fall and Rise of the Communists', in *Foreign Affairs*, no. 73 (November/December 1994), pp. 7–13.
15 For instance, the Hungarian-American billionaire philanthropist George Soros told the US House Sub-committee on International Security and Human Rights in August 1994: 'I do not find the recent electoral victories of former communist parties like [those in] Hungary, Poland or Lithuania disturbing at all. These are reform communists who want to get away from communism as far as possible.' Why these parties should cling to their leftist legacy and the name of socialism if their anxiety was to reject their Marxist past was not explained, but for Soros 'their re-emergence constitutes a welcome extension of the democratic spectrum'. He argued that 'Communism as a dogma is well and truly dead. The real danger is the emergence of would-be nationalist dictators.'

socialists in 1994: 'Socialists' win in Bulgaria lifts hope for reform'.[16] The
paper's analysis fitted the news from Sofia into a general pattern of welcome:
'Bulgaria now has an opportunity for stable government by a socialist party
which is ... likely to be dominated by pragmatic reformers who accept the
need for a market economy and privatisation. In this, Bulgaria is following a
pattern in central Europe.' But in practice the Bulgarian socialists produced
worse results for the economy, as even their Western admirers had to admit
by late 1996.[17]

Just like the Foxites, who saw the Directory's greed as a guarantee of its
peaceful intentions in 1795, modern apologists for the great share-out of state
assets among a tiny clique of 'new Russians' are confusing possession with
property. Despite the much-acclaimed death of Marxism, Karl Marx's insistence that ownership determines everything befuddles the mind of most
Western observers of the post-Soviet East. Burke would not have accepted
the crude Marxian notion that privatisation of any kind is a step towards the
kind of economic system that he favoured. Owing to Jacobin legitimisation of
confiscation – and the mass murder of former owners – the restoration of
property is no longer feasible in most cases, but its transference into the hands
of its former administrators does not constitute the establishment of legitimate property. From the tragedy of revolutionary violence and dispossession
there is no easy escape.

16   *Financial Times*, 20 December 1994. For other examples of the *Financial Times*'s hos-
     tility to anti-communists, see Jonathan Sunley, 'Post-Communism. An Infantile
     Disorder' in *The National Interest* (Summer, 1996).
17   *The Economist* has gone further, approving of the new rôle of former KGB officers
     in the nominally private economy. In April 1995 it noted the restoration of many
     powers to the renamed KGB before endorsing them: 'The KGB is back and Russia
     is becoming a police state. That was the conclusion that many card-carrying liberals
     leapt to when, on 5 April, Boris Yeltsin signed ... a decree returning to Russia's se-
     curity services many of the powers once wielded by the Soviet KGB ... It would be
     a mistake, however, to assume that this attempt to revive the KGB is a desperate bid
     by an increasingly unpopular government to prop itself up by Soviet-style subterfuge
     and intimidation. It may just be a populist measure.' *The Economist* informed its
     readers that some of the 'best' former-KGB officials were already working for banks.
     However, what such men have to say about why they are considered assets to new
     private enterprises suggests that they owe their employment more to past perfor-
     mance than to any newly-learned capitalist tricks. (*The Economist*, 15 April 1995.)
     Former KGB chief Victor Ivanenko is now vice-president of the Yukos oil concern.
     His business methods resemble the mafia's rather than BP's – one hopes: 'When the
     subsidiaries don't listen I usually talk to them. They're afraid of me, because of what
     I used to do for a living.' See 'Despite iffy finances, Russian oil companies draw
     Western dollars', *Wall Street Journal*, 29 March 1996.

CONCLUSION

In East and West alike there has been a convergence of élites producing a common cult of aimless greed which is the doctrine of the New World Order. All the braying 'bourgeois triumphalism' of reborn capitalists in the 1990s cannot drown out the social and economic consequences of the widespread acceptance in the West of Jacobin and Marxist values, and the proliferation of unholy alliances in politics and business between Westerners and former Soviet communists makes a depressing coda to Burke's posthumous struggle for morality and property regulated by the rule of law.

Burke would surely have considered the subordination of all policy to the selfish interests of individuals as not just short-sighted in the extreme, but as the denial of the proper rôle of statesman and merchant. The interpenetration of élites, post-communist and post-Burkean, across the northern hemisphere is not producing the well-ordered society and economy advocated by Burke. The threat of nuclear war may have been banished and the ideological competition between East and West resolved, but it is not clear what ideas really won the Cold War. It may already have been true in 1790, but, surveying the post-communist moral malaise today, Burke would hardly withdraw his conclusion that 'the age of chivalry is gone. That of sophisters, economists and calculators has succeeded; and the glory of Europe is extinguished forever.'

Edmund Burke and the British Constitution

Jim McCue

Edmund Burke was a staunch defender of the British constitution, which he believed was 'placed in a just correspondence and symmetry with the order of the world'. Different principles were represented in the mixed constitution by the monarchy, the Lords and the Commons, each of which offset the powers and shortcomings of the others. None of these estates was sovereign, for the nation had outgrown the doctrine of divine right.

This constitution accorded with man's permanent and fallible nature, because it blended several kinds of authority, from above and below, and prevented any one from becoming a new absolutism. Authority from below, the authority of the people, was expressed through the Commons, on juries, and through free association in clubs, guilds and so forth. But not everything was a matter of personal or majority choice. Some values in society had been immemorially understood or decided, such as moral imperatives, taboos and the sanctity of property. These values were maintained by authority from above, expressed through the monarchy, the aristocracy and the Church.

This stable constitution of things accorded also with what was 'second nature' to the British people: the conventions, traditions and prejudices that had arisen from the conditions of living in a particular place, and which expressed themselves in particular institutions.

The word 'constitution' means the nature of things. The human constitution is what cannot be changed, or can be changed only with the utmost difficulty over a long period. A national constitution is the same: it should be descriptive, not prescriptive. The phrase 'the British constitution' can mean either the character of John Bull (which has to do with roast beef and hearts of oak) or the arrangements of his politics – and as the phrase tells us, the two naturally coincide. To constitute is, according to the pleasing tautology in Johnson's Dictionary, 'to make anything what it is', not to make it something else. The constitution acknowledges the existing make-up of a people and a country.

In defence of the constitution, Burke at different periods of his career opposed the overweening ambitions both of the monarchy, when George III attempted to dictate policy to Parliament, and of the masses, when the

French Revolution threatened general anarchy. For him, the crucial thing was restraint and the avoidance of tyranny. Self-restraint was best, but people and powers should also be checked by mutual restraint.

Burke's political wisdom was based not upon documents, charters and declarations, but upon magnanimity and consent – 'that great and only foundation of government, the confidence of the poeple'. He shunned the kind of political philosophy that looked for the ultimate source of sovereignty or the perfect formulation of political rights and freedoms. His thinking begins always from present practicalities – from men as they are – and never from the realms of legal or constitutional speculation. 'Men are not tied to one another by paper and seals,' he wrote. 'They are led to associate by resemblances, by conformities, by sympathies.'

Writing after the overthrow of France by the revolutionaries, Burke argued that 'the pretended Republic', with its tangle of rights and constitutional innovations, was not France, but a usurpation:

> The body politic of France existed in the majesty of its throne; in the dignity of its nobility; in the honour of its gentry; in the sanctity of its clergy; in the reverence of its magistracy; in the weight and consideration due to its landed property in the several bailliages; in the respect due to its moveable substance represented by the corporations of the kingdom. All these particular *moleculae* united, form the great mass of what is truly the body politic in all countries. They are so many deposits and receptacles of justice; because they can only exist by justice. Nation is a moral essence, not a geographical arrangement.

Burke's model of society was utterly different from that generally accepted today. He knew that what constitutes the spirit of a people is precisely what cannot be written down. His model was based upon man's better nature, upon families, convention and manners, the feelings he famously encompassed under the word 'chivalry', which gave society its tone.

'Manners are of more importance than laws,' he wrote. 'Upon them, in a great measure the laws depend. The law touches us but here and there, and now and then. Manners are what vex or sooth, corrupt or purify, exalt or debase, barbarise or refine us, by a constant, steady, uniform, insensible operation, like that of the air we breathe in. They give their whole form and colour to our lives.' Manners regulate not simply how we behave, but how we think: Johnson defines 'Manners' as 'character of the mind'. In contrasting them with law, Burke was emphasising that they dictate not what is permitted by others, but what we permit ourselves. If we have the discipline of manners, morals and conventions, we may be allowed more legal freedoms. But if the restraints that would once have made some things unthinkable are endlessly questioned or flouted, then the rigidity of the law has to be applied. What is not observed voluntarily has to be enforced, and the state is strengthened in the name of – but at the expense of – the people.

Burke wished to deflect men from the new fashion of casting politics in terms of their rights and claims. Instead he wanted men, and particularly their leaders, to abide by chivalry's concessive and selfless codes. 'The question with me is not whether you have a right to render your people miserable,' he told Parliament, 'but whether it is not your interest to make them happy.' As the antithesis in his sentence shows, people's supposed rights can be the opposite of their true interests.

In 1774, hoping for conciliation with America, Burke urged ministers not to press the 'right' to tax to its disastrous conclusion: 'I am not here going into the distinctions of rights, nor attempting to mark their boundaries. I do not enter into these metaphysical distinctions; I hate the very sound of them.' Burke realised that the colonies could be retained only with their consent, and that abstractions are dangerous because they encourage an unaccommodating, fundamentalist habit of mind. No degree of exactness can anticipate every circumstance. Governing well, like being a good father or a good teacher, depends upon tact, sympathy, give and take, mutual interest and respect much more than upon fixed rules. But the administration pursued its proud rights and lost the colonies. Ever since, people have continued the struggle over such metaphysical distinctions. Like Burke, we should wince, and consider instead their true interests.

Burke's friend and sparring partner Dr Johnson warned: 'Things modified by human understandings, subject to varieties of complication, and changeable as experience advances knowledge or accident influences caprice, are scarcely to be included in any standing form of expression, because they are always suffering from some alteration of their state' (*Rambler* No. 125). This is the reason why Burke would have opposed a written, inflexible constitution for Britain.

Written constitutions pretend always to know best, and to judge before the event. But the supposed finality of written constitutions rarely holds in practice, so they can be detrimental to the very values they were intended to enshrine. As changing circumstances and technologies make their limitations plain, they are liable to accrue ever more technical amendments. So instead of being statements of broad principle, they tend to decline into cumbersome charters of law which are especially rigid because supposedly above politics. A constitution written today would inevitably be couched in the too-specific, too-narrow and yet indefinitely extendable terms of human rights, with all the 'mumping cant' that Burke abhorred.

Burke shows us that Britain has no need of a written constitution, because it is governed within the rule of law. We are not ruled by despotic caprice.

Judges can and do tell ministers if they are exceeding their powers. The government must operate within the law, although it can change the law with the assent of the necessary parliamentary majorities – which are now too easily whipped, and insufficiently jealous of their conscientious independence. Instead of a written constitution, we have a spirit of compromise. Britain's system of jurisprudence relies heavily on precedent, yet the principle stands that no Parliament can bind the Parliaments of the future. The present is bound to the past, but not by it.

A few years ago, the newly appointed editor of a national newspaper made the radical mistake of throwing away a house style guide that had been compiled over decades, and writing his own. He issued directions on matters that scarcely arose, while omitting to rule on genuinely crucial points. Nor could he know the reasons – of consistency, literary convention or legal propriety – why successive sub-editors had adopted and passed on particular practices. He looked for system, and did not find it; what he overlooked was a series of working methods. The newspaper had not been publishing since the age of Edmund Burke without considering stylistic issues. The paper's previous style notes had been compiled and adjusted in response to circumstances; the new guide was written all at once and imposed (aptly enough in the form of a little red book). It did not work, and had swiftly to be rewritten. What had previously been second nature had been so much investigated and discussed that the paper had become self-conscious, and in some cases pedantic and unidiomatic.

To attempt to write a constitution from scratch (or even from the terms of alien documents) would be to make the same mistake. For like the style book, Britain's unwritten constitution is, in Burke's phrase, 'the result of the thoughts of many minds, in many ages'. The style book of a newspaper is a trivial thing by comparison with a constitution; and if the serviceable elegance of such a painstakingly compiled *vade mecum* was not apparent to the reformer, the moral and practical dimensions of an ancient constitution are not likely to be apparent either. And how much greater are the consequences of misunderstanding them.

Burke had a particular contempt for the kind of self-appointed, self-validating claques who claim to represent a public desire for thoroughgoing reforms. In *Observations on the Conduct of the Minority* (1793), he warns that the danger from groups such as the Revolution Society (then) or Charter 88 (now) is that 'without legal names, these clubs will be led to assume political capacities; that they may debate the forms of the constitution; and that from their meetings they may insolently dictate their will to the regular authorities of the kingdom, in the manner in which the Jacobin clubs issue their mandates to the National Assembly.' What would he make of opposition parties that set up a quasi-official commission to investigate the constitutional position of Scotland or Northern Ireland? The constitutional position is known: they are part of the United Kingdom. But when such a body begins to talk of a Scottish parliament, and deciding where this fiction might sit, it is presumptuously attempting to change the constitution without any authority. The danger is that the talk may prove self-fulfilling, because newspapers and broadcasters take such bodies, and such fictions, at their own estimation. Journalists have a reckless and unaccountable influence over such matters, and an inherent interest in change, because it is news.

In one of the funniest metaphors in the *Reflections*, Burke warns his French friend against taking agitators to be representative of the general opinion:

> The vanity, restlessness, petulance, and spirit of intrigue of several petty cabals, who attempt to hide their total want of consequence in bustle and noise, and puffing, and mutual quotation of each other, makes you imagine that our contemptuous neglect of their abilities is a mark of general acquiescence in their opinions. No such thing, I assure you. Because half a dozen grasshoppers under a fern make the field ring with their importunate chink, whilst thousands of great cattle, reposed beneath the shadow of the British oak, chew the cud and are silent, pray do not imagine that those who make the noise are the only inhabitants of the field; that of course, they are many in number; or that, after all, they are other than the little shrivelled, meagre, hopping, though loud and troublesome insects of the hour.

These masterly sentences not only mock the shrillness of malcontents and intriguers, but demonstrate the placid power and weight of the settled, contemplative majority. The agitators are busily puffing one another (always with the risk that the balloon will burst). Like crickets talkin' back and forth in rhyme, they resort not only to 'mutual quotation', but to mutual quotation, emphatically, 'of each other' – as if platitudes might improve by repetition and tautology. But though they in their squeaking laugh contemn, these are but insects. Their doctrines are slight, fragile and short-lived, in contrast to the long-established principles of tenancy. The true occupants, the great somnolent cattle, need only swish their tails. After Burke's first, 52-word sentence about the cabalists, six brisk words of dismissal suffice: 'No such thing, I assure you.'

There may be times when it is necessary to write a new constitution or code of laws, but this, as Burke says, is likely to be after a national cataclysm, such as defeat in war or a declaration of independence. Then the task will be hard enough; but to write a new constitution for a country that is living consensually by long-standing arrangements is harder yet, and an invitation to controversy and bitterness. It is to declare an emergency when there is none.

The oldest national written constitution still in use, that of the United States, had the advantage of being framed by sagacious leaders consolidating a nation. But noble though it is, the American Constitution has undergone periodic revision and reversion. An amendment ratified in 1913, for instance, was needed before Congress could impose income tax, whereas in Britain the tax was simply passed into law. Nor can the supposedly transcendent authority of the Constitution put an end to political wrangles, or ameliorate bad policies. The furore over abortion continues, and the notorious amendment prohibiting alcohol, ratified in 1919, had to be repealed in 1933. This was not truly a constitutional matter, but a law.

The American Constitution has become a battlefield of contradictions over which rights shall prevail. It takes power away from the government and gives it to judges, who necessarily become politicised. For instance, the states have seen their power to impose the death penalty first arbitrarily abolished and then arbitrarily restored by the Supreme Court as a constitutional question, without Congress having a vote on the matter at all.

To define British liberties under a charter or bill of rights or written constitution would be to confine them. Yet at the same time, if the American experience is any indication, such a document would require an interpretative court and would not be a permanent apolitical fixture, but a recurrent political fix. The idea that introducing a written constitution for the United Kingdom would put an end to constitutional wrangling is naïve and incredible. The inevitable disputes over the writing of a new constitution would signal that the whole system was contingent and subject to revision. The pressure for alterations to suit passing fancies would be enormous. This would be a grave concession to meddlers who, in Burke's words, 'think they have no liberty, if it does not comprehend a right in them of making to themselves new constitutions at their pleasure'.

Nations resort to written constitutions when ill at ease. A nation constantly referring to one is akin to a couple continually discussing the state of their relationship instead of living it. Nation and relationship are both liable to be made unhappy and less stable by worrying away unnecessarily at matters which might never trouble them in practice.

The analogy has been taken farthest by a couple from – obviously – the United States, who drew up for themselves a marital constitution, which lays out what are to be their life aims, their separate responsibilities, how often they are to have sex and when they shall have children. Well, by his fifties Tristram Shandy's father had come to regulate his married life so that he wound the house-clock on the first Sunday night of every month, and 'had likewise gradually brought some other little family concernments to the same period, in order, as he would often say to my uncle *Toby*, to get them all out of the way at one time' – but this was in a novel. One can only pity a couple so lacking in spontaneity that they must regulate their lives by charter. By living to an agenda, they hope to overcome their absence of imagination, tolerance, flexibility and trust. Doubtless the divorce will be for breach of contract.

Burke argues that a contented society (like a contented relationship) does not crave theoretical underpinnings. 'The bulk of mankind on their part are not excessively curious concerning any theories whilst they are really happy; and one sure symptom of an ill-conducted state is the propensity of the people to resort to them.' Such questions are raised only when a tacit faith is violated, as America's independence began to be demanded only when Parliament began to tax the colonies: 'The same cause which has introduced all formal compacts and covenants among men made it necessary. I mean habits of soreness, jealousy, and distrust.' A written constitution is not a victory, but an admission of defeat, of soreness, jealousy and distrust. Burke understood that just as people's wishes, needs and interests should be addressed directly, rather than escalated into 'rights', so political problems should not be escalated into 'constitutional issues' if this can possibly be avoided.

Those keenest to impose upon us a written constitution – with its worthless guarantees of Liberty, Equality and Fraternity – are generally those keenest also to subject the nation to an unmitigated sovereignty of the European Union, in which the people have no restraining powers at all. 'They must be worse than blind who do not see with what undeviating regularity of system, in this case and in all cases, they pursue their scheme for the utter destruction of every independent power,' wrote Burke in 1796. A written constitution and the European treaties that we have sleepwalked into are both inflexible forms of power from above. Any British constitution written at present would not be freely entered into by a free people, because it would be constrained by our subjection and supposed obligations to European bodies. The writers of a constitution would not, for instance, feel able to determine the nature of the highest court of appeal, or the extent of the powers of Parliament. These are already under the control of foreign powers. This would make it impossible to compose a free constitution.

Burke's comments on the nature and aims of the post-revolutionary Directory in France offer parallels to the constitutional attitudes of the European bureaucracies, which insist they must be the final arbiters. Power is not to be dispersed, divided and balanced, as in the constitution for which Burke fought to his last breath, but must be newly concentrated in a true and foreign sovereignty. Furthermore, the basis of European laws is precisely the kind of metaphysics that was propounded during the French Revolution. The European Court of Human Rights is the direct descendant of the 'rights of man', which claimed a universal jurisdiction. And the European Commission, like the revolutionary French Directory, asserts that it is empowered to overrule national laws, courts and parliaments.

The Directory of 1796 believed that it had not just a right but a duty to impose its laws upon Europe. As Burke wrote, it insisted that, being 'charged by the Constitution with the execution of the laws, it cannot make or listen to any proposal that would be contrary to them. The constitutional act does not permit it to consent to any alienation of that which, according to the existing laws, constitutes the territory of the Republic.' Burke went on to expound this, in his *Letters on a Regicide Peace*:

> Their will is the law, not only at home, but as to the concerns of every nation. Who has made that law but the Regicide Republic itself, whose laws, like those of the Medes and Persians, they cannot alter or abrogate, or even so much as take into consideration. Without the least ceremony or compliment, they have sent out of the world whole sets of laws and lawgivers. They have swept away the very constitutions under which the legislatures acted, and the laws were made ... whatever they have put their seal on for the purposes of their ambition, and the ruin of their neighbours, that alone is invulnerable, impassible, immortal ... In other words, they are powerful to usurp, impotent to restore; and equally by their power and their impotence they aggrandise themselves, and weaken and impoverish you and all other nations.

The case is the same today, with the European Union adamant that it can take on new powers – over money, defence, foreign policy – but can never relinquish any. Eventually, quite possibly, Britain will be told that she may not have a monarchy, and may not have an unelected Upper House, on the grounds that these are not democratic (and our new masters would hardly be receptive to the argument that this is their point).

'If we once place ourselves in a state of inferiority,' wrote Burke in a letter of 1 March 1797, 'they will now, and at all times, in effect, name a [prime] minister to this country. There never has been a superior power who would suffer a dependent province substantially to name its own minister.' It may be that the European Union will continue to allow Britain to choose figurehead prime ministers, but it is likely that it will try to 'harmonise' the domestic legislative arrangements of its member states. It would be peculiar if we were made to conform in litres and metres, in fridges and bridges, without there being an eventual attempt to standardise and homogenise our parliamentary system too.

Twenty-five years of European entanglements have dangerously weakened the British constitution. Worse even than the loss of legislative and judicial powers has been the loss of confidence in Parliament. The self-sufficiency of the nation has bled away. And the means of sapping national confidence are the same as they were 200 years ago. 'First,' wrote Burke in 1796, the foreign usurpers 'more directly undertake to be the real representatives of the people of this kingdom: and on a supposition in which they agree with our parliamentary reformers, that the House of Commons is not that representative, the function being vacant, they, as our true constitutional organ, inform his Majesty and the world of the sense of the nation.' Once Parliament ceases to be the agreed focus of 'the sense of the nation', because its powers have been exported or arrogated, the plausibility of all kinds of systematic reforms is dangerously increased.

Even leaving aside the European disaster, Britain's political system is not working well, and Burke's writings help to explain why. People who over-emphasise things that can be counted (money, votes) or written down (rights, entitlements) are liable to underestimate or even scorn values that are unquantifiable (experience, wisdom) or magnanimous (loyalty, leniency). As Burke remarked of 'the tribe of vulgar politicians', in his *Letters on a Regicide Peace*, 'They think there is nothing worth pursuit, but that which they can handle; which they can measure with a two-foot rule; which they can tell upon ten fingers.'

For two centuries, constitutional reforms have all been in the direction commended by Burke's antagonist Thomas Paine, towards greater and simpler democracy, and embracing what Burke described as 'that grand magazine of offensive weapons, the rights of man'. This has had the effect of weakening and further weakening the non-democratic, immeasurable elements of the state, so that now the Left can truly say that the constitution needs strengthening. The system does need reform, but any conservative, or Burkean, must hesitate to say so, because all schemes of reform that are on offer would make matters worse. The nation does not need to abolish the monarchy, or the voting rights of hereditary peers (with no idea of how to replace their restraining influence), or to introduce proportional representation or regional parliaments or 'citizens' juries'. To avoid a sovereign tyranny of apparatchiks, claiming their mandate from majorities of the manipulated mass, it is now necessary to stand up, as Burke did, for a restrained constitution of varied parts. The nation needs not an extension of democracy, but new counterbalances to democracy. It should not have fewer anomalies, but more – for many anomalies are correctives in disguise. Rather than the British constitution being judged (and found wanting) by the purist criterion of democracy, democracy should be judged by criteria of consent and contentment. As Burke would have clearly seen, most current proposals for change are attempts to correct a system too reliant on a biddable popular opinion by relying upon it still further. Instead of refining our democracy, he would have us pause to ask, is democracy enough?

Edmund Burke and New Labour

Lord Plant of Highfield

Comparisons between thinkers and situations divided by two hundred years must be approached with a good deal of caution. One of the major advances in political thought over the past twenty years has been sensitivity to the context and circumstances in which a particular thinker operates. Ideas, values and principles on this view are not perennial, nor are they Platonic forms standing behind and instantiating themselves in particular contexts and discourses. Their meaning, rather, is given in the discourse of a particular time and place, and as those discourses change or are forgotten, so, too, ideas change and cease to count.

Nevertheless, Burke is taken as an icon of Conservatism (in both the upper and lower cases) and many of his ideas, to a degree abstracted from the context in which they were developed, are still part of a living debate in politics. The Conservative Party has been the vehicle whereby some elements of Burke's thought have been transmitted into contemporary political discourse; but it is possible to identify certain themes in that legacy which are now more fully embodied in the outlook of the modern Labour Party.

On the face of it, it seems very unlikely that a party of the Left should be able to learn from Burke or to integrate any of his ideas into its own political practice. After all, Burke's most familiar political doctrines were formulated largely in response to the French Revolution, an event which Burke saw as calling forth the need for a more systematic defence of the prevailing order than most politicians at that time felt comfortable with. Tradition, habit and prejudice now needed a defence because their authority could no longer be presumed as a sort of second nature. In a sense, then, it could be argued that the French Revolution precipitated the formulation of conservatism as a doctrine rather than just as a set of habits and dispositions, despite the fact that Burke's arguments were designed to secure the authority of habits and dispositions. Since the French Revolution, which presented the possibility of a radical reform of society based upon rational and universal principles, was the quintessential event in radical politics, how can counter-revolutionary doctrines conceived in such circumstances be thought to be relevant to a party of the Left?

I

There are two aspects of Burke's critique of the French Revolution which can throw light upon the present position of the Labour Party. Burke was strongly opposed to the pursuit of rationalism in politics and he saw the French Revolution as embodying such a pursuit. Rationalism was defective in a number of ways: human knowledge was too dispersed, too limited, too fragmented to provide a basis for a radical transformation of society. 'A man is never in greater danger of being wholly wrong,' Burke wrote, 'than when he advances far in the road of refinement; nor have I ever that diffidence and suspicion of my reasonings as when they seem to be most curious, exact and conclusive.' Not only this, but human action is fraught with unintended consequences which would lead to outcomes which would probably not have been chosen by the radical if he had been in a position to choose. In *Reflections on the Revolution in France*, Burke stated: 'The science of constructing a commonwealth, or renovating it, or reforming it, is, like every other experimental science, not to be taught *a priori* ... Very plausible schemes, with very pleasing commencements, have often shameful and lamentable conclusions.'

Rationalism also purports to deal in universals such as ideas of natural rights. Just because they are natural and universal, such rights are held by all, and thus doctrines about rights do not deal with people as situated members of communities, traditions and groups. The propensity of human beings, however, is to define themselves in terms of particular descriptions – a member of this nation, religion, gender, culture, ethnic group – rather than in terms of some universal principles such as rights, which, because they are presumed to be held equally by all human beings, can only carry their moral force by being abstracted from precisely the particulars which give human beings a sense of dignity, worth and identity. People are moved in politics by things close to them, not by universal principles which depend for their degree of power on the degree of their abstraction from the particular.

The manifold defects of political rationalism mean that the basis for political authority and activity has to be found in tradition, practices, habit and prejudice in Burke's sense – the 'untaught feelings' – rather than in some kind of overarching systematic theory. Political action should not be founded on theory so much as on the political contours of a lived political tradition.

Socialism in both its Marxist and social democratic forms has been rationalistic in the objectionable sense that Burke described. Marxism presupposed a whole theory of history and a complex account of the evolving relationships between means of production, relations of production and their corresponding ideological and political forms. Social democracy – particularly in its mid-twentieth-century variants – prescribed a set of goals for political action: the pursuit of greater social justice and social equality, coupled with a consequential set of rights and entitlements in political, civil and socio-economic life. Greater social equality was to be achieved by Keynesian demand management techniques which, it was believed, would yield increased fiscal dividends to government to improve the relative position of the worst off. This, in turn, implied a substantial rôle for the state in intervention in the economy.

Both of these rationalistic (in Burke's sense) paradigms of left-wing political thought have collapsed. Marxism has collapsed in a more complete way as a practical political option because of the colossal planning failures of Marxism/ Leninism in the Soviet Union and Eastern Europe. Planning as practised in those countries was itself a hubristically rationalistic enterprise which neglected both the dispersed and the fragmented nature of human knowledge and which ignored the unintended nature of the consequences of collective action. Social democracy, in its mid-century, Croslandite form, is also widely seen as being irrelevant, based upon unusually favourable economic circumstances in the fifties and sixties. It is assumed, however, that it cannot adjust itself to the impact of free markets and the global economy and is not compatible with the degree of deregulation that markets require to compete effectively in today's world: how can a country pursue a policy of social justice and greater social and economic equality, with all that this implies for taxation and expenditure, in the context of a global economy in which our competitors are doing no such thing? Keynesianism in one country cannot work any longer in the global market-place, as François Mitterand found out in the early years of his presidency in France.

The acute difficulties at the heart of these two paradigms of the Left – both committed to social justice, but each adopting a different strategy for its attainment – have necessitated a rethinking of the moral and intellectual basis of the politics of the Left. It can be argued that in this post-modern world, where confidence in large-scale intellectual theories in politics has been lost, and grand narratives such as Marxism seem to have little salience, the only possible basis for left-wing politics is a clear analysis and interpretation of where we are now in society and a view of the possibilities arising out of that interpretation. Such an analysis must take into account history as a way in which our fellow citizens have developed a sense of identity and as a source of the moral values underpinning the society on which the Left seeks to operate.

This is not just a message for the Left. It also applies to many on the free market Right who seem to take as rationalistic a view about the economy as the Left has done about politics. If one takes a good deal of the writing by free market economists about market reform in the former Soviet Union for example, there is an assumption that the market is a technical device which can somehow be grafted onto what is in each case a unique history and culture, and that what works well in one place can be expected to work in another, whatever the differences of circumstance. Here there is also little recognition of historical singularity, little recognition of the assumed universality of the market as a mechanism, little recognition of the problems of collective action which Burke predicted would arise in an attempt to implement a universalistic approach, and little sense of the unintended consequences of a collective decision to introduce markets without taking any real notice of the cultural and historical context. There can be a hubristic rationalism of the Right as well as of the Left. In defending 'ancient opinions and rules of life' against the rationalist 'rights of men' theories of the French revolutionaries, Burke made it clear that he regarded the market, as much as any other area of social life, to be based upon those historical values: 'Even commerce, and trade, and manufacture, the gods of our economical politicians, are themselves perhaps but creatures; are themselves but effects, which, as first causes, we choose to worship.'

So if we are to think about the relative rôles of state, market, community and private life in modern society, we should not be guided by general theories of either the Left or the Right, nor should we be guided by historically specific models and assume that US-style capitalism is the only form that a mature capitalist economy can take. Rather, we need to consider the range of ways in which the market can be embedded in a society such as ours, with its history and values. If we are to think about the limits of the state or the limits of the market, we should not assume, for example, that the only justification for state action lies in some general market-based theory where the state's rôle is only to provide the legal framework for the market together with a set of public goods (in the economist's sense). Burke did indeed say that 'the moment that government appears at market, all the principles of market will be subverted' – but these principles are not those shared by our contemporary libertarian economists and calculators.

II

In this sense, New Labour may well implicitly embody a more Burkean approach to understanding the appropriate relations between state, market, community and individual than the modern Conservative Party. Many ideologues of the Right pledge their allegiance to Burke while their political practice belies their devotion. A few specific examples may serve to illustrate this.

First, there has been the tendency of Conservative governments since 1979 to seek to extend markets or quasi-markets (as in the NHS) for reasons which have as much to do with economic theory as they have to do with reasons drawn from the ways in which ordinary people think about and value things. This has had two consequences. In the first place, Conservative governments have tended to see the citizen in terms of the economic category of 'consumer'.

Now, undoubtedly citizens are consumers and they do seek good services and value for money; but we do not therefore have to think that a consumerist ethos has to pervade all institutions and that all institutions have to be run on this basis. Two examples might make this point clearer. There is no doubt that the introduction of quasi-markets has altered fundamentally the values of the NHS, and yet this is an institution whose values ran quite deep in British society. One can understand why a politician driven by a belief in the supremacy of market theory over instinct might well believe that the NHS is a standing contradiction to the values of the market. First, it emphasises need rather than want or preference and this takes it out of the range of categories with which market theorists usually operate. Secondly, it emphasises both equality of access and free access at the point of delivery, the first of which is now threatened by the two-tier approach that comes from the way fund-holding is actually developing. Even some conservative followers of Burke now accept that in defending the values of the NHS, which seem to lie deep within the contemporary value system, the Labour Party is operating in a more Burkean fashion than the Conservatives. The economy of Burke's time precluded modern systems of welfare, of course, but Burke's strictures on the limits of rationalism and the need to take into account what is implied in a particular political tradition mean that we have to be as sensitive to those values in the society which favour collective provision as to those that don't, and must not assume, on the basis of economic theory, that, as far as possible, collective values should be displaced in favour of private ones.

At this point it is also worth stressing the central rôle in Burke's thought of society as a natural provider for the needs of individuals. Society, he once said, 'gave alms to the indigent, defence to the weak, instruction to the ignorant, employment to the industrious, consolation to those who wanted it, nurture to the helpless, support to the aged, faith to the doubtful, hope to those in despair, and charity to all the human race.' The practical economic limitations of his own time should not obscure the principle behind these words in an age when some people are prepared to question the whole concept of 'society'.

The second example is local government, whose rôle, status and powers have been very severely attenuated after seventeen years of Conservative government. A good deal of this attenuation has been justified by invoking the one-dimensional idea of the citizen as almost wholly a consumer. On this view, a long tradition of local self-government can be overturned and re-placed by other mechanisms because it is assumed that the citizen is only interested in outcomes and is not in the slightest bit bothered about functions for local government other than that of service-provider. So the rôle of the locality, its political identity, local civic leadership, and the constraint on centralised power represented by local authority, is rejected in favour of what needs to be put in place to satisfy this abstraction called 'the consumer'. It is part of Burke's teaching, though, that people have multiple identities mediated through different institutions through which they grow and develop to maturity: 'Men come ... into a community with the social state of their parents, endowed with all the benefits, loaded with all the duties, of their situation. If the social ties and ligaments, spun out of those principal relations which are the elements of the commonwealth, in most cases begin, and always continue, independently of our will; so, without any stipulation on our own part, are we bound by that relation called our country, which comprehends ... "all the charities of all".'

The idea that these various social relationships can all be collapsed into that of consumer seems as much an abstraction as the French republican view that the only category that mattered was *citoyen*. Again, Labour policies to restore local government to a more traditional rôle in British society seem to be more in tune with the spirit of Burke than the consumerist-driven philosophy of public institutions espoused by recent Conservative administrations, as does the recognition that people have multiple ways of thinking about themselves and their needs, which should be reflected in a range of different institutions embodying different values.

This reshaping of institutions to fit the model of a market and the extension of the market philosophy to more and more areas of life means that Britain is moving increasingly towards what Graham Mather (approvingly) calls the 'contract society'. In the same way that status and the mutual obligations which went with it formed the central model of feudal relations, so contract is the central relational category of capitalist market society. As with the consumer, contract is indispensable to modern society, and nothing in the following argument should be taken as detracting from that; but there are two major dangers in moving towards a contract society. The first is that contractual relations are just too simplistic to serve as a foundation for social relationships and interaction. Burke was very clear about this, as is seen in his famous passage in the *Reflections*:

> the state ought not to be considered as nothing better than a partnership agreement in a trade of pepper and coffee, calico or tobacco, or some other such low concern, to be taken up for a little temporary interest, and to be dissolved by the fancy of the parties ... It is a partnership in all science; a partnership in all art; a partnership in every virtue, and in all perfection. As the ends of such a partnership cannot be obtained in many generations, it becomes a partnership not only between those who are living, but between those who are living, those who are dead, and those who are to be born.

To work, contractual arrangements have to be embedded in a culture which is not itself contractual in a straightforward way, as Burke's remarks about the cross-generational nature of the cultural and moral contract imply. This leads to the second point about a contract society. A contractual relationship depends on a moral order of trust, promise-keeping, integrity, truth-telling and reputation. In proportion as society becomes more and more defined by contractual relationships, so it is likely to lose sight of these moral roots. A contractual culture cannot be free-floating, and yet, if relationships are seen primarily in contractual terms, where is the sense of shared moral community to come from which itself underpins a contractual culture? As Durkheim says, and as Burke might well have said, 'not everything in the contract is contractual'. Here, too, the Labour Party now has a deeper sense not just of the necessity of markets and therefore the indispensable rôle of contract and the consumer, but also of the moral limits of these categories and the need for a range of public as well as private market-based institutions to serve the complex moral characters which real people – as opposed to the individualised rational economic men of economic theory – have.

The point about contract can be put in another way too. In the public sector, contract has displaced more and more the service ethic which was once seen as a central feature of public sector institutions – and again this might be thought of as something that runs deep in British political culture. This has been displaced by the emphasis on the consumer and on contract, but also by something more deep-seated. When Conservative politicians such as Nigel Lawson and Nicholas Ridley became convinced of the Public Choice School's approach to understanding the behaviour of bureaucracies, the Thatcher government sought to displace the service ethic in the public sector by a more market-orientated approach. Nigel Lawson wrote about these issues in *The New Conservatism*: 'We are all imperfect – even the most high-minded civil servant. Academic work is still in its infancy on the economics of bureaucracy; but it is already clear that it promises to be a fruitful field. The civil servants and middle-class welfare administrators are far from selfless Platonic guardians of public mythology: they are a major interest group in their own right.'

The academic work to which Lawson refers is that developed by Niskanen, Buchanan and Tullock among others, in which it is assumed that the public sector bureaucrat is driven not by an ethic of service but by the same motives that drive people in markets, namely utility maximisation. Maximising utility outside a market by bureaucrats will lead to the growth of the bureaux, increasing budgets, increasing pay and status for the bureaucrats, an increase in the scope of their responsibility and a decrease in their accountability. These problems can be countered only by either privatising and therefore 'marketising' public sector bodies or by introducing market or quasi-market mechanisms in the public services. Again, this seems to be largely a theory-driven approach with a theory-driven solution. It takes a one-dimensional view of human motives and will lead again to human nature and human society being understood in simplistic ways in which the categories of consumer and contract will be dominant.

III

The modern Left, having lost confidence in large-scale theories, has nowhere else to go for political inspiration other than an understanding of the society in which it is a part, the complexities of that society, and the political possibilities within it. This has led New Labour nearer to a Burkean position not so much in terms of practical policy – that cannot be stressed too much – but in terms of the roots of its political position and the kinds of things that count in politics. At the same time, oddly enough, the Conservative Party seems to be much more in the grip of theoretical models that have led it to prefer proposals for reform which do not seem deep in the instincts of British society.

The area in which it might seem obvious that the Labour Party is a long way from Burkean is that of constitutional reform. The Party is committed to a programme of constitutional reform which will include a parliament for Scotland, assemblies for Wales and the regions of England, the incorporation of the European Convention on Human Rights into UK law, the reform of the House of Lords and a referendum on the electoral system for the House of Commons. If this programme is carried through, it will be one of the most comprehensive reform programmes ever carried through Parliament. In addition, there will be greater use of referenda – as for the new bodies for Wales and Scotland, the electoral system and for a European Monetary Union. Again, when considering these issues, we need to distinguish the particular political positions to which Burke thought his own traditionalism committed him at the end of the eighteenth century and the ways in which his own views of the sources of political principles and action might nowadays underscore different forms. It will not do just to assume that a Burkean perspective on the sources of political action would disallow constitutional change. After all, it was Burke himself who argued that 'Circumstances (which with some gentlemen pass for nothing) give in reality to every political principle its distinguishing colour, and discriminating effect,' and who was consequently led to declare that he dismissed 'no form of government merely upon abstract principles'.

Labour's proposals for constitutional reform are certainly more rooted in circumstances than theory. Indeed, if they were rooted more in theory they would in some ways be more abstractly coherent than they are. As it is, there are loose ends – for example over Scottish representation at Westminster, about the desirability of a nominated chamber as an interim reform of the House of Lords and about the rôle for any regional assemblies in England (which, at least in some parts of the country, do not seem to be strongly supported by popular opinion). The Labour Party perceives compelling circumstances for these incremental reforms. If the people of Scotland and Wales do desire a parliament and an assembly respectively – a sentiment which will be checked by a referendum on the specific proposal – then this would surely constitute a compelling set of circumstances and therefore, for Burke, the legitimate basis for political action. Burke was not opposed to constitutional change, as we see in his discussion of the Glorious Revolution of 1688:

> A state without the means of some change is without the means of its conservation. Without such means it might even risk the loss of that part of the constitution which it wished the most religiously to preserve. The two principles of conservation and correction operated strongly at the two critical periods of the Restoration and the Revolution, when England found itself without a king. At both those periods the nation had lost the bond of union in their ancient edifice; they did not, however, dissolve the whole fabric. On the contrary, in both cases they regenerated the deficient part of the old constitution through the parts which were not impaired ... They acted by the ancient organised states in the shape of their old organisation, and not by the organic *moleculae* of a disbanded people.

In many respects, what Labour is proposing fits very well with this understanding of constitutional change. It is concerned to preserve the union of the Kingdom, but it firmly believes that pressing circumstances mean that, as far as devolution is concerned, there is a significant demand for it (which, after a referendum, will not be a matter of conjecture). This demand has to receive a response if the forces of Scottish separatism in particular are not to grow even stronger.

Devolution also fits with Burke's ideas about loyalty to smaller scale institutions, the famous little platoons. In a global economy with enormous forces working for homogenisation and cultural similarity, people are likely to value more what is local and particular, and this will eventually require some kind of political recognition and expression.

Considering the proposals for the incorporation of the European Convention of Human Rights into the law of the United Kingdom, at first sight this looks doubly un-Burkean with its extra-territorial nature and its emphasis on rights. But Burke was not against the recognition of rights so long as they are not based upon supposed metaphysical claims about the natural rights of

man. Rights, Burke argued, are 'in a sort of middle', arising out of and in-
telligible only in terms of a particular set of cultural and political practices.
It is because there is no recognition of these rights under UK law, while
there is an individual right to appeal to the Strasbourg Commission and Court,
that the Labour Party is proposing the incorporation of the Convention to
which we are in any case a free signatory. Once incorporated, these rights
could then be made justiciable against the background of jurisprudence by
British judges. So incorporation could be regarded as a repatriation of powers to the United Kingdom from the Strasbourg Court.

Again, therefore, when we look at New Labour's proposals for constitutional reform, we need to distinguish between principles and circumstances:
what we might regard as the philosophical basis of Burke's theory, and the
particular political positions which Burke himself believed followed from his
own assumptions. This method of argument should not be too procrustean.
There are many areas, particularly in relation to welfare, where there would
be big differences, with Burke approving only very modest provision for the
most indigent, but again, given that the rôle of the welfare state is now well
entrenched in the British political tradition, the reforms New Labour is
proposing could be seen as responding to circumstances within that Burkean
tradition in contrast to political opponents who are taking a wholly rationalistic standpoint from the outside.

Edmund Burke and Modern Conservatism

John Redwood

Conservatives have never been afraid of evolution, but they are deeply suspicious of revolution. They do not expect their politicians to be reactionary, but they do believe that the greatest political virtue is prudence. They expect governments to use authority sparingly, as a trust, not vigorously, as a power.

Edmund Burke viewed society as an organism of extraordinary complexity, constantly developing and transforming itself, both shaping and reacting to shifting circumstances with a wisdom beyond the understanding of the keenest social scientists. Change he welcomed, as a law of nature, not only unstoppable but desirable, a challenge and opportunity to be faced with confidence and optimism. Men, he argued, have needs for which society must cater and for which the state was created. In the modern world we can exploit technology and experience to achieve these same goals more effectively and to a higher degree.

But Burke also saw that people require stable institutions and constant values in their lives if their diverse needs are to be brought together peacefully. They need rules to regulate relations with others, from the firm parental guidance of the family to the political wisdom of our British constitution. These things, he believed, must not be sacrificed to modern fads and theories, or we cast ourselves off into dangerous experiments, heedless of consequences which we have not foreseen. Furthermore, he argued, our liberties are secured precisely through conserving, for liberty is doing what we may and what we ought, not what we please. He warned against the French Revolution because it promised liberty through total innovation, shaking off the wise restraining hand of past generations. It was a warning that many failed to heed. In this century Marxism is the obvious example of reckless revolution producing tyranny rather than liberty; but we can see similar effects in our own society as we try to wrestle with the consequences of post-war 'Jerusalems' and sixties' Utopias.

Burke's insights into the difference between gradual change and radical innovation, the complex nature of our liberties and the importance of finding the right balance between continuity and adaptation make him a worthy, even if unwitting, founder of modern British Conservatism. His writings added intellectual backbone to the resilient pragmatism of Pitt the Younger; they underlay the message of Peel's Tamworth Manifesto, with its commitment to combining 'the firm maintenance of established rights [with] the correction of proved abuses and the redress of real grievances'; they helped to shape Disraeli's One Nation Conservatism; they sanctioned the determination of Margaret Thatcher to push back the arrogant schemes of the state planners. The modern Conservative Party, as the party of prudence and liberty, should always aim to promote Burke's great contribution to British political thought – at home, and, ever more urgently, in the European Union.

There are three strong foundations of modern Conservatism. The first is popular capitalism. Conservatives believe that liberty in economic policy underpins freedom. It is the surest way of generating prosperity, which was always Burke's test for the well-ordered and truly liberal society. On this sound basis, but harnessing the evolving potential of technological change, Conservatism has developed a tradition of care and concern for those who are sick, old or in need through far-reaching social legislation, because some of the wealth generated by society should be redistributed by the state for the benefit of those unable to compete. Burke's state, after all, was a partnership of interests and a moral community.

The second foundation of modern Conservatism is a sense of time and space – a belief in the wisdom of a community that evolves with a clear sense of its own past, and of veneration for what is best in its inheritance. Burke, of course, saw this wisdom as superior to that of the sophisters, economists and calculators who chose to spurn the untaught wisdom of ordinary people for their own revolutionary schemes. He condemned the politically correct before their agenda was formed.

The third foundation is the establishment and defence of political freedom. Deep in the Anglo-Saxon tradition is the right of every individual man and woman to be governed by representative institutions and the right of everyone to a fair trial under an independent judicial system. The state must be prepared to defend those rights and defend a world order based upon them. Burke's commitment to restrained and responsible government was at the heart of all his political crusades, and he fought arbitrary government wherever he found it – in America, in India and in France.

I. POPULAR CAPITALISM

Popular capitalism is a direct response to the advance of all-embracing schemes of government, such as Marxism, which have attempted to dismantle our inherited institutions and values and then reconstruct society according to a supposedly rational plan. The stated aim has usually been to secure a list of vague, abstract rights. Burke faced the first of such attempts in the schemes of the Jacobins of the French Revolution (who were, of course, idolised by the communists in Russia and China), and he warned that when governments began to shape communities instead of listening to them, all the glittering promises would result in the opposite of what was expected.

Popular capitalism, in contrast, recognises that secure, effective change, which conserves our liberties and rights and doesn't endanger them, must emerge from the activities and needs of communities – the ordinary round of daily business, and the demands of the market-place. This requires, first, a firm, enduring basis of sound money, established through the abolition of exchange controls. Monetary policy should be prudent and the state debt and borrowing controlled. It is the duty of every national authority to pursue a monetary policy designed to keep inflation under control. To do this, governments have to be realistic about their own levels of debt and borrowing. In every case where governments overspend and decide to borrow too much, monetary control proves difficult. The government inevitably resorts to printing money to get itself out of temporary difficulties. The result is a fraud on the saver through rapid inflation. Those countries that have done best in controlling the level of state debt and new borrowing are also those that have been the most prosperous, led by Japan and Switzerland. During the period of debt repayment in the 1980s in the United Kingdom, the economy experienced its fastest rate of growth and improvement for many a long year. People need to have confidence in the currency; the precondition is that it remains free of exchange controls.

On this strong foundation, the interference of the state can be cut back with safety and communities can be given room to breathe. Popular capitalism has achieved that through a number of initiatives. The drive to broaden ownership of land and of commercial and industrial enterprises was undertaken with the vision of making every man a property-owner and a shareholder; the sale of council houses, privatisation and the development of personal equity plans and portable pensions all strengthened the links between individuals and ownership of the wealth of the country. Everyone should have a financial stake, because, as Burke wrote, 'the property of the nation is the nation'.

Popular capitalism also aims to stimulate wealth through the introduction of broader, freer markets and pricing. It advocates the abolition of monopoly boards for the sale and purchase of products, the freeing of prices, and the development of stock exchanges. In Britain, much has been achieved in the wake of privatisation by promoting competition, through the successful development of a proper market-place in telecommunications and in electricity. In agriculture, the Common Agricultural Policy, which currently imposes a £20 a week levy or extra tax upon the average family in the UK in the form of dearer food bills, is in urgent need of reform. It is an irony of life that the systems of both East and West Europe decided, in the Cold War years, to intervene substantially in agricultural markets. The West has set prices that are too high, with the result that it produces surpluses: the East set prices that were too low, with the result that it became chronically short of food. Both types of intervention have vindicated Burke and those like him who argued that free markets and price should play the central rôle in bringing supply and demand into balance.

Conservatives believe in lower rates of income tax. This tax was originally introduced as a special levy to pay for a war, but the habit caught on and governments now rely on substantial income tax revenues for normal peacetime expenditure. Those countries which have the fastest growing standards of living and the most successful enterprise economies, such as Hong Kong and Singapore, also have the lowest rates of income tax. But the tax issue is more than that – it emphasises the vital distinction between the private and public spheres in society. In a letter to Thomas Mercer in 1790, Burke made this telling point about the temptation of governments to invade private property for what they decide is the public interest: 'I do not find myself at liberty, either as a man, or as a trustee for men, to take a *vested* property from one man and to give it to another, because *I* think that the portion of one is too great, and that of another too small.' Burke held the belief that the state does not exist primarily to redistribute possessions from one class to another, but to help all people to maximise and develop what they have by ensuring security in their possession. Public and private interests are mutually dependent, not contradictory. Modern Conservatives agree with rather more income redistribution through the tax and benefit system.

The United Kingdom has changed from being a relatively highly taxed to being a relatively lowly taxed economy in the last fifteen years. Conservatives argue that further progress at all levels is essential, and one way to achieve this is to raise the interest and participation among people in the wealth required to guarantee future security through pensions. Everyone should enjoy basic insurance protection against unemployment, sickness and old age from a state scheme, and the state should continue to take care of the basics, ensuring that no one in a rich, advanced capitalist society should be in real want but may be helped through a system of national insurance. 'Pay as you go' is not a satisfactory way of providing the additional levels of pension most people now expect in their retirement; future generations cannot rely on future generations of politicians to do the right thing in voting them the monies they think they have earned, or to which they believe they are entitled. It is a much better guarantee to have a pool of money clearly held in trust for each individual or for each group of employees in a company so that they know that their pensions can be paid on time and at the right level. Such responsibility can only be expected on the basis of the state respecting the private possessions of its citizens.

II. A SENSE OF TIME AND SPACE

The fundamental problem of distributive justice is that, in the name of bringing social cohesion and unity, it can actually divide people. In his *Thoughts and Details on Scarcity*, Burke argued against a system of relief that divorced poverty from the realities of fluctuating markets and created an eternal class of the 'poor', antagonistic to, and irreconcilable with, the 'rich' in society. It was as if poverty were an inevitable result of wealth, and as if this situation were an injustice that only deeply intrusive state action could (and should) rectify. Burke was afraid that this approach provided the justification for the public authority to invade private property in a way that would endanger liberty for everyone. When he recommended, instead, charity, or compassion 'to be shown in action, the more the better, according to every man's ability', he was partly restricted by the realities of the economy of his time, but he was also emphasising that public responsibilities arise out of private interests, which remain the source of liberty even in times of hardship and dearth. This distinction takes us beyond economic matters to the very fabric of social life, where the relationship between what is private and what is public is equally significant.

It is local, private activities that build communities. Individual interests become public compromises, and people become aware of their interdependence in a way that cannot happen when the state takes so much responsibility for daily life upon itself – even when it is in a good cause. Burke placed great stress on the little platoon, and the various associations that he called the 'inns and resting-places' by which our immediate interests are brought into gear with the greater good of our community. This process is not achieved through government diktat, or even through law, but it evolves through experience and the wisdom inherent in our everyday manners and customs. It is this wisdom that Burke saw as the regulator of change: and we should not meddle with the associations and groups by which it is passed to us. Their wisdom, not contracts or written constitutions, is the guarantee for our liberty.

The principle of pluralism, which is an essential aspect of popular capitalism, ensures the vibrancy and independence of these communities and associations. Pluralism is important to modern Conservatism, at home and abroad, and it testifies to the continued confidence of Conservatives in the abilities of people to work out their own interests in a fair and ordered way, without interference. It is our political faith in Burke's 'untaught feelings'. It is rooted in the broader conservative sense of place, and of the past and our culture. Conservatives believe in tradition and evolution. They are not social revolutionaries wishing to undertake major upheavals of every aspect of our way of life. They believe in building on what is best in the past and in blending the old with the new – in evolution, not revolution.

This is apparent, for example, in Conservative attitudes towards planning and the built environment. The social engineers and socialists of the 1960s bulldozed whole streets of Victorian terrace houses and replaced them with the stark, modern tower blocks of Le Corbusier's vision. The result was an architecture out of sympathy with the wishes of individual families and people, which has bequeathed us great problems. The rotting and decaying fabric of these badly constructed buildings complements the social turmoil they created, and exemplifies the danger of innovation.

The Conservative approach to the built environment, on the other hand, is to preserve the best of the past, and to recognise individual aspirations for houses and gardens rather than apartment blocks. It is to accommodate change in line with the needs and wishes of our communities. New buildings can be added to the street scene as long as they are in keeping with the style and scale of the buildings around them. Sometimes comprehensive redevelopment behind existing façades is sensible; sometimes demolition and clearance should take place; sometimes adding new buildings on the fringe of the town is the way to proceed. Each judgment is made pragmatically, in relation to the wishes of individuals and those who propose to carry out developments. Each is based upon aesthetic and community judgments of what is acceptable. Build too much and people will feel swamped. Build nothing, and the town or village may become a museum.

This attitude is consistent with modern Conservative policy where larger communities are concerned. We may consider it, for example, as it applies to Britain's relations with the European Union, where the Conservative government has sought a decent deal for Britain while developing those aspects of cooperation with our European partners which seem to it to make most sense. Eight hundred years of English constitutional development should not be overthrown in a few hectic years, and it is no business of Conservatives to help in creating a European super-state which takes over from the well tried, balanced powers within the British unwritten constitution and which dictates programmes of behaviour to us. On the other hand, Conservatives accept that in the modern world a growing number of government matters require collaboration on an international scale. The development of a world market-place requires a response by the government of more than one country to regulate the market, to see fair play and honest dealing. Our defence and security require cooperation with a range of like-minded countries on both sides of the Atlantic. In these, and other, areas, Britain is happy to cooperate and to extend the process of collaboration with other nation states, embracing evolution in Europe, but resisting political and financial revolution.

In a similar way, when Burke responded to the events in France after 1789, his writings showed both affection for the common inheritance of European civilisation and a refusal to stand back and allow a centralised political system to extend a uniform control over diverse cultures and societies.

Conservatives believe that a large number of decisions and actions should be made by individuals, families, companies and private organisations rather than by government. A healthy and strong democracy flourishes through a variety of different institutions, communities and social groupings interacting and achieving compromise. Diversity begets unity as private interests create public ones: the sequence cannot be reversed, and, at the same time, the distinctions must be preserved. Render unto Caesar that which is Caesar's and leave to the churches, clubs, companies, neighbourhoods, councils and other organisations those functions which they can carry out best for themselves. It is a habit of the socialist mind which says that all problems require government solutions and that every injustice should be put right by government intervention.

Communities cannot be created by government action any more than by architects. They come about through culture and traditions, the shared inheritance of individuals living together in neighbourhoods, towns and localities. Before it is objected that Burke lived and wrote in a much more parochial and circumscribed world than modern Conservatives, we should recognise that a sense of local loyalty is an increasingly important feature of modern life. The more relentless and remorseless the pace of economic change becomes, the further people can travel, the easier it becomes to span the world by telecommunications and air travel, the more people look for comfort and solace in their local roots. Loyalty to the village pub or the town cricket team, loyalty to the local charity, club or church are important focuses of life. An individual who may be just a small cog in a large industrial machine somewhere can be a leading light in the local dramatics society or a good tennis player. A director of BP may be a sidesman at his local church and a railway porter the chairman of the local residents' association.

Pluralism, then, must thrive, so that the power of the state is counterbalanced by the interests, opinions and activities of hundreds of independent communities and institutions.

III. THE DEFENCE OF POLITICAL FREEDOM

In a mature democracy such as Britain, the habits of self-help and local associations are deeply ingrained. The sense of history is inherent: as a Russian visitor said to me on his first visit to Britain, the thing that struck him most forcefully was that Britain is at peace with her past. Everywhere he went he saw the loving care and attention devoted to preserving old buildings, to ex-

plaining the story of the peoples who had lived in them, to showing community pride in what had gone before. This is not possible for many other
peoples in the world, whose histories have been deeply scarred by alien
creeds and violent revolutions in comparatively recent years.

The main rôle of the state now becomes apparent. Our communities must
be protected, not invaded, by strong defence and strong law and order, so that
the principles of freedom may thrive. The rule of law and the defence of the
realm are therefore fundamental to modern Conservative policy and philosophy. The Conservative sense of past and community makes us proud of our
country, and keen to see our island nation maintain her place in the world.
In the post-war period, only Conservatives have been consistently pledged to
the firm protection of the United Kingdom and its interests abroad – not
least in defending the retention of nuclear weapons in order to provide an effective deterrent against potentially hostile powers. Burke saw in the days of
the empire that imperial power was always in danger of corrupting these
principles and enlarging the interference of government. He fought against
this, and we see in the Commonwealth a tribute to his success in emphasising the moral responsibilities of power.

External vigilance is required for the defence of freedom. Whilst the outcome of the Gulf War and the collapse of the Soviet Union have been positive
signs, no one looking at the world in the 1990s can suggest that democracy
and freedom are now safe forever. So Britain must continue to play an important rôle in the international community. Our moral and political standing is high, based on the economic renaissance of Britain in the 1980s, the
proof we have given of our willingness to resort to arms in the Falklands and
the Gulf when countries were invaded, and the example of democracy and of
long-standing, balanced constitutional development that we offer. Many countries in the world and many persecuted dissidents look to Britain to provide
a lead in introducing and sustaining democratic systems of government and
fair play in international relations. Britain also has a unique rôle within
Western Europe through its special relationship with the United States of
America. It will therefore be up to Britain more than any other country to
ensure that the successful formula of Nato, in adding American power to the
self-help of the European states for their mutual defence, remains at the
heart of Western defence strategy.

At home, Conservatives believe in the rule of law as the corner-stone of
our democracy. We are conscious heirs of the long democratic tradition of
the British peoples. Through Magna Carta in 1215 the strong power of the
Crown was first limited by agreement with the principal landowners of
England. Written into charter form were basic and specific rights of individuals to have a fair trial, of towns and cities to have free navigation and trade,
and of parliaments to be summoned for the redress of grievances and the

voting of taxation. The rise of Parliament through the fifteenth, sixteenth and seventeenth centuries, culminating in the major advances made for parliamentary democracy as a result of the Civil War, led to one of the earliest democratic settlements anywhere in the world. The 1689 Bill of Rights is the forerunner of the American Declaration of Independence and of the central canons of the American Constitution.

Burke understood this and fought hardest where he saw threats to the British constitution: at times against the power of the Crown, or the corrosive impact of corruption, or the radicalism of British supporters of the French Revolution. In the 1980s there were times when the left-wing challenge to the authority of government took undemocratic and unparliamentary forms – when there was, in short, a challenge to democracy itself. Conservatives had to face down that challenge. Great issues of the day must be brought before Parliament for debate. Parliament must remain the fount and origin of our liberties. Every imposition on the British people must be debated and voted through Parliament. Grievances must be brought to Parliament for redress. Parliament is, and must remain, the very expression of the political nation.

The British parliamentary tradition, based upon the direct challenge of Opposition to the Government – the cockpit battle between personalities representing authority and challenge to authority – is so much better than many of the wooden, formal parliamentary institutions elsewhere. It is through the incessant, day-to-day challenge of those in authority that the executive can be curbed and the reality of policy successfully exposed for good or ill.

Burke once defined the quality of the statesman as 'a disposition to preserve, and an ability to improve'. The preservation of our liberties depends upon the actions, ambitions and abilities of private individuals as represented through our parliamentary system. True parliamentarians – among whom Burke stands prominent – seek one thing above all as their epitaph: that they believed in that parliamentary system.

This essay is an adaptation of the author's pamphlet *Conservative Philosophy in Action* (Conservative Political Centre, 1991) and is reproduced here with the kind permission of the author and of the Conservative Political Centre.

Edmund Burke and Contemporary American Conservatism

Mark C. Henrie

I

The American political and intellectual landscape after 1945 was remarkably inhospitable to anyone professing conservative principles. The apparent success of New Deal measures in overcoming economic depression and the costly struggle against fascism (generally misunderstood as a phenomenon of the Right) had placed conservative ideas at a distinct disadvantage. In 1950, Lionel Trilling notoriously wrote: 'In the United States at this time liberalism is not only the dominant but even the sole intellectual tradition.' By 1955, Harvard political theorist Louis Hartz would trump Trilling by contending that, in fact, there never had been nor could be anything but a Lockean liberal tradition in America, because America had been bourgeois from the beginning.[1] His maxim was, *no feudalism, no socialism*: but a necessary corollary was, *no feudalism, no true conservatism either*.

Of course, Hartz was wrong. There *was* an American tradition of conservative political thought; but that tradition was problematically 'American'. T.S. Eliot had emigrated to England. Irving Babbit and Paul Elmer More were united in their humanistic refinement and divided between Buddhism and Anglo-Catholicism. Henry Adams gazed longingly back to the civilisation which produced Chartres and with disdain at his own country's culture of the dynamo. Any genuinely popular conservative 'party' within the American polity had to be sought in the region of the old Confederate South. The conservative cause seemed a lost cause in America. It is true that the work of antebellum Southern political thinkers was significantly more impressive than that of their more famous Northern antagonists; but insofar as these Southern conservatives had European antecedents, they were a strange amalgam of radical political economists and reactionary theorists of the organic state.[2]

---

1 Lionel Trilling, *The Liberal Imagination* (New York, 1950), p. ix. Louis Hart, *The Liberal Tradition in America* (New York, 1955).

2 The ex-Marxist historian, Eugene Genovese, has recently worked to revive the reputation of Southern conservative social thought as an appropriate form of anti-liberal reflection for a post-Cold War world. See *The Southern Tradition: The Achievements and Limitations of an American Conservatism* (Cambridge, Mass.: Harvard University Press, 1995).

Consequently, after 1945, those liberal critics who bothered to notice America's new would-be conservatives at all contended that these must either admit their descent from European defenders of feudal privilege (and so admit to being essentially un-American) or else must devote themselves to a programme of conserving authentically American institutions – that is, the institutions of American liberalism. The conservative's proper rôle would then be a bit-part in the Whig story of left-liberal progress.

In the face of such intellectual challenges, Edmund Burke appeared as one solution to the problem of American conservatism, a solution discovered or invented – it is sometimes difficult to tell – by Russell Kirk. In his book *The Conservative Mind: From Burke to Santayana* (1953), Kirk first introduced Burke's anti-revolutionary, anti-ideological and relatively anti-modern political thought and then recounted the views of a line of thinkers who bore a family resemblance to this author of the *Reflections*. These later thinkers need not have mentioned their debt to Burke to be, in Kirk's view, 'Burkeans'. Conversely, in assembling his particular family of Burkeans, Kirk created an archetype through which to discern the true structure of Burke's ideas, and, with that, an autonomous set of conservative principles ready for application in contemporary America. Kirk's Burke was a solution because he articulated substantive political and social principles – not simply a disposition to conserve whatever may exist, but also a critique of modern forms of political rationalism, a novel account of the origin of political rights and duties, an implicit view of the relationship between state and society, an argument about the rôle of élites in popular government, a concrete sense of whence dangers arise under modern social conditions, and a unique position regarding the cultivation of political virtue. Yet although he went beyond sentiments into the realm of argument and ideas, Burke was not at all like such continental theorists as de Maistre, Bonald or Müller; he was very much an English political thinker who spoke in the language of freedom, contract and the common law. Thus, making non-Lockean arguments in a Lockean idiom, and presenting unheard-of thoughts to liberal America in a very familiar language, Burke seemed uniquely suited to serve as the inspiration for an American conservatism that was more than attitudinal.

The success and influence of Kirk's *Conservative Mind* has been frequently recounted, notably in George Nash's seminal study, *The Conservative Intellectual Movement in America since 1945* (1996). Nash notes that the American conservative movement from the early 1950s, and indeed throughout the Cold War, was fundamentally a coalition of three distinct political positions, united negatively by their common proximate enemy, American left-liberalism, rather than by any positive agreement in principle. Free-enterprise, *laissez-faire* libertarians who had opposed the statist programmes of the New Deal claimed allegiance to Adam Smith and championed an often extreme (though very American) individualism. Anti-communists, often themselves former members of the Communist Party, focused their attention on the threat to the American way of life presented by a revolutionary totalitarian ideology which made inroads both at home and abroad in the name of a false understanding of justice. The traditionalists were perhaps the most unusual party in the coalition. These men of humanistic learning were devoted simultaneously to an austere, vaguely aristocratic personal ethic and to a nostalgic affection for the decent, small-town and/or agrarian life which had been eclipsed in the first half of the twentieth century by the emergence of the rootless anomie of the great American cities and then by the development of a more subtle form of alienation with the suburbanisation of the 1950s.

Russell Kirk, the dean of the traditionalists, proffered Burke to all these branches of American conservatism as the common father. This proposal was both plausible and politically astute. For while Kirk's Burke was fundamentally a traditionalist – an opponent of innovative schemes based on abstract theories and a defender of settled, if ramshackle, social practices – there were elements of Burke's thought which could appeal to each of the parties of the conservative coalition. Burke's *Thoughts and Details on Scarcity* seemed to show greater allegiance to the unimpeded free market than even Smith's *Wealth of Nations*, and his statements in the *Reflections* and the *Letters on a Regicide Peace* were a rich mine of arguments against the modern *'armed doctrine'* of communism. Advocating from 1790 to the end of his life what amounted to a policy of 'rollback' against the Jacobins, Burke was a model cold warrior for those who saw in the American policy of containing Soviet communism merely a species of appeasement.

Nonetheless, the penetration of Burke's thought into American political life was limited, seldom extending beyond the conservative intellectual élite. America, after all, was the inheritor of a revolutionary tradition of its own; as a society it was in significant ways the product not of prescription and prejudice but of deliberation and choice. The founding myth of America as *novus ordo seclorum*, the 'city set on a hill', and the re-founding myth of an America 'dedicated to a proposition', were too deeply ingrained in American public consciousness for Burke's pragmatic, anti-utopian traditionalism to elicit widespread sympathy. Ronald Reagan was a diligent and convinced student of America's post-war conservative intellectual movement, yet during his Presidency he quoted Thomas Paine far more often than Edmund Burke.

Even within the American conservative élite, while Burke was frequently quoted with reverence, his actual prescriptions found only a precarious home. Few free-marketeers could follow Burke's polemic against speculative stock-jobbing, much less his preference for an economy in which large-scale landed property-holding predominated over any creative magic of the market-place.

And faced with the solidaristic rhetoric of Soviet Marxism, anti-communists often found greater utility in Lockean or Jeffersonian accounts of individual liberty than in the subtle rejoinder to Locke found in Burke's writings. Within the political horizon of the Cold War, it often seemed that Burke only obscured the issues at stake. Thus, while it is true that in Kirk's hands Burke's status in American intellectual life moved from that of being the author of a set-piece in old-fashioned high school rhetoric textbooks (*Conciliation with the Colonies*) to that of a potential source of insights into contemporary political problems, the appeal of explicitly Burkean political and social principles remained limited. Indeed, so peculiar was Burke's style of thought for Americans that even among those scholars most intent on learning from him – the (often Roman Catholic) traditionalists – Burke's texts were usually combed, with uncertain success, for restatements or affirmations of the 'tradition' of natural law. This attempt to align Burke with a mid-century revival of scholasticism ironically hindered appreciation of Burke's stronger links with the tradition of Catholic social thought – his understanding of the rôle of culture and society in modern political life.

If we step back from the dynamics of Cold War party politics, we can see that it was not *prima facie* unrealistic or fanciful for American conservatives to have sought to use Burke to orientate an authentic conservatism in their country. Nor did this effort of ideological appropriation necessarily generate a distorted understanding of Burke's teachings.[3] For if there is such a thing as universal history, then the two centuries since the French Revolution may rightly be called 'the age of ideology'. Whereas ancient political thinkers believed that the permanent divisions in human societies lay between the rich and the poor and between the wise and the unwise, the primary political division during our era has been between the partisans of the Left and the Right. This is a far murkier division, a division quite novel historically, a dynamic division, and yet a division which has persisted for two hundred years. Arrayed on the Left have been the advocates of reason, progress, the future, equality, freedom, the individual, secularism and the sovereign state. On the Right have been defenders of tradition, the past, ordered hierarchies, duties, the sacred, and historically evolved communities both above and below the level of the state.

All practical European politics before the eighteenth century might be characterised as conservative, but only equivocally so. For prior to the Enlightenment's assault on tradition, political and social practices were either undefended because unchallenged, or, if challenged, were defended on

3   *Contra* Conor Cruise O'Brien's dismissive contention in *The Great Melody* (London and Chicago, 1992), pp. lxi–lxix.

grounds which are best described as pre-conservative.[4] Conservatism is the *second* Western ideology, appearing only after and in response to the liberal ideology of the Enlightenment when it had become regnant in France.[5] Burke was the first great thinker to speak for the Right after this decisive event; indeed, it is no exaggeration to say that his *Reflections on the Revolution in France* called into being that which we have for two centuries understood to be the Right. Insofar as the course of our political life continues to proceed within terms of the age of ideology, conservative thinkers rightly return to Burke as a perennial source of political wisdom. Despite the differences between eighteenth-century England and twentieth-century America, therefore, it was natural and appropriate for American conservatives after 1945 to seek to ground their own reflections on Burke's thoughts, for those American men of the Right faced parties of the Left both at home and abroad which, while new in some respects, were themselves authentic inheritors of that great movement of 'progress' launched by the *philosophes* and the Jacobins.

II

But what about today? Even if Burke's political thought was rightly marshalled by American conservatives during the Cold War, are his teachings still relevant now? With the collapse of the Soviet tyranny, and the slow emergence of the European Community, some commentators have claimed that we have reached the end of the age of ideology and, indeed, the end of history.[6] For these people, the fall of communism signifies that the conflicts of the human psyche which generated the ideological struggle of two centuries have at last been resolved and that the political history of mankind has reached its *telos*. What is 'natural' or 'normal' for man is revealed to be the

4 For example, Filmer and Bossuet defended monarchic absolutism in part with the claim that the ruling dynasties of their respective states inherited (literally by biological descent) their respective right to rule from God's grant to Adam of the ownership of the earth. Burke had no truck with the 'exploded' defenders of the divine right of kings, but defended limited monarchy on at least two grounds: monarchy's symbolic value in reminding citizens that they are inevitably subject in part to laws to which they could not have consented, and monarchy's fundamental relationship to the aristocratic social form, which Burke believed to be socially beneficial.

5 Dating conservatism from the time of the French Revolution is conventional. However, clearly 'Burkean' themes are already evident in the works of Justus Möser, writing as early as the 1770s against Enlightened reforms in the German states. From the conservative perspective. the key division does not lie between revolutionary and non-revolutionary forms of Enlightenment liberalism but between rationalist and non-rationalist approaches to political and social life.

6 Francis Fukuyama, 'The End of History?', *National Interest* no. 16, Summer 1989. pp. 3–18.

benign individualistic materialism of liberal democratic capitalism, techno-
cratically administered – a system that is purportedly *beyond* ideology. As we
are all post-modern now, it would be argued, so our -isms can only be neo-
isms. Consequently, those social scientists – be they called neo-conservative
or neo-liberal – working with the latest methods of their disciplines to discover the most efficient social forms for achieving the social ends about which
'we all agree' have nothing to learn from the likes of Burke. If this is true, if
the issues which Burke discussed are now cut off from us in a never-to-be-
retrieved past, then the study of Burke is a matter only for historians. For
the purposes of practical politics, Burke's arguments and insights would be
as useless to us as those of Filmer and Bossuet.

But *have* we reached the end of the age of ideology and the end of history?
After all, a form of the original Western ideology of liberalism (precisely
that against which Burke rallied Europe) still stands, and is still an ideology.
When liberal technocrats claim that at the end of history their views are
beyond (and therefore above) ideology, that the decisive political questions
have all been answered (and they have the answers), there appears in such
assertions a recurrence of the liberal's familiar manoeuvre of consigning all
opposition and counter argument to the intellectual dustbin of history. Just
as Louis Hartz, two years after the publication of *The Conservative Mind*,
could detect no intellectual alternative to the liberal tradition in America, just
as the *philosophes* claimed exclusive possession of the categories of reason and
nature, throwing their conservative opponents into the night of irrationality
and myth, so once again the current variety of liberalism constructs itself as
the exclusively natural, rational or normal organisation of man in society.
After all, it is tirelessly repeated, we cannot turn back the clock.

Prescinding for a moment (if we may) from liberalism's prior ideological
commitments, *why* can't we turn back the clock? Or, rather, to be more faithful to Burke, who was himself no believer in simple reaction, why may we
not address publicly and politically the negative social and cultural effects
which follow from the normal operation of liberal political, economic and social institutions – especially when, as in contemporary American jurisprudence, these institutions are understood as expressing a theory rather than as
embodying a tradition? In other words, how may we heal a society that has
overdosed on liberalism?

This is emerging as the great question of our time, as is evident from several recent developments: the appearance of communitarian critics of liberalism and now of a communitarian movement; the new academic alarm about
the depletion of social trust and 'social capital',[7] and the increasing conflict

7   The theorising of 'social capital' has in the past several years proceeded largely among
    neo-liberal academics who trace their work back to Tocqueville, who is understood to

in our political life over issues which would formerly have been understood as non-political, such as education, the family and culture. What has not yet been appreciated is that the presence of these key items on America's current political agenda is nothing new, nor are they evasions of real political issues. Rather, these sorts of concerns have been at the heart of conservative thought from the time that they first appeared in the writings of Edmund Burke. Thus, what liberal heralds of the end of history conveniently fail to notice is that the collapse of the Marxist-Leninist alternative does not leave liberalism in exclusive possession of the field of political ideas, for Western conservatism remains.

Moreover, with the social disintegration long predicted by Burke and his disciples now evident to all but those few who are wholly blinded by ideology, conservative criticisms can no longer be dismissed as illusory. In short, we live in an age better prepared than any heretofore to receive Burke's thought favourably.

III

The effects of social disintegration are well illustrated in three areas of contemporary political debate, where American conservatives are engaged in challenging the liberal consensus: culture, education and the family.

Burke initiated what may rightly be called the conservative preoccupation with the question of culture. Time and again in the *Reflections* we may be surprised to see Burke's hottest judgments arising from aesthetic and cultural concerns which we have now been taught to consider non-political and fundamentally private matters. This reveals a significant theme at the core of

---

be a 'chastened liberal'. So fashionable has been this new concept that the Clinton administration has expressed concern about the depletion of America's 'social capital'. But it must be observed, in fairness, that the term seems to mean precisely the same thing as *geistliche Kapital*, a term already coined in the early nineteenth century by Adam Müller, Burke's disciple among the German Romantics and an implacably hostile foe to the political economy of Adam Smith. Müller believed himself to be developing Burkean views when he observed that more than a commitment to lawful self-interest is required for men to associate profitably in economic corporations, that some kind of pre-contractual and largely unconscious habit of cooperation (or subordination, or trust) must exist within a culture as a precondition for any consciously voluntary association, and that the development and progress of liberal economic and political life appeared to erode this *geistliche Kapital*. Because of the ideological narrowness of American university life, to the best of my knowledge no one has understood that this fashionable concern about depleting 'social capital' has a tradition of almost two centuries in conservative writing.

Burke's project: a re-evaluation of the distinction between the public and the private. The full implications of this distinction are evident when he takes the language of liberalism – accepting willingly in the *Reflections*, for example, that 'Society is indeed a contract' – but subverts both its Lockean and its Rousseauvian meaning so as to recover a lost insight: that every political system is sooner or later transformed into a complete way of life. The *social* contract truly understood, he writes, 'is to be looked on with ... reverence because it is not a partnership in things subservient only to the gross animal existence of a temporary and perishable nature. It is a partnership in all science; a partnership in all art; a partnership in every virtue, and in all perfection. As the ends of such a partnership cannot be obtained in many generations, it becomes a partnership not only between those who are living, but between those who are living, those who are dead, and those who are to be born.'[8]

This point was obvious to Greek philosophers reflecting on the life of the *polis*. But early-modern liberal thinkers reflecting on the life of much larger political units – European monarchic states – devised a new understanding of politics which deliberately limited the public sphere, leaving men free in private to pursue whatever ends they might desire so long as they respected the fences that law placed around their freedom. For thinkers such as Locke, society could surely not be a partnership in 'every virtue and in all perfection', for did not Catholics and Protestants fundamentally disagree over what constituted virtue and perfection? It was far safer to understand society as a partnership merely in the preservation of life, liberty and property and to remain publicly agnostic about any higher human Good.

Liberals to this day boast that they alone fight to protect large spheres of life from the public coercive power of the state. But their 'conquering empire of light and reason' is falsely modest: it claims to be agnostic with regard to the Good, but then goes on to hold that because this is so, it must insist unalterably on a general public commitment to the primacy of the right to the Good. That right, which is effectively arbitrary freedom, naturally becomes itself the absolute public standard of the Good. After all, it has been enshrined at the heart of our common life. This in turn implies a certain notion of human flourishing, of human virtue, which has a public standing above that of all commitments to substantive theories of the Good which might persist in certain spheres of private life.[9] Burke grasped this situation from the beginning, and furthermore he knew that the public valorisation of such an

8   *Reflections*, 194–95.
9   Moreover, in this binary distinction between the public and the private. there is a built-in tendency for the private to be understood as what relates only to the individual, opening up in principle every social relation (every intermediate association) to potential public regulation.

inverted form of virtue would necessarily have a disintegrative impact on human societies and on that sphere of culture which lies beyond the competence of the state.

In this sense Burke may be said to have discovered *culture*, even as he discovered *society*. He discovered that many relations and routines of human life heretofore thought to exist simply in the realm of necessity are actually products of human art, and have now become subject to an unprecedented revolution. He discovered the value of culture in the experience of its loss, which was the loss of something dearly loved, 'the unbought grace of life'. Hence, his great lament: 'But the age of chivalry is gone ... and the glory of Europe is extinguished forever.'[10] The note of lost love here is significant, for whereas liberal theory may be broadly seen as following Cicero in asserting that the commonwealth is constituted by an agreement about *justice*, Burke follows St Augustine's rejoinder to Cicero in holding that the commonwealth is constituted by an agreement about the *objects of love*. What goes unacknowledged in liberal theory is that public devotion to the justice of individual rights constitutes a form of love which excludes other loves by means of their radical subordination. Moreover, the publicly protected exercise of individual rights at the expense of a common culture slowly erodes the loveliness of a country, undermining a necessary prerequisite for patriotism. And, Burke contends, a common devotion to public justice is simply not an adequate tie for binding a society together. The ultimate foundation for a society so bound is not justice but the police power: 'In the groves of *their* academy, at the end of every vista, you see nothing but the gallows. Nothing is left which engages the affections on the part of the commonwealth. On the principles of this mechanistic philosophy, our institutions can never be embodied ... so as to create in us love, veneration, admiration, or attachment. But that sort of reason which banishes the affections is incapable of filling their place. These public affections, combined with manners, are required sometimes as supplements, sometimes as correctives, always as aids to law.'[11]

In the lengthy passages on taste and elegance which are found throughout his writings after 1790, and which often echo his early work on *The Sublime and Beautiful*, Burke is reiterating a simple point: though liberal ideologues may believe themselves uniquely to have limited the power of the state, much of European social life has in fact always been regulated not by the force of law but by custom, habit and the whole informal realm of culture. But the cultural realm is never wholly independent of the political régime, and the public law generated by liberal ideology necessarily has a corrosive effect on the myriad means by which a healthy culture polices its norms. A rereading

10 *Reflections*, 170
11 Ibid., 171–72.

of Burke confirms the conservative conviction that liberal theory must be corrected or supplemented so that the institutions of modern societies can begin to recognise the common goods of a culture which we are losing through our exclusive devotion to the protection of individual liberty.

Closely related to culture, of course, is the question of cultivation – education and the rearing of new generations. This was always the central political problem for ancient philosophers, and the definitive political solution. Accounts of educational regimens are found at the heart of Plato's *Republic* and at the culmination of both Aristotle's *Ethics* and his *Politics*. But as we have seen, modern political writers attempt to disengage politics from private life and from controversial commitments to any account of the Good. In constructing political institutions which purportedly operate to achieve just outcomes regardless of the virtue of citizens and statesmen, liberal theorists have generally eliminated the question of education from their political works. For Locke, since all education must ultimately take some position with respect to irresoluble (religious) claims about man's *summum bonum*, education is effectively removed from public life into the operation of the 'free' private sphere. A usually unremarked irony of the American experience is that our political system is legitimised by a form of Locke's theory, but nonetheless we maintain at enormous public expense a vast state-privileged educational apparatus. And while this apparatus has proved quite unable to ensure basic literacy and numeracy in its graduates, it has taken upon itself the responsibility of inculcating a set of 'civic virtues' which extends on the one hand to such evidently private matters as sexual ethics, and on the other hand to the incitement of vague moral sentiments concerning 'global' issues such as race, gender, human rights, and the environment. In other words, America's educational régime has progressed beyond Locke to Rousseau and has thus arrived at a state quite similar to that of Jacobin France.

Burke argues that every civilised society must be concerned with the formal curriculum through which its rising generation will pass: 'Nothing ought to be more weighted than the nature of books recommended by public authority. So recommended, they soon form the character of the age.'[12]

Public *commendation* is especially important in a country which does not practise public *condemnation*, or censorship. But Burke is also alive to the power of subtler engines of sentimental education – for example, the selection of heroes who are publicly venerated. Not only do the French read Rousseau in their schools, but, Burke exclaims, church bells are melted down to construct statues in honour of this bold experimenter in morality: 'His blood they transfuse into their minds and into their manners. Him they study; him

12 *Works*, II, 535.

they meditate; him they turn over in the time they can spare from the labo-
rious mischief of the day ... Rousseau is their canon of holy writ.'[13] Moreover,
Burke recognises a moral (and therefore political and social) danger in the
powerful, unreflective emotions which can be conjured up by such public enter-
tainments as the theatre – especially as he sees that the French theatre is now
saturated with the naturalistic sentiments of Rousseau.[14]

For Burke, such a libertine sentimental education inevitably undermines
the virtues necessary for responsible government. He writes that 'men are
qualified for civil liberty, in exact proportion to their disposition to put moral
chains upon their own appetites'.[15] But France's Rousseauvian educational
scheme pursued a precisely contrary programme: 'All other people have laid
the foundations of civil freedom in severer manners and a system of more
austere and masculine morality. France ... doubled the licence of a ferocious
dissoluteness in manners and of an insolent irreligion of opinions and practice.'[16] So too in America: in a land of unsurpassed civil liberties, our modern educational system has worked to expand the imagination and sense of
individual possibilities beyond all limit, to free the mind of prejudice, superstition, and the outmoded moral hang-ups of the past. The novels on standard high school curricula almost invariably develop the theme of the young
individual's conflict with the expectations of society, and his eventual liberation from society's injustice or hypocrisy. In our theatre – television – the
same subversive *leitmotif* is evident: consider how often we are presented with
images of wise children needing to correct the moral views of their out-of-
touch parents. But, as Burke notes, an education consisting of 'metaphysical
speculation, blended with the coarsest sensuality' is not one for the rearing
of citizens.[17]

It may be objected here that Burke's attacks on Rousseau should not be
confounded with an attack on a liberalism which looks back to Locke. The
American system, it might be argued, was intended as a Lockean régime, and
the American conservative's aim should be to return the country to Locke,
not to reject him: in other words, our goal should be to return from late, left-
liberalism to early liberalism. But the attraction of liberal – Lockean – societies
to Rousseauvian moral sentimentality is not something contingent, it is essential. As Plato's Socrates knew well, every régime tends to raise up a generation
ill-equipped to perpetuate its principles, and such seems to be the case with
democratic liberalism. Much of the burden of Burke's argument is to show

13 Ibid.
14 See *Reflections*, 176.
15 *Works*, II, 555.
16 *Reflections*, 125.
17 *Works*, II, 540.

how the lacunae of early liberal theory invite the later left-liberalism. Any theoretical return to an unmodified Locke would only set the stage for a new development towards Rousseau.[18]

The widespread cult of authenticity and spontaneity evident among Americans today is probably traceable in theory to Rousseau and in practice to the experience of everyday life in a liberal political order: formality, manners, deference, restraints are rejected in favour of the expressivism of natural men, or noble savages, who are each in principle the equal of all others. Artificial distinctions are stripped away as nature is laid bare: 'On this scheme of things,' Burke writes, 'a king is but a man, a queen is but a woman; a woman is but an animal, and an animal not of the highest order.' While the moral notion lying behind Rousseau's view is that man has spoilt the simple nature which the good God has given us, in Burke's darker view of the human condition, what lies beneath the artificiality of our manners and morals is nothing noble, nothing truly human, but mere gross animality. Man's truly human nature is found in manners, culture, art: 'art is man's nature'. Thus, particularly under conditions of great civil liberty, the moral example which ought ever to be before our eyes is not the noble savage, but the *gentleman*.

Burke's imaginative ideal, which forms the basis of his educational programme, is the age of chivalry, a culture – from the Enlightenment's point of view – more artificial or contrary to nature than any in history; in reality a culture organized by courtly manners into giving a more-than-human respect to what is all too-human; a culture in which self-interest extends to the honour of living up to an ideal of civilised behaviour rather than in living 'down' to the unhindered satisfaction of natural desires; and a culture which knows it stands on the shoulders of giants, and so habitually seeks for moral wisdom in the past rather than positing it in the future. Burke does not (usually) support censorship or formal programmes of indoctrination, but he does believe that public authority – society – has an immediate interest in fostering some forms of art, learning and spectacle at the expense of others. Burke's educational programme amounts to a return to the classical curriculum, modified, however, by the inclusion of exemplars from the Christian centuries and, in particular, of modern works romantically evocative of chivalric manners. He does not advocate turning back the clock to the days of feudal Europe – a charge sometimes hurled against him – any more than Renaissance thinkers wanted to return to the days of slave-holding ancient Athens. Rather, he seeks to furnish the contemporary moral imagination with the material of Christian

18 It may be noted that America shows another moral face to the world: a quite tyrannical puritanism concerning smoking and drinking, for example. This, however, is merely the other side of Rousseau: the admirer of ancient Sparta.

chivalry. His medievalism is pedagogical, not institutional.[19] In this sense, his principles of the gentlemanly ideal are directly relevant as American conservatives pass beyond a critique of our society's educational régime to present concrete proposals for change.

Another contemporary phenomenon traceable to Rousseau and his pseudo-virtue of humanity is the popularity of moral crusades concerning global issues such as the environment or human rights. The Rousseauvian moralist, seeking in the name of justice to overcome restricting attachments to contingent particulars, 'melts with tenderness for those only who touch him by the remotest relation'.[20] Yet this exalted virtue seems not to require morally responsible behaviour with respect to those who are most *one's own*: Rousseau, the father of several abandoned children, is thus 'a lover of his kind, but a hater of his kindred'.[21] Those who search for rationalist, ideological conceptions of universal justice likewise search for moral wisdom anywhere but in *their own* tradition. This is the root of contemporary multiculturalism, which might more accurately be called *xenocentrism*.[22]

Against this habit of focusing our moral attention on the abstractly universal and the distant – and in so doing, losing sight of the importance of the concrete and the local – Burke famously drew up his little platoon, 'the first link in the series by which we proceed towards a love to our country and to mankind'.[23] In Burke's thought, the good society is not achieved by working politically for a change in unjust structures of the whole, but by living uprightly in one's own private life, and in seeing to it that one's neighbours do the same. Of course, the primary little platoon, the first element of every society and culture, and the seedbed of virtue, is the family. Already, in 1790, what alarmed Burke most of all in his reflections on events in France was the evidently revolutionising effect Jacobin principles were having on the family: a concern about family values has *always* been at the heart of American conservatism.

Burke believed that the debilitation of the family tie is an inevitable effect, and perhaps even a deliberate tactic, of the Jacobin ideology. Writing to a member of the French National Assembly he notes: 'As the relation between parents and children is the first among the elements of vulgar, natural morality ... Your masters [the Jacobins] reject the duties of this vulgar relation, as contrary to liberty; as not founded in the social compact; and not binding ac-

---

19 Russell Kirk's devotion to the novels of Sir Walter Scott can be understood as one faithful embodiment of Burke's project.
20 *Works*, II, 537.
21 Ibid., 538.
22 My thanks to Professor Philip E. Devine of Providence College for this apt coinage.
23 *Reflections*, 135.

cording to the rights of men; because the relation is not, of course, the result of free election; never so on the side of the children, not always on the part of the parents.'[24]

In part, Burke continues, the Jacobins – like our contemporary liberal ideologues – destroy the family through a revolution in manners. Rousseau, their honoured human exemplar, is hardly a family man, nor is responsible family life held out today as an integral element of human flourishing in our own youth culture. The 'decent pride' and 'salutary domestic prejudice' which were traditional cultural supports for the family are pushed away into the private sphere by the public values of liberal society. Also, virtually all modern states, like revolutionary France, have introduced a public law of marriage and divorce purporting to be grounded in nature or reason alone. In so doing, they follow Locke more than Rousseau. For although the status of the family in common law is unique and ambiguous, liberal theory is more coherent. That theory cannot comprehend the family as in any way a genuine unity. Rather, Locke had to, and his successors must, understand the family as formed by a contract between free individuals: there is no such thing as a family, only a man and a woman. Were such a contract to be indissoluble it would amount to slavery, and Locke has clearly demonstrated to his own satisfaction that it is impossible (short of actual military conquest) for a rational man to enter a binding contract of enslavement. Thus, according to Locke, the marriage tie naturally or rationally is always a revisable contract between a man and a woman for mutual temporal advantage. From this perspective, for the public authority to forbid divorce would be a profound infringement of liberty. After all, it would be argued, if you are personally opposed to divorce, you are free not to divorce; but it would be wrong to impose this view on others trapped in bad marriages.

Burke had, here, already glimpsed what we have now come to know too well: introducing even the possibility of divorce for some people alters the cultural meaning of marriage for all. From his eighteenth-century perspective, Burke focuses on the general cultural protection of a woman's virtue, before and in marriage, which is lost when both law and custom are interpreted in a liberal way. If marriage is forever, there can be no excuse for the would-be adulterer; but if marriage rests on free election alone, then any step towards adultery may well be justifiable. Thus every woman (and every man) is culturally unprotected from what might be called occasions of sin.

24 *Works*, II, 538.

CONCLUSION

The political achievements of liberal societies – which might more simply be termed representative democracies or parliamentary governments – are obvious to all, and were so not least to that great parliamentarian Edmund Burke. However, because ideological liberalism began as a self-consciously partial theory, and because liberalism further boasts that its institutions amount to a machine that will run by itself, then children – their family, education and introduction to adult culture – are originally missing from liberal theory. Yet, as Burke saw in a revolutionary way in France and we have seen in an evolutionary way over the decades, the liberal state never really leaves the private sphere alone, but sooner or later it works with carrot and stick to reshape all social relations into its image of freely contracting individuals. Unresisted, political liberalism drives to totalism, and consequently it produces an untenable atomism which ends either in political collapse or in the bureaucratic paternalism of democratic despotism. Understanding this, Burke sounded an alarm which has echoed down the years and across the oceans. He sought to provide arguments, which even modern liberals might understand, to prove the legitimacy of such non-political, essentially non liberal institutions and practices as the traditional family, gentlemanly responsibility tied to personal honour, and educational cultivation in local traditions. In so doing, he offered a way of saving liberalism from itself, or, at least, of rescuing the practical advantages of parliamentary political institutions from liberal theoretical meanings that actually tend to the apotheosis of freedom. This fundamentally different understanding of the meaning and value of modern social institutions makes Burke's conservatism an alternative to liberalism rather than a codicil to it. In an America plagued by ever-increasing social pathology, this is Burke's great contribution to conservatism: it is also his enduring legacy in political theory.

Contributors

MARK ALMOND is Lecturer in Modern History at Oriel College, Oxford, and author of *The Rise and Fall of Nicolae and Elena Ceausescu*; *Europe's Backyard War: the War in the Balkans* and *Revolution*. He is preparing a study on *The Peculiarities of Post-Communism*.

NORMAN BARRY is Professor of Social and Political Theory at the University of Buckingham. He is a specialist in the political philosophy and political economy of classical liberalism, the theory of welfare and business ethics. His books include *Hayek's Social and Economic Philosophy*; *An Introduction to Modern Political Theory*; *On Classical Liberalism and Libertarianism*; *Welfare* and *The Morality of Business Enterprise*. He is a member of the Academic Advisory Boards of the Institute of Economic Affairs (London) and the David Hume Institute (Edinburgh).

STEVEN BLAKEMORE is Assistant Professor of English at Florida Atlantic University and author of *Burke and the Fall of Language: The French Revolution as Linguistic Event*. His book *Intertextual War: Burke and the French Revolution in the Works of Mary Wollstonecraft, Thomas Paine and James Mackintosh* is published this summer.

YVES CHIRON teaches in Niherne, France. He is the author of a number of works on the history of political ideas including, *Maurice Barres*; *Edmund Burke et la Revolution française*; *La Contre-Révolution* and *La Vie de Maurras*.

IAN CROWE is a member of the Edmund Burke Society and has been teaching History and Politics in schools and colleges for fifteen years. His research interests include counter-revolutionary thought at the time of the French Revolution, and he is at present working on a thematic introduction to the writings of Edmund Burke.

L.M. CULLEN is Professor of Modern Irish History at Trinity College, University of Dublin. His publications include, *An Economic History of Ireland since 1660*; *The Emergence of Modern Ireland, 1600–1900* and *The Hidden Ireland: Reassessment of a Concept*.

BRUCE FROHNEN has taught at Reed College, Cornell College, Oglethorpe University and Emory University. He has published articles in a number of journals, including the *George Washington Law Review*, the *American Journal of Jurisprudence* and several journals of political science. He is the author of two books, *Virtue and the Promise of Conservatism: the Legacy of Burke and Tocqueville* and *The New Communitarians and the Crisis of Modern Liberalism*. He is currently a lecturer in the Politics department at the Catholic University of America.

MICHAEL GOVE writes for *The Times*. His publications include *Michael Portillo: The Future of the Right*, which appeared in 1995.

MARK HENRIE holds degrees from Dartmouth, Cambridge and Harvard, and he is currently engaged in Catholic theological studies leading to priestly ordination. His numerous articles and reviews have appeared in such journals as *First Things*, *Crisis*, *Modern Age* and the *Intercollegiate Review*.

JIM MCCUE writes the 'Bibliomane' column for *The Times*, and has edited *The Selected Poems of Arthur Hugh Clough* for Penguin. His book *Edmund Burke and Our Present Discontents* is published by Claridge Press.

P.J. MARSHALL is Professor Emeritus of History at King's College, London. He is Associate Editor of the Oxford University Press edition of the *Writings and Speeches of Edmund Burke*, for which he has edited volumes V and VI. His other publications include *The Impeachment of Warren Hastings*; (ed.) *The Correspondence of Edmund Burke, vol. VII* (with John A. Woods); *The Great Map of Mankind* (with Glyndwr Williams) and (ed.) *The Cambridge Illustrated History of the British Empire*.

CONOR CRUISE O'BRIEN has had a distinguished career in teaching, the diplomatic service, journalism and politics. He was a member of the Dáil, 1969–77, serving as Minister for Posts and Telegraphs in 1973–77, and was a member of the All Ireland Forum. He edited the Penguin Classic edition of Burke's *Reflections on the Revolution in France* and his most recent publications include, *God Land: Reflections on Religion and Nationalism*; *The Great Melody: A Thematic Biography of Edmund Burke*; *Ancestral Voices* and his controversial book on Thomas Jefferson, *The Long Affair*.

JOSEPH PAPPIN III has taught in the Department of Philosophy and Religious Studies at the University of Arkansas and he is now Dean at the University of South Carolina at Lancaster. He is author of *The Metaphysics of Edmund Burke*.

LORD PLANT OF HIGHFIELD is Master of St Catherine's College, Oxford and Labour spokesman on Home Affairs in the House of Lords. He is the author of many books and articles on political theory, including *Hegel, Community and Ideology*; *Philosophy, Politics and Citizenship: The Life and Thought of the British Idealists* (with A. Vincent); *Conservative Capitalism in Britain and the United States: A Critical Appraisal* (with K. Hoover) and *Modern Political Thought*.

JOHN REDWOOD was head of the Prime Minister's Policy Unit in Downing Street from 1983 to 1985 and has been Conservative MP for Wokingham since 1987. He has served as Minister of State for Corporate Affairs, 1990–92, Minister of State for Local Government and Inner Cities, 1992–93, and Secretary of State for Wales, 1993–95. He was made a Privy Counsellor in 1993. He has written several books on free enterprise and democracy, including, *The Global Market Place* and *Views from Wales*. His most recent publication is *Our Currency, Our Country*.

SIR ROBERT RHODES JAMES was Conservative MP for Cambridge for sixteen years, a Chairman of the House of Commons, 1987–92, and Chairman of the History of Parliament Trust, 1983–93, of which he remains a Trustee. His extensive publications include biographies of Lord Randolph Churchill, Rosebery and Eden. He is a Fellow of the Royal Society of Literature and of the Royal Historical Society, and a Fellow of Wolfson College, Cambridge.

JAMES SACK is Associate Professor in the Department of History at the University of Illinois at Chicago. His publications include *The Grenvillites, 1801–1829: Party Politics and Factionalism in the Age of Pitt and Liverpool*, and *From Jacobite to Conservative: Reaction and Orthodoxy in Britain, c. 1760–1832*.

PETER J. STANLIS has taught in various American colleges and universities for over forty years, and has been a guest lecturer in four European universities. In 1969 he was one of the six founders of The American Society for Eighteenth-Century Studies and in 1982 he was appointed by President Ronald Reagan to the National Council for the Humanities. Since 1988 he has been Distinguished Professor of Humanities, Emeritus, of Rockford College. His publications on Burke include twenty-six articles, and he edited *The Burke Newsletter* and *Studies in Burke and his Time* for thirteen years. His books include *Edmund Burke and the Natural Law; Edmund Burke: A Bibliography of Secondary Studies to 1982* (with Clara I. Gandy) and *Edmund Burke: The Enlightenment and Revolution*.

Index